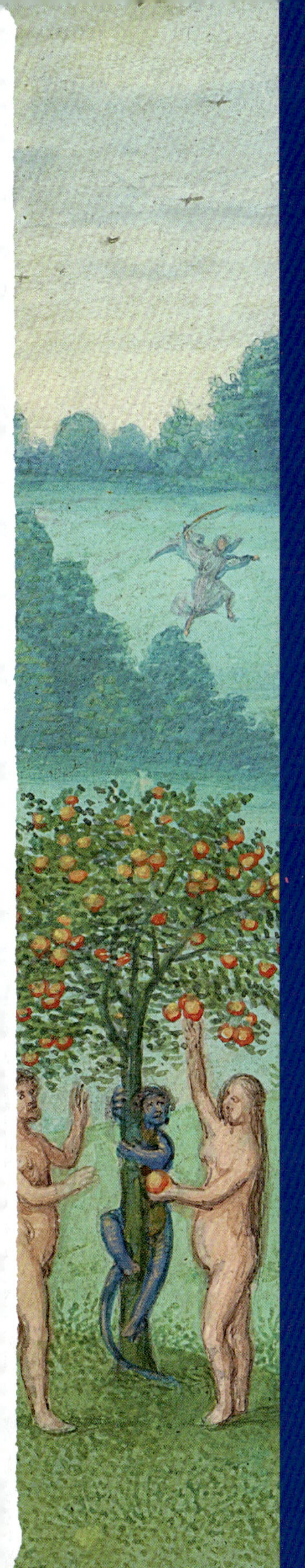

SACRED LANDSCAPES

NATURE IN RENAISSANCE MANUSCRIPTS

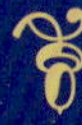

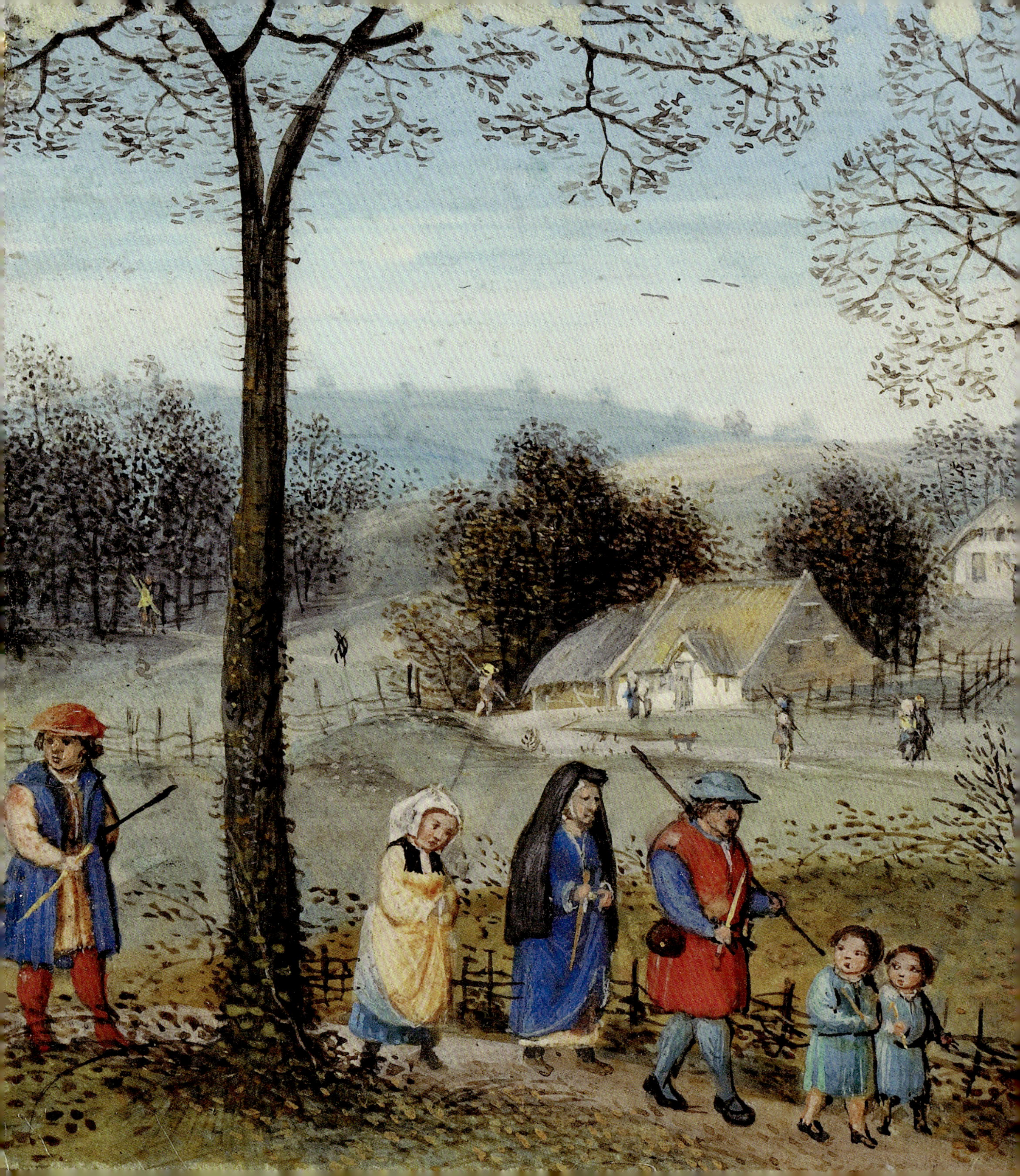

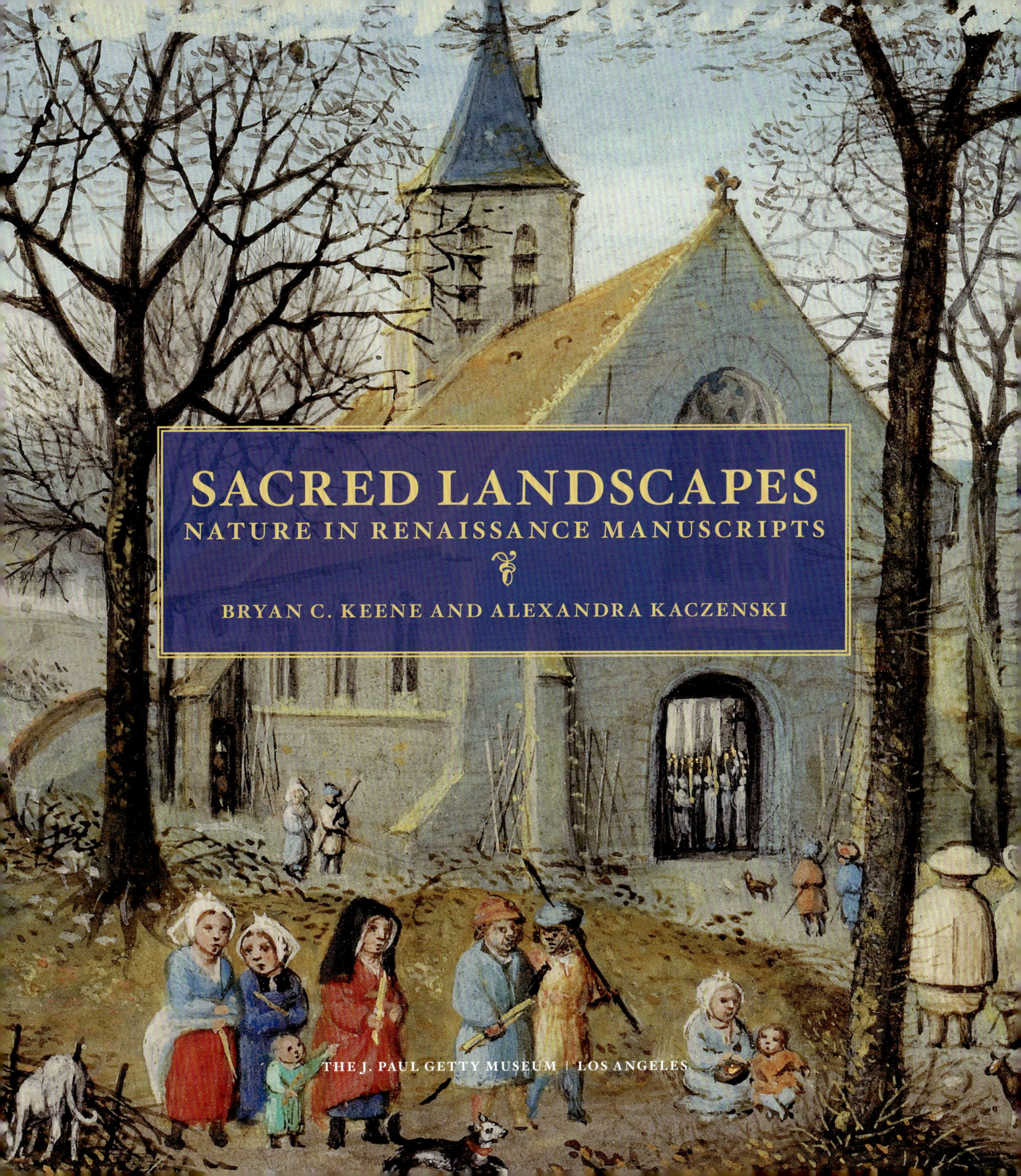

SACRED LANDSCAPES
NATURE IN RENAISSANCE MANUSCRIPTS
BRYAN C. KEENE AND ALEXANDRA KACZENSKI
THE J. PAUL GETTY MUSEUM | LOS ANGELES

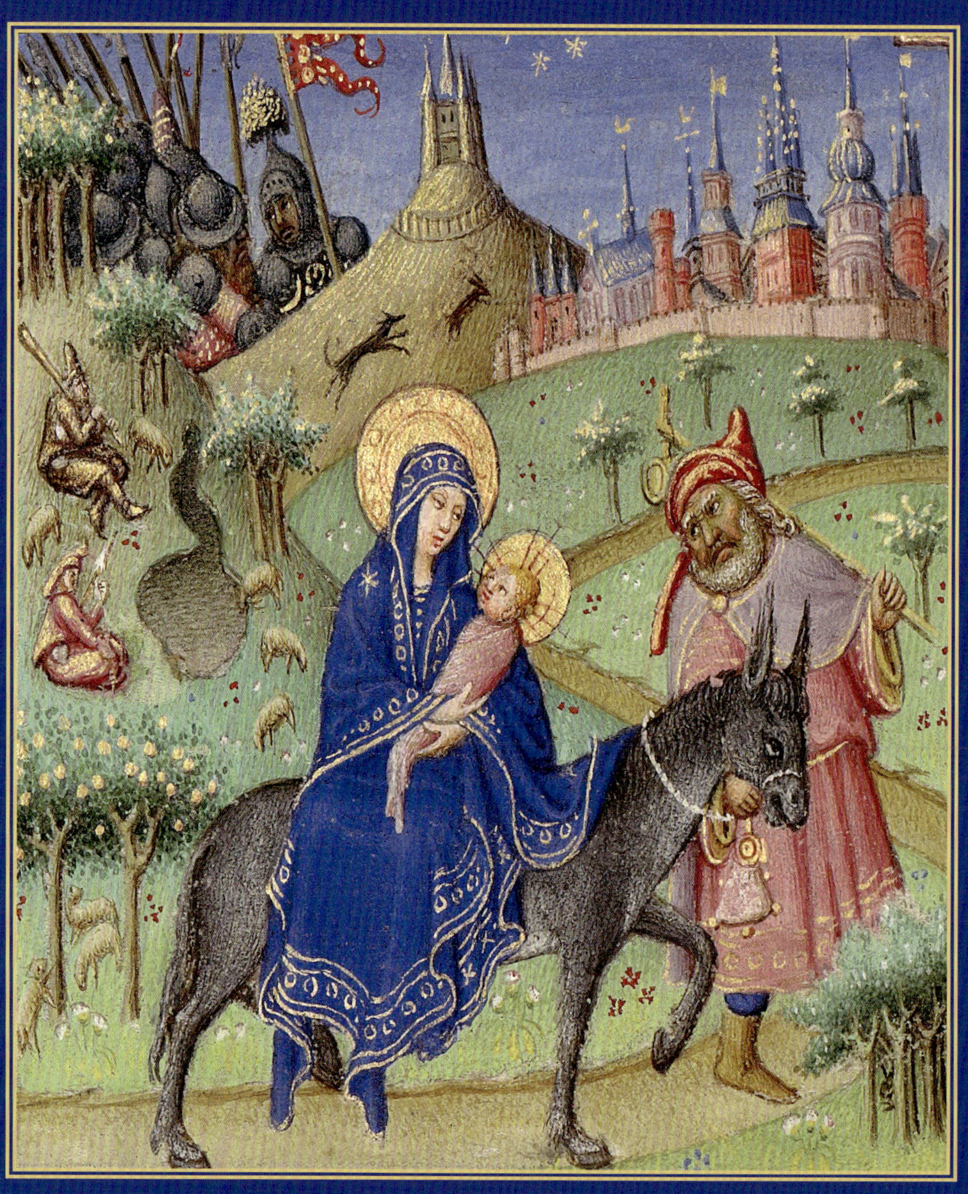

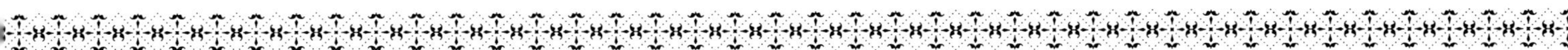

CONTENTS

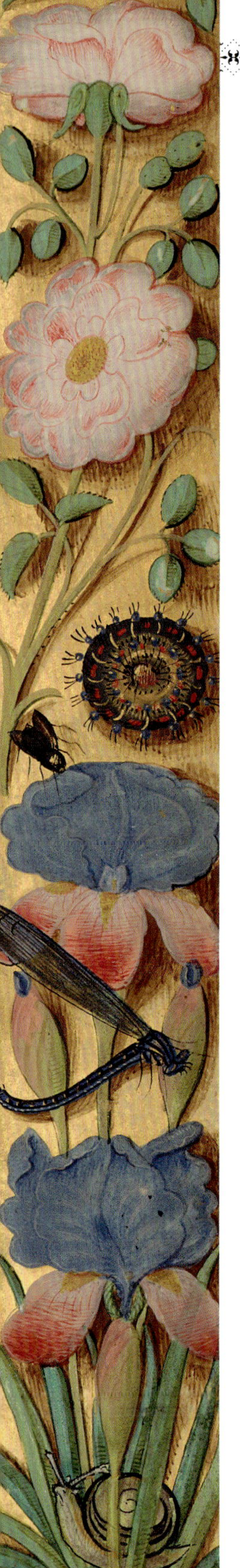

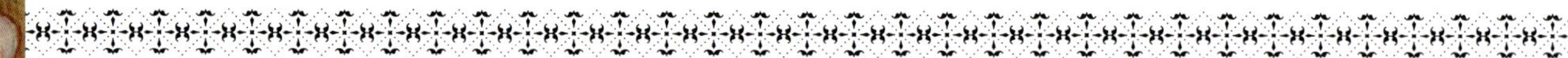

FOREWORD

THE MAJESTY OF NATURE HAS A UNIVERSAL APPEAL, BOTH AESTHETIC AND spiritual, that is deeply rooted in the human condition. A distant mountain range, a vast and darkening sky, the awesome force of the sea—these have inspired wanderers, poets, and artists of every culture across time and space. For some, the wonders of the natural world reinforce religious convictions; for others, they evoke the essence of being and the passage of years; and, for a growing number of people today, they elicit concern for the welfare of the planet.

During the Renaissance, European artists painted spiritually uplifting landscapes to exhilarate viewers and enhance religious experience. This volume presents some of the most impressive examples of this art, gathering a wide range of illuminated manuscripts made between 1400 and 1600, as well as panel paintings, drawings, and decorative arts, primarily selected from the permanent collection of the J. Paul Getty Museum. The keen observer will see here the influence that Albrecht Dürer, Jan van Eyck, Leonardo da Vinci, Piero della Francesca, and other Renaissance painters had on the book arts and will gain new appreciation for manuscript illuminators such as Simon Bening, Joris Hoefnagel, Vincent Raymond, and the Spitz Master, who were revered throughout the early modern period for their equally innovative contributions to the early development of landscape painting.

We are grateful to Bryan C. Keene, assistant curator, and Alexandra Kaczenski, former curatorial graduate intern in the Getty's Manuscripts Department, for giving this aspect of Renaissance art the focused attention it deserves, both in this publication and in the accompanying exhibition at the Getty Museum. Other departments at the museum have supported this project by sharing additional works relevant to this study, notably the departments of Drawings, Paintings, and Sculpture and Decorative Arts.

This beautiful, verdant volume invites us all to take a moment to consider the splendor of nature, whether encountered outdoors or on the exquisitely illustrated pages of a book.

Timothy Potts
Director, J. Paul Getty Museum

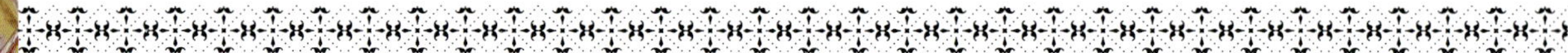

ACKNOWLEDGMENTS

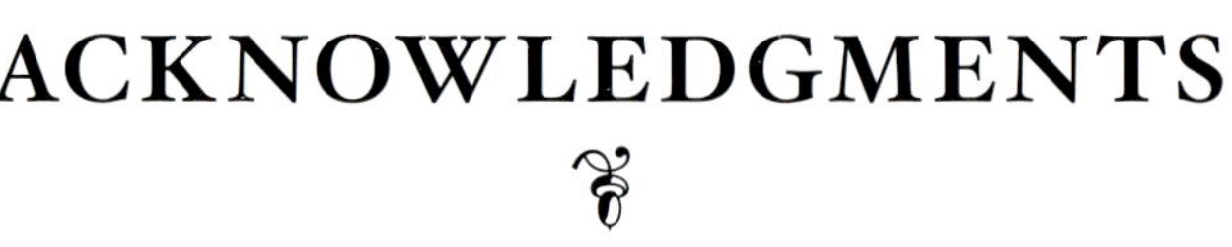

IN 2006, THOMAS KREN (FORMER SENIOR CURATOR OF MANUSCRIPTS AND associate director for collections at the J. Paul Getty Museum) organized the exhibition *Landscape in the Renaissance*, which considered the emergence of the genre of landscape painting in European art. We found inspiration in this project and are grateful to Elizabeth Morrison, senior curator of manuscripts, for continuing to expand the Getty's manuscript collection with numerous books and leaves filled with lush green spaces. Kristen Collins, curator of manuscripts, and Nancy Turner, conservator of manuscripts, have provided especially useful guidance during this project, offering invaluable suggestions for refining the exhibition and extending the scholarly arc of the book. Davide Gasparotto, senior curator of paintings, has been an ideal partner in organizing an exhibition dedicated to landscape painting in the Renaissance; many of the themes in his show *Giovanni Bellini: Landscapes of Faith in Renaissance Venice* (October 2017–January 2018) have been explored herein. Christine Sciacca, associate curator of European art, 300–1400 CE, at the Walters Art Museum and former assistant curator of manuscripts at the Getty, generously collaborated with us on overlapping objects in her exhibition *Illuminating Women in the Medieval World* (June–September 2017), which opened prior to *Sacred Landscapes: Nature in Renaissance Manuscripts*. For all logistical matters related to the book and exhibition, we relied on the organization and timeliness of staff assistants Andrea Hawken and Morgan Conger, the latter of whom assisted with identifying flowers, downloading images, preparing presentations, and editing bibliographies, at times aided by summer undergraduate intern Isabel Diaz-Brady.

We thank Rheagan Martin, past curatorial assistant and graduate intern of manuscripts, and photographers Sara Rivers and Kayla Kee for digitizing numerous manuscript images, and Johana Herrera, senior imaging technician, for ensuring that each illumination is stunning in print.

To our curatorial colleagues Davide Gasparotto and, in the Department of Drawings, Julian Brooks, senior curator, and Stephanie Schrader, curator, we offer our gratitude for generous loans to the exhibition and suggestions for material to include in the book. We greatly appreciate the insights shared by Deirdre Larkin, horticulturist emerita of the Met Cloisters and Gardens of the Metropolitan Museum of Art, New York.

At Getty Publications, we thank Karen Levine, editor in chief, Elizabeth Nicholson, senior editor, and Rachel Barth, assistant editor, for their constant support during this project and especially for their enlightened suggestions for an innovative format and their sharp editorial eyes, which have allowed our subject to flourish on these pages. Thanks also to manuscript editor Jane Bobko for ensuring clarity throughout the text. Particular thanks are due to senior designer Catherine Lorenz for her attention to every exquisite detail throughout this volume, and to senior production coordinator Amita Molloy for her organization of this publication and the high quality of its images.

On behalf of Bryan, this book is dedicated to Mark Mark and Alexander Jaxon Keene, for being evergreen sources of love, joy, and inspiration.

On behalf of Alexandra, this book is dedicated to her loving and supportive family and friends, without whom she would be—well—lost in the wilderness.

Bryan C. Keene
Alexandra Kaczenski

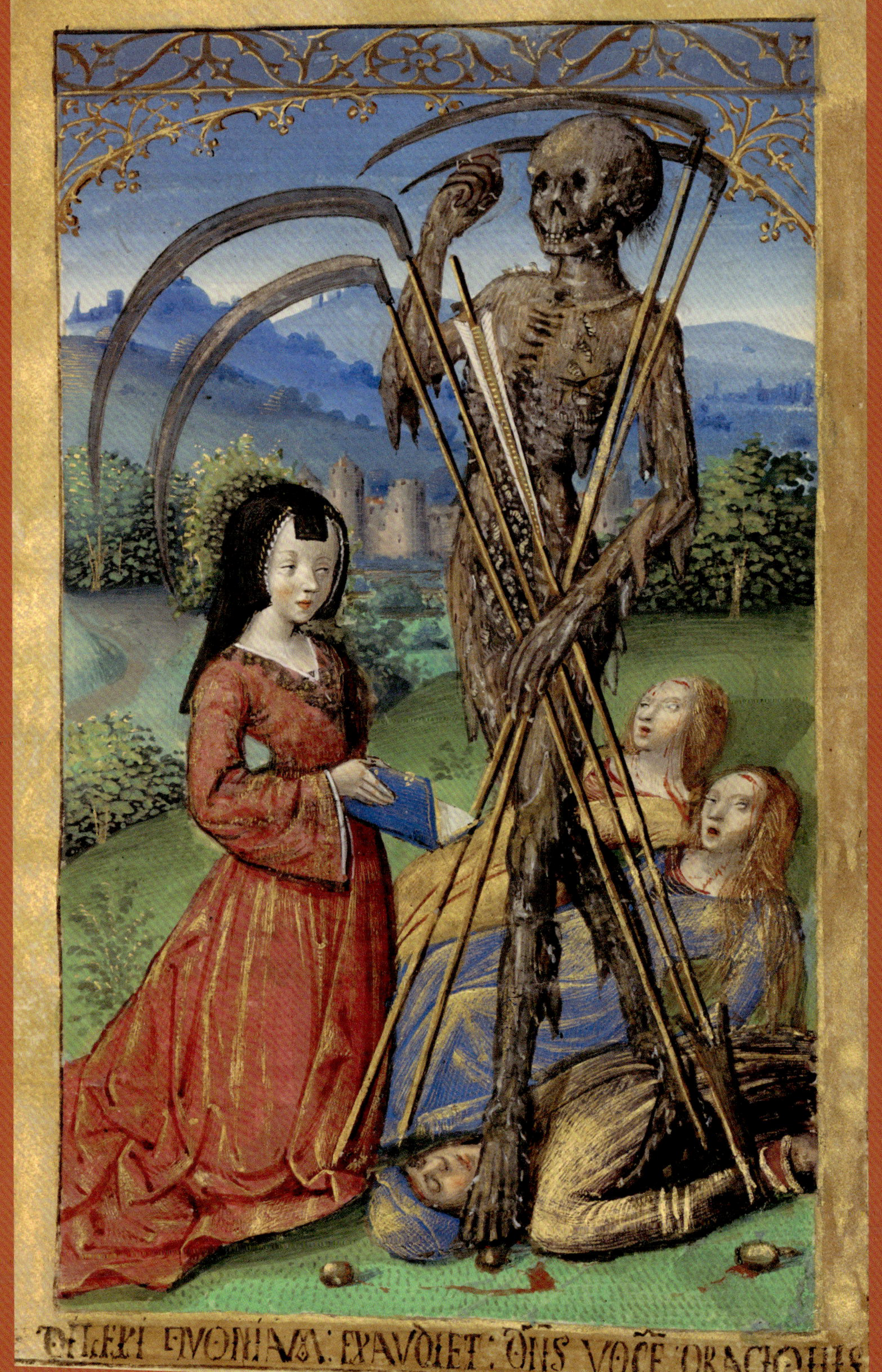
DILEXI QVONIAM EXAVDIET DNS VOCE ORACIONIS

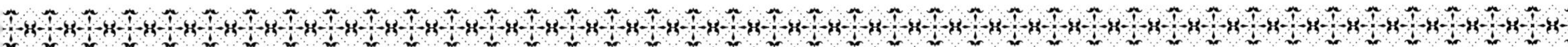

PROLOGUE

young woman named Denise Poncher kneels in prayer (fig. 1). She appears
serene, though she is threatened by the macabre specter of Death, which
has vanquished three other souls. Immersed in the splendor and mystery of
God's creation, Denise has achieved a state of grace, and her piety saves her.
The scene is a reminder that death can come at any moment and that daily
prayer is one pathway to salvation.

This image appears in a book of hours, a type of manuscript intended for private use, that was especially made for Denise Poncher around 1500,
at the height of the Renaissance. The portable book contains prayers appropriate for different times of the day, and Denise would have kept it close
at hand and referred to it frequently from morning until evening, every day
throughout the year. The gold tracery arch at the top of the frame indicates
that the image is a window onto a sacred and evergreen realm, immune from
the changes of the seasons and time's inevitable decay. Whether outdoors
or within the city walls in the darkest heart of winter, Denise could lift her
spirits by meditating on this painting of verdant fields, rushing streams, and
skies of heavenly blue.

The exquisitely illuminated manuscript now known as the Poncher
Hours includes many paintings of idyllic natural settings, such as *Noli me
tangere* (fig. 2). Far beyond turreted city walls more reminiscent of fifteenth-
century Paris than first-century Jerusalem, Mary Magdalene kneels among
green trees tinged with gold. She is visiting Christ's tomb and is horrified
to discover it empty, until a risen Christ appears to her. She reaches out to

FIGURE 1 | *Denise Poncher before
a Vision of Death*, Paris, ca. 1500,
Master of the *Chronique scandaleuse*,
Poncher Hours, 13.8 × 9.8 cm
(5⁷⁄₁₆ × 3⅞ in.), Ms. 109 (2011.40),
fol. 156

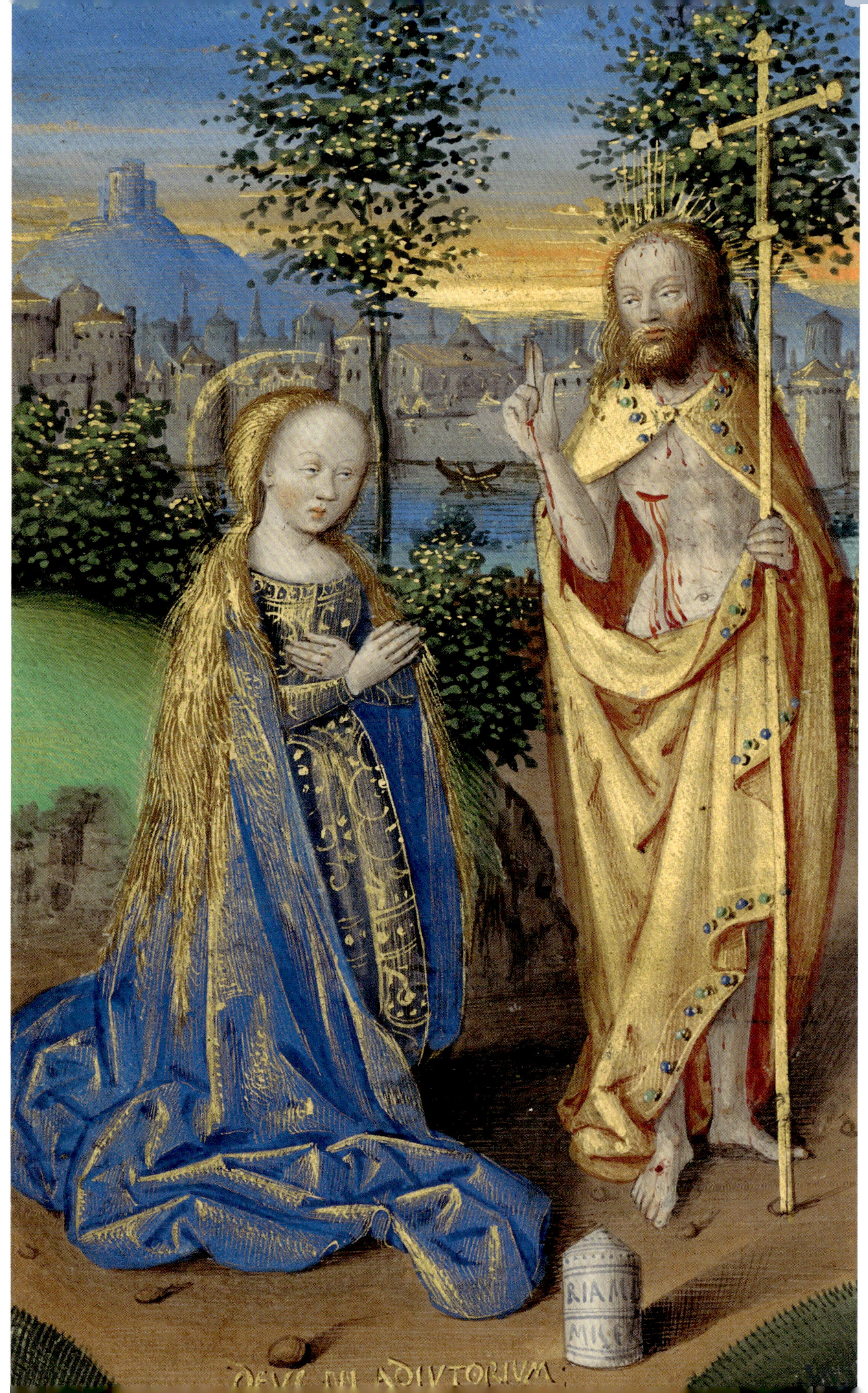

DEVS IN ADIVTORIVM

him, but he admonishes her, "Noli me tangere" (Do not hold on to me; John 20:17).[1] Contemplating this religious scene set within a verdant landscape would have allowed Denise Poncher not only to connect with a centuries-old story of faith but also to seek transcendence through the beauty of the natural world.

The veneration of nature in religious art is revelatory and reflective of the values of the day. From the fifteenth through seventeenth centuries, artists from France and Italy to Flanders and Germany elevated the art of landscape to new artistic and spiritual heights. Devotional manuscripts for personal or communal use—from small-scale prayer books to massive choir books—were filled with some of the most illusionistic landscapes and nature studies of this period. 🌿

FIGURE 2 | *Noli me tangere*, Paris, ca. 1500, Master of the *Chronique scandaleuse*, Poncher Hours, 13.8 × 9.8 cm (5⅞₆ × 3⅞ in.), Ms. 109 (2011.40), fol. 130v

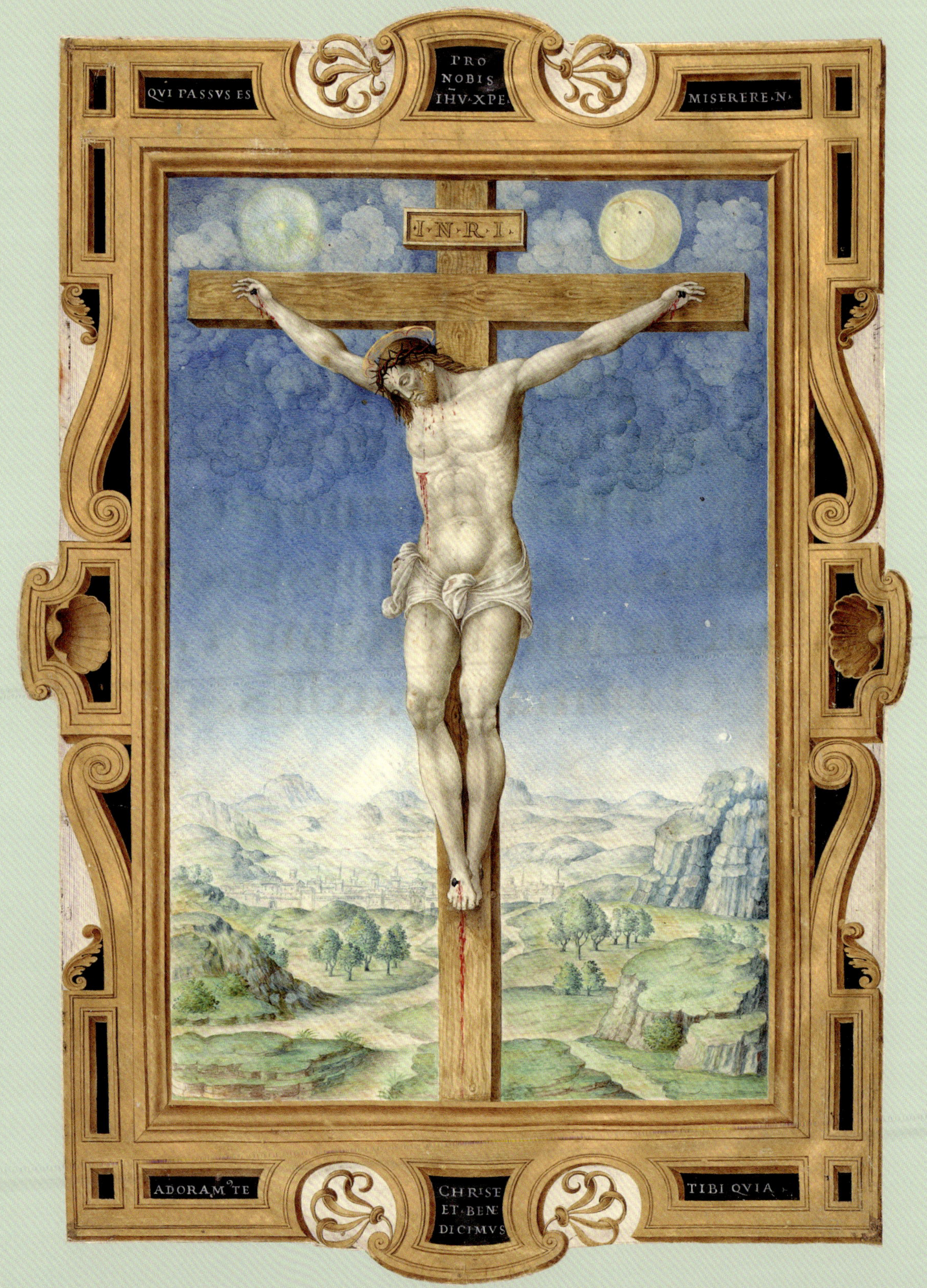
QVI PASSVS ES
PRO NOBIS IHV XPE
MISERERE N
I N R I
ADORAM TE
CHRISTE ET BENEDICIMVS
TIBI QVIA

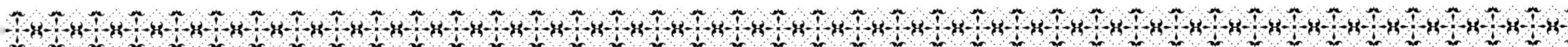

INTRODUCTION

THE ENVIRONMENTAL CONCERNS OF THE POSTINDUSTRIAL WORLD TO preserve nature's verdancy are not so distant from the attitudes of artists, intellectuals, and pious members of society in Renaissance Europe. Nature within the walls of the city and beyond provided inspiration and guidance for spiritual pursuits and contemplation of the divine, even during a period often characterized by humanist ambitions, an interest in the classical world, numerous advances in the natural sciences, and a general secularization of society where faith was no longer the sole or the dominant cultural currency. At this time, gardens and other cultivated plots of land reminded Christians of the biblical accounts of Adam and Eve or of Mary Magdalene and Christ, and humanists made associations with the Golden Age, an era of idyllic abundance in antiquity. As physical spaces, gardens facilitated rest and sustenance. The wilderness and untamed or unexplored land beyond the city demonstrated the natural riches and wonders of creation. Hermits and other ascetics sought solitude in these sylvan or desolate spaces in order to achieve authentic spiritual experiences.[2] The elements of nature—rocks, trees, flowers, waterways, mountains, and even atmosphere—could be combined in paintings, drawings, and manuscript illuminations to create expansive landscapes and vistas, which often formed the settings for epic romances, historical accounts, and religious texts and gradually became a genre in their own right. The objects in this book and in the exhibition that it accompanies invite close looking to witness this phenomenon during one of the most fertile periods in the history of art.

The decades between the creation of the Poncher Hours (ca. 1500; see figs. 1, 2) and that of the impressive leaf (ca. 1545; fig. 3) from the Missal

FIGURE 3 | *The Crucifixion*, Rome, ca. 1545, Vincent Raymond, miniature from the Missal of Pope Paul III, 37.2 × 26 cm (14⅝ × 10¼ in.), Ms. 85 (2003.116), recto

of Pope Paul III (r. 1534–49) saw the rise of landscape as a worthy genre of painting. Enclosed by an illusionistic frame inscribed with Latin phrases recited on the feast of the Exaltation of the Holy Cross, Christ's body has been rendered by the papal illuminator Vincent Raymond (active 1535–57) with heroic musculature reminiscent of that of male nudes by Michelangelo (1475–1564). The monumental cross is positioned with a high vantage point and dominates a vast, sweeping landscape, with the sun and moon overhead, recalling the eclipse at the moment when Christ breathed his final breath after suffering on behalf of humanity and symbolizing God's creation and dominion over the whole universe. In order to fully appreciate the significance of atmospheric perspective (a suggestion of depth or distance achieved by rendering the background view with colors lighter than those in the foreground) in this work, it is necessary to briefly examine proto-landscapes in manuscripts from the high Middle Ages and to keep in mind that, for about one thousand years before the Renaissance, European artists actively remembered the Greek and Roman visual, literary, and scientific traditions (of Zeuxis and Apelles or Theophrastus and Galen) they had inherited.

The Gothic period (1200–1400) witnessed a renewed interest in nature as a source of artistic inspiration, a phenomenon beautifully visualized in a *bas-de-page* scene from an early fourteenth-century manuscript: standing next to a lush tree, a youth gestures toward an ape seated on a rock nearby (fig. 4). The Latin phrase *ars simia naturae est* means "art is the ape of nature": art imitates the perfection inherent in all flora

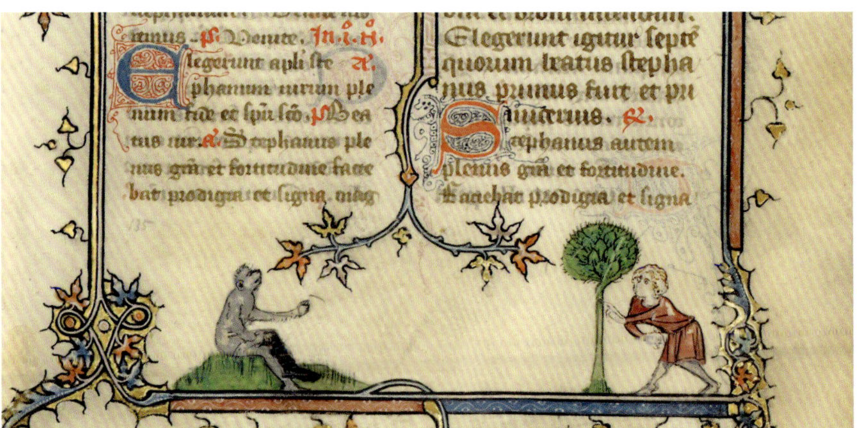

FIGURE 4 | *An Ape and a Youth*, Paris, ca. 1320–25, breviary, 16.7 × 11.1 cm (6⁹⁄₁₆ × 4⅜ in.), Ms. Ludwig IX 2 (83.ML.98), fol. 135 (detail)

and fauna in the same way that simians mimic humans. Likewise, artists emulated God through design, form, color, and composition. The individual elements of nature and the ever-changing landscapes depicted in illuminated manuscripts afforded reader-viewers a sense of transcendence well into the Renaissance. The sections that follow will briefly trace the development of landscape painting as a recognizable genre and the role of nature in the art of France, Italy, the Burgundian Netherlands, and Germany. These overviews will culminate in the mid-sixteenth century, when academies across Europe began to establish a hierarchy of genres for painted arts and humanist circles started to commingle with religious spheres.

THE FRENCH RENAISSANCE

In France, landscape painting emerged in the early fifteenth century, drawing on an earlier precedent. An illuminator working in Paris in the mid-thirteenth century incorporated a landscape in a *bas-de-page* scene from a psalter, showing four holy women wandering through a field of flowers while reading their manuscripts (fig. 5). One of the scrolling vines of the groundline grows to become a dragon, which flies in the company of music-making angels. This heavenly orchestra accompanies King David's harp-song within the initial *E*. Here, the ascenders and descenders of letterforms become mini-landscapes that enjoin marginal subjects with a musical interlude above, all of which complement the spiritual context of the psalmic writing. Just a few pages earlier, the author of the psalms had made a proclamation that echoed across the Middle Ages: "The earth is the Lord's, and everything in it, the world, and all who live in it" (Psalms 24:1).

The illuminator known as the Spitz Master (active ca. 1415–25) recognized the role played by physical environments in the narratives of biblical or apocryphal stories and incorporated a range of settings, verdant and architectural alike.[3] The artist imagined the Holy Family's quest for safety in Egypt as a journey through winding hills, past fruiting groves and shepherds grazing herds of sheep (fig. 6). Graceful figures, delicately rendered fabrics, and natural environments with cityscapes looming in the distance in a Parisian book of hours suggest that the artist was familiar with the oeuvre of the Limbourg brothers, arguably the greatest illuminators of the early fifteenth century.

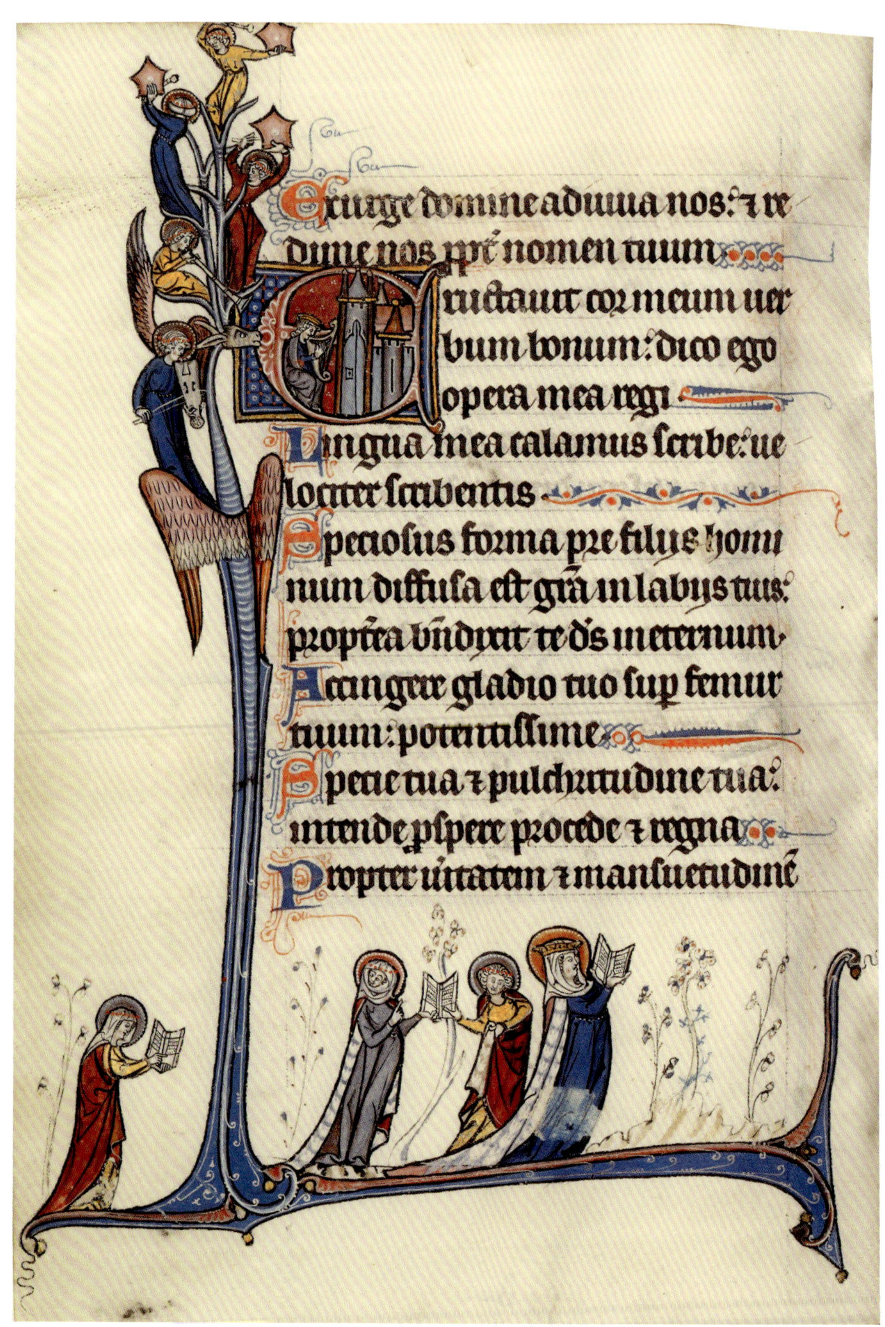

FIGURE 5 | Initial E: *David Playing the Harp*, northeastern France, ca. 1270–80, Bute Master, Bute Psalter, 17 × 11.9 cm (6¹¹⁄₁₆ × 4¹¹⁄₁₆ in.), Ms. 47 (92.MK.92), fol. 61v

FIGURE 6 | *The Flight into Egypt*, Paris, ca. 1420, Spitz Master, book of hours, 20.5 × 15.9 cm (8¹⁄₁₆ × 6¼ in.), Ms. 57 (94.ML.26), fol. 103v

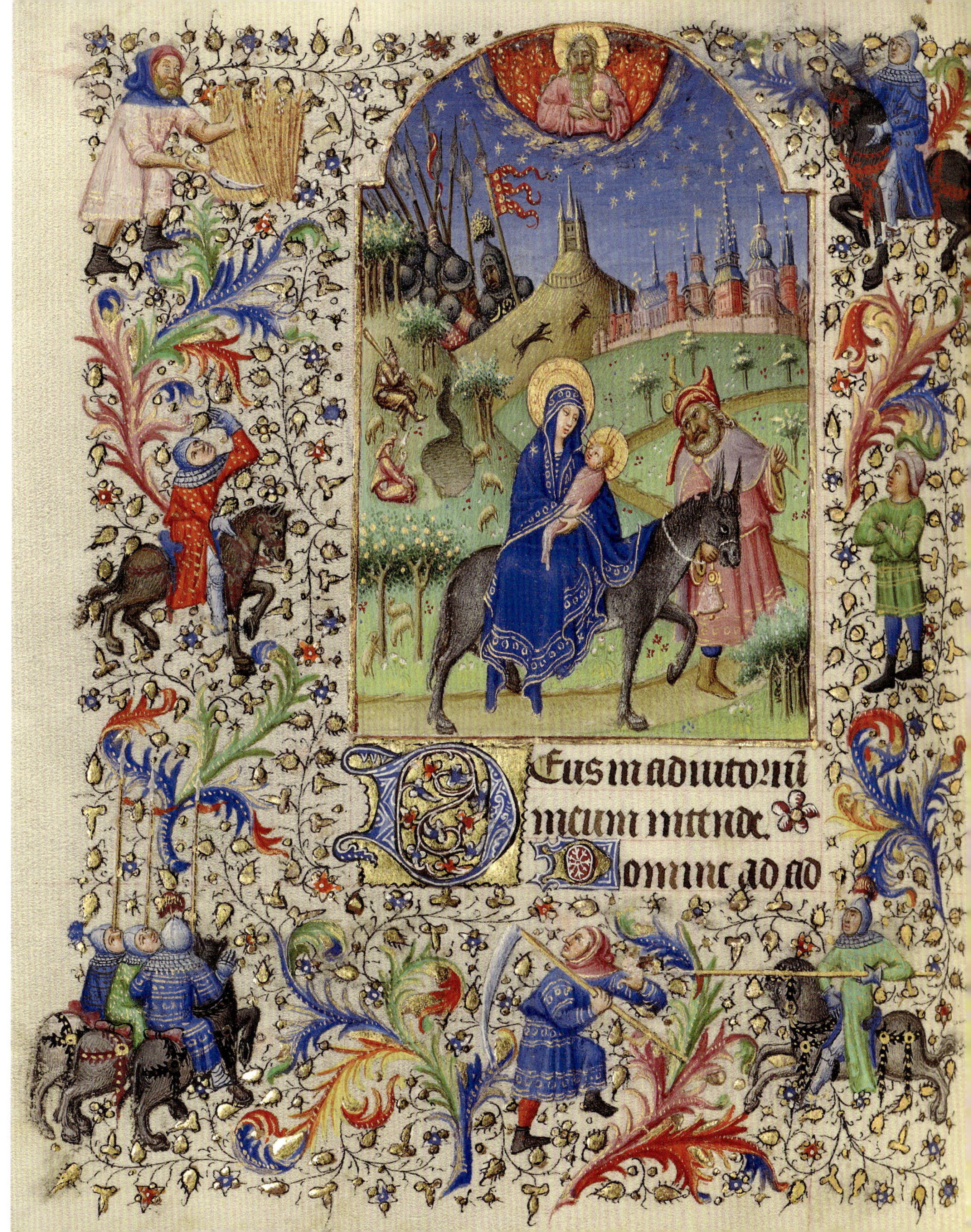

Eus in adiutorium
meum intende.
Domine ad ad

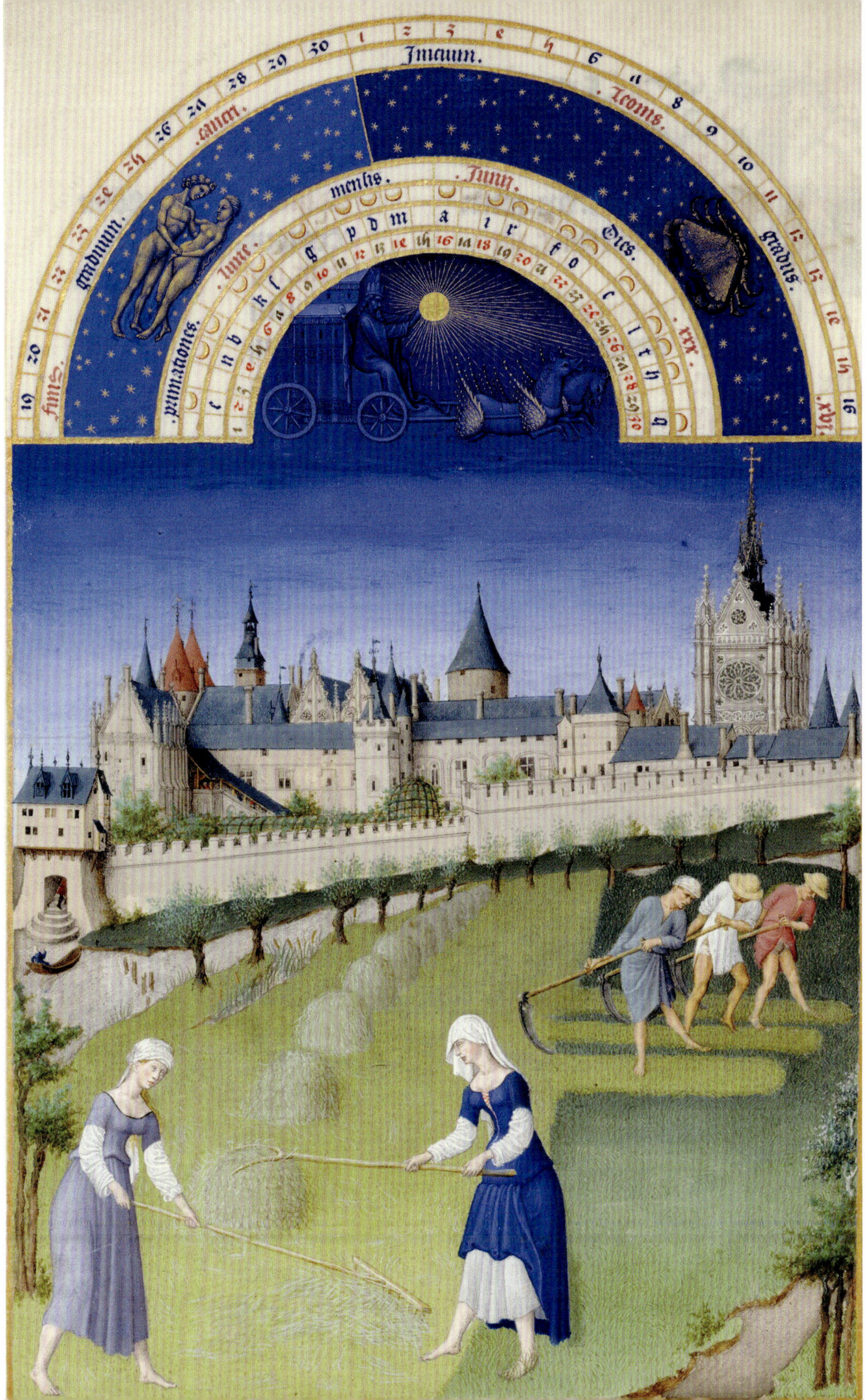

Although left incomplete after the sudden deaths of both the patron and the artists, the *Très Riches Heures* remains one of the treasures of French late Gothic illumination. The three Dutch Limbourg brothers (Jean, Herman, and Paul; active ca. 1385–1416) worked in Paris at the beginning of the fifteenth century and fulfilled the commission for Jean de France, duc de Berry (1340–1416). At the start of the manuscript is a calendar of important Christian feast days, decorated with representations of the zodiac and seasonal occupations. These full-page scenes break with traditional calendar designs by setting the activities representative of the months in real locations that would have been familiar to the patron. On the page for June (fig. 7), five peasants work the fields outside the Île de la Cité (the spire of Sainte-Chapelle is visible within the walls).[4] Each dynamic calendar landscape reflects seasonal changes and shows a developing sense of proportion and accurate spatial relationships. At the end of the calendar section is a full-page image of a nude figure within a mandorla containing the twelve zodiacal symbols; these symbols are also arranged on the figure's body (fig. 8). Medieval medicine was

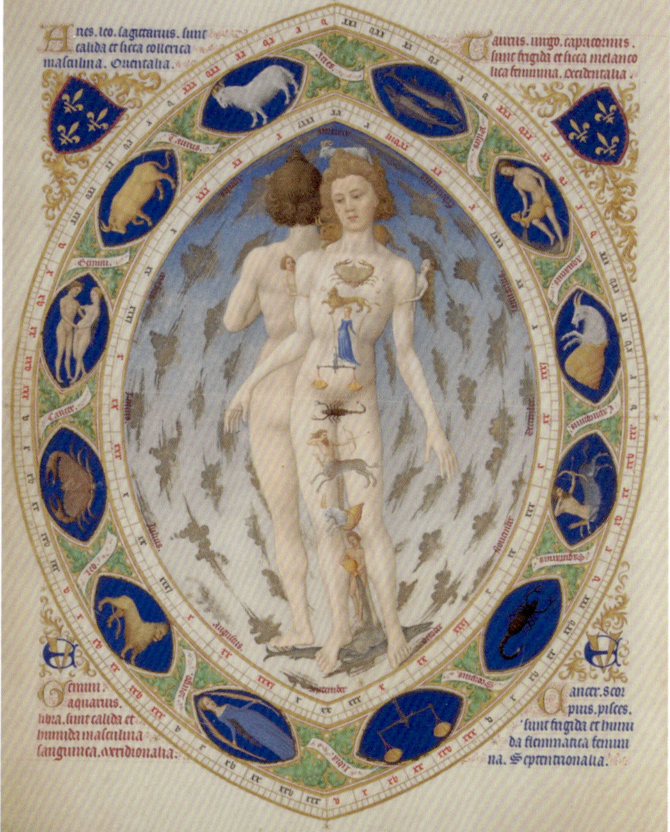

FIGURE 7 | *June* (Palais de la Cité and the Sainte-Chapelle), probably Paris, ca. 1412–16, Limbourg brothers, *Très Riches Heures*, 29 × 21 cm (11⅜ × 8¼ in.). Chantilly, Musée Condé, Ms. 65, fol. 6v

FIGURE 8 | *The Zodiacal Man*, probably Paris, ca. 1412–16, Limbourg brothers, *Très Riches Heures*, 29 × 21 cm (11⅜ × 8¼ in.). Chantilly, Musée Condé, Ms. 65, fol. 14v

often guided by the belief that planetary and other astral movements affected the body by altering the humoral fluids (blood, phlegm, and yellow and black bile);[5] these relationships influenced every action, including one's devotional life.[6] By mapping the cosmos onto the body, the illuminators suggest an empirical approach to the universe whereby human beings perceive and know the world through their senses. The Limbourg brothers laid the groundwork for artists such as Jean Fouquet (ca. 1425–1478), whose delicate figures, subtle use of light, and direct observations of the natural world made him one of the most celebrated painters in Renaissance France. In the Hours of Simon de Varie, made for a knight and treasurer at the court of Charles VII (r. 1422–61), Fouquet's three-dimensional figures stand on a simple green patch surrounded by trellised bluebells (fig. 9).[7]

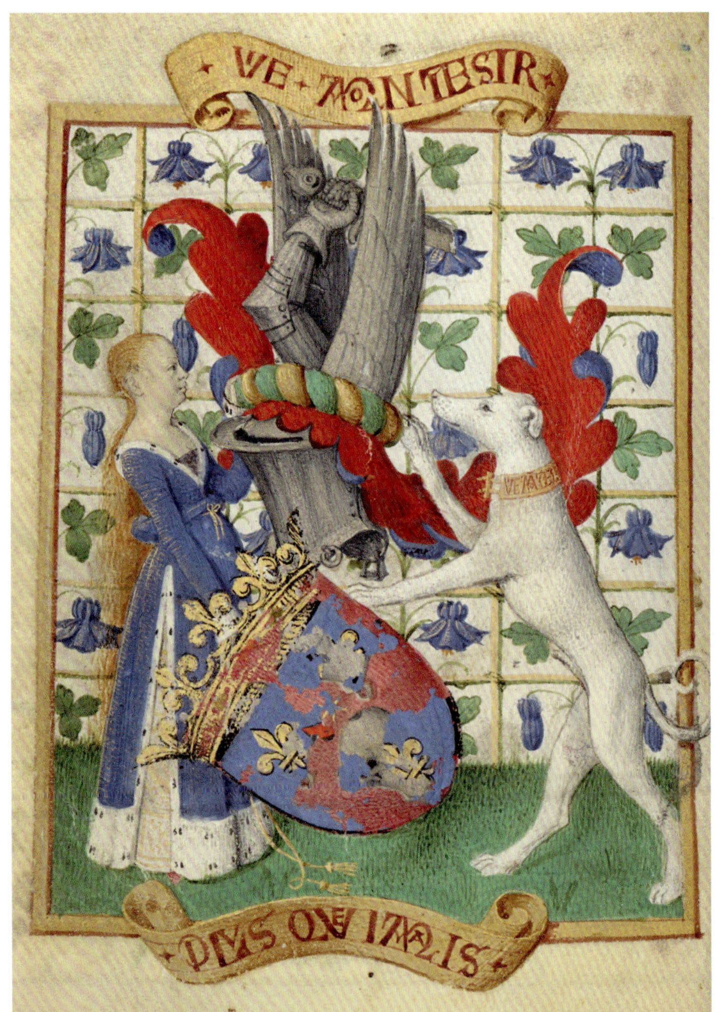

FIGURE 9 | *Coat of Arms Held by a Woman and a Greyhound*, Tours or Paris, 1455, Jean Fouquet, Hours of Simon de Varie, 11.4 × 8.3 cm (4½ × 3¼ in.), Ms. 7 (85.ML.27), fol. 2v

By the mid-sixteenth century, artists in France looked not only to Italy but also to Flanders and Germany for inspiration. The majestic illuminations by the Master of the Getty Epistles (see fig. 72), for example, betray the influence of Flemish drawings in their intricately rendered scattered borders, and of German prints in the delineation of the background where human architecture meets the realm of nature.

FROM TRECENTO THEATRICS TO HIGH RENAISSANCE HUMANISM IN ITALY

Beginning around 1340, a group of laymen and laywomen known as the Compagnia di Sant'Agnese gathered each year in the church of Santa Maria del Carmine in Florence to stage a theatrical performance of Christ's ascension. The sets likely included a Jerusalem landscape and a mechanical device that raised an actor high into the vaulted rafters of the church that simulated heaven. The *compagnia* commissioned an artist from the orbit of Pacino di Bonaguida (active ca. 1303–47) to render the dramatic biblical event in a *laudario*, or book of hymns of praise, and the illumination includes two of the group's members kneeling as supplicants in the lower roundel, serving as models of perpetual devotion (fig. 10).[8] In the miniature above, Christ's followers stand in awe amid a green landscape that today appears quite sparse but that once abounded in small flowering plants (now visible only under ultraviolet light). The two olive trees on the tiny peak below Christ foreshadow an event in the book of Revelation when two witnesses represented as two olive trees are killed by the Antichrist on the Mount of Olives—from which Christ ascended to heaven—before the Antichrist himself is slain there by Christ at the Second Coming (Revelation 11:4).

Toward the end of the fourteenth century, illuminators in Florence at the Camaldolese monastery of Santa Maria degli Angeli began decorating what would become the most celebrated multivolume choir-book set of the Renaissance. Lorenzo Monaco (ca. 1370–ca. 1425) provided many drawings for these volumes, and his *Ascension of Christ*—composed similarly to the Pacinesque scene in the *laudario* just mentioned—was later painted by followers of Fra Angelico (ca. 1395–1455; fig. 11).[9] Here, again, the two trees atop mountainous peaks and the olive branches held by the angels at the upper

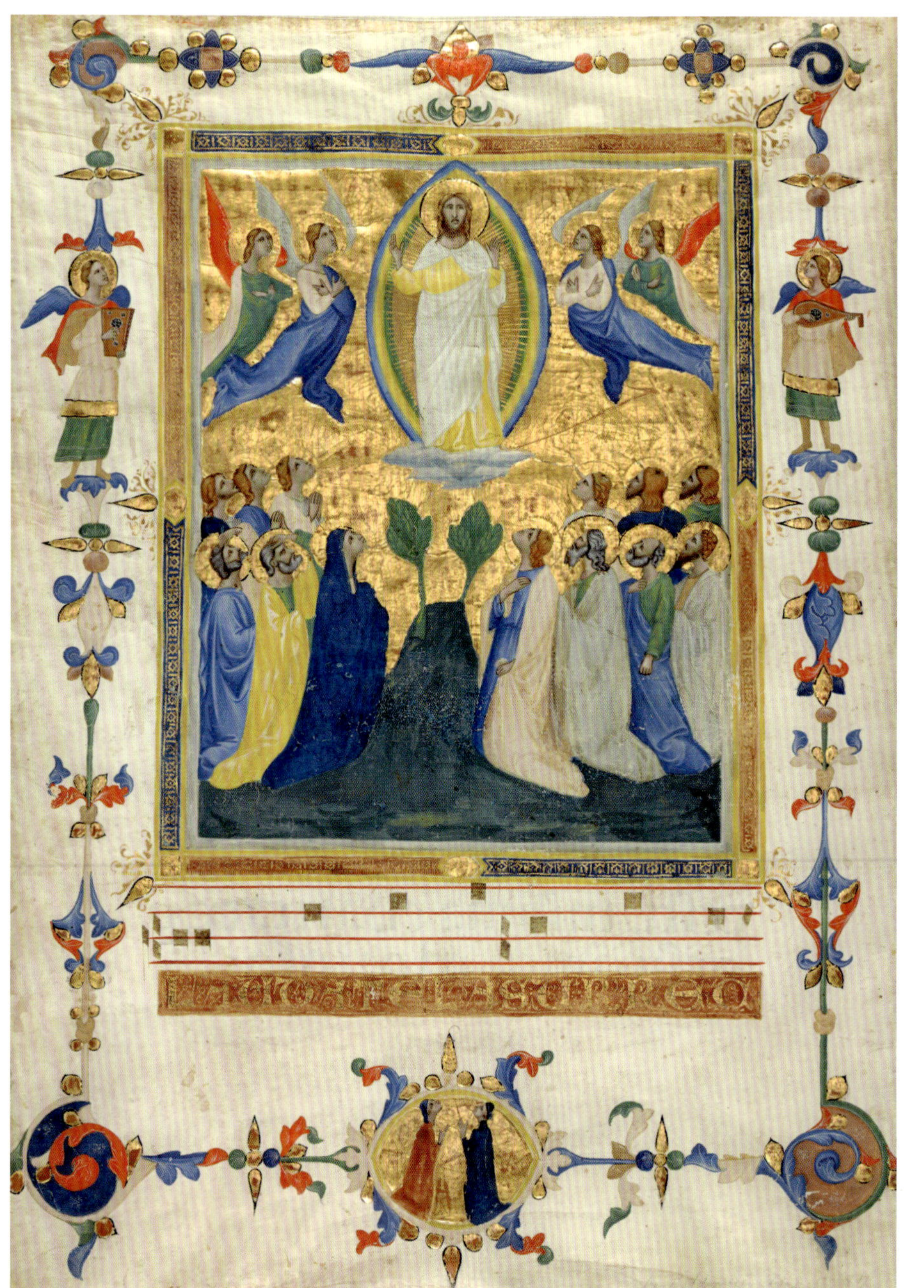

FIGURE 10 | *The Ascension of Christ*, Florence, ca. 1340, Pacino di Bonaguida, leaf from the Laudario of Sant'Agnese, 44.4 × 31.8 cm (17½ × 12½ in.), Ms. 80a (2005.26), verso

FIGURE 11 | *The Ascension of Christ*, Florence, designed ca. 1410, completed ca. 1431, Lorenzo Monaco, Zanobi di Benedetto Strozzi, and Battista di Biagio Sanguini, cutting from a gradual, 40.2 × 32.7 cm (15¹³⁄₁₆ × 12⅞ in.), Ms. 78 (2003.104), recto

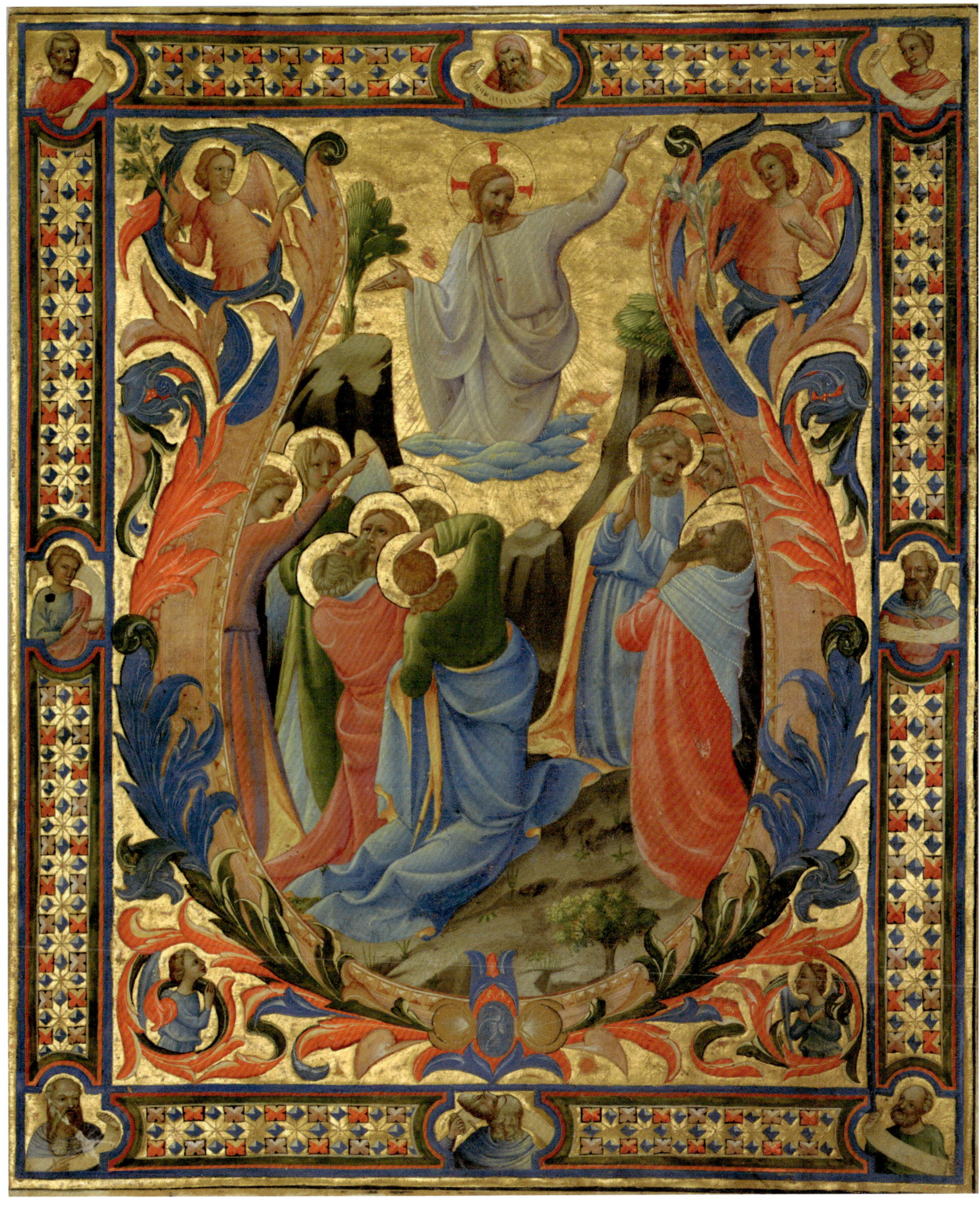

terminals of the initial *V* remind the faithful choir of Christ's Second Coming. Until about the second half of the fifteenth century, a tension existed between an artist's meticulous brushwork, or ability to simulate objects as if directly observed from life, and the desire for imagination, creative expression, or *capriccio* (an expression of individual whim, at times a mixture of fantasy and reality), including, in some instances, a radiant but flattening gold background.

To witness this tension, one need only turn to the northern Italian courts. In Milan, for example, the lord and later duke Gian Galeazzo Visconti (r. 1395–1402) commissioned a book of hours from Giovannino dei Grassi (ca. 1350–1398) and his son Salomone (active ca. 1397–ca. 1400), both of whom produced luxury copies of texts on natural history and medicine filled with carefully rendered flora and fauna; each also compiled model books with dynamic examples of *naturalia*. A generation later, Duke Filippo Maria Visconti (r. 1412–47) and his wife, Marie of Savoy (1411–1469), employed Belbello da Pavia (active 1430–70) to complete the volume, and one immediately notices Belbello's penchant for vibrant colors and fantastic, even vision-like scenes of biblical subjects. The Dei Grassis' ability to naturalistically realize life-size insects that appear to crawl across the page, as well as the clever approach to representing God separating the water from the land, stands in stark contrast to Belbello's display of refined splendor and golden nocturnal light on the facing page (fig. 12).[10]

In nearby Mantua, a talented artist known as Pisanello (by 1395–ca. 1455) was held on retainer by the Gonzaga family, which valued his remarkable ability to render surfaces with elegant patterning and his spellbinding studies observed directly from life, studio models, and pattern books.[11] In a small historiated initial *S* once part of a large choir book (fig. 13), Pisanello's hand is recognized in the miniscule strokes of paint in the flowing manes and fur that delineate muscular equine bodies and in the fanciful rider's portrait features, perhaps those of Ludovico III Gonzaga, Marquis of Mantua (r. 1444–78). Certain other details, such as the atmospheric perspective and landscape, may have been assigned to the illuminator known as the Master of the Antiphonal *Q* of San Giorgio Maggiore (ca. 1440–ca. 1470), who at the courts in Lombardy and the Veneto developed a refined ability to depict expansive vistas.[12]

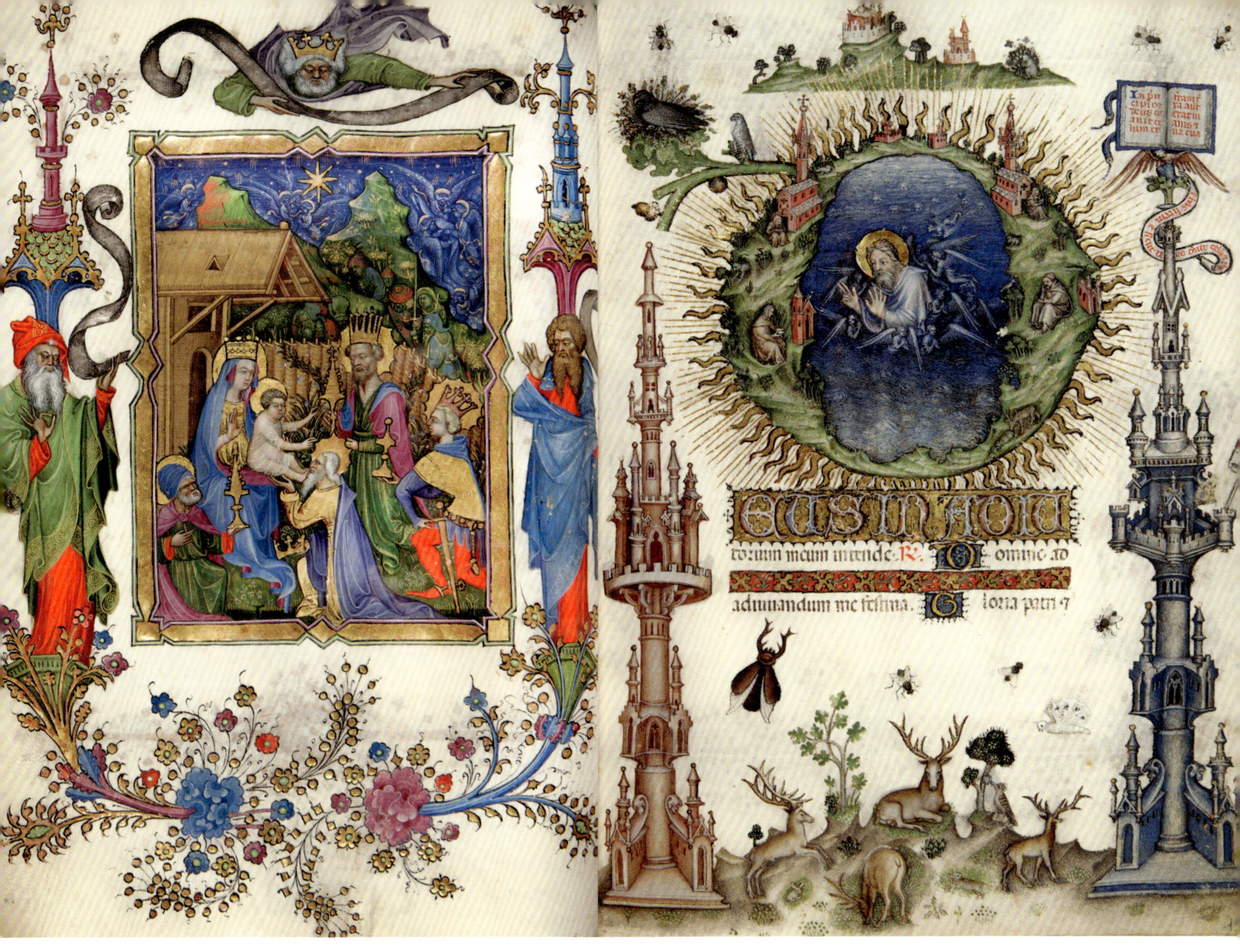

FIGURE 12 | *The Adoration of the Magi;
Creation of the World*, Milan, ca. 1390,
completed ca. 1430, Giovannino and
Salomone dei Grassi and Belbello da
Pavia, Visconti Hours, 24.7 × 17.9 cm
(9¹¹⁄₁₆ × 7¹⁄₁₆ in.). Florence, Biblioteca
Nazionale Centrale, LF 18v–19

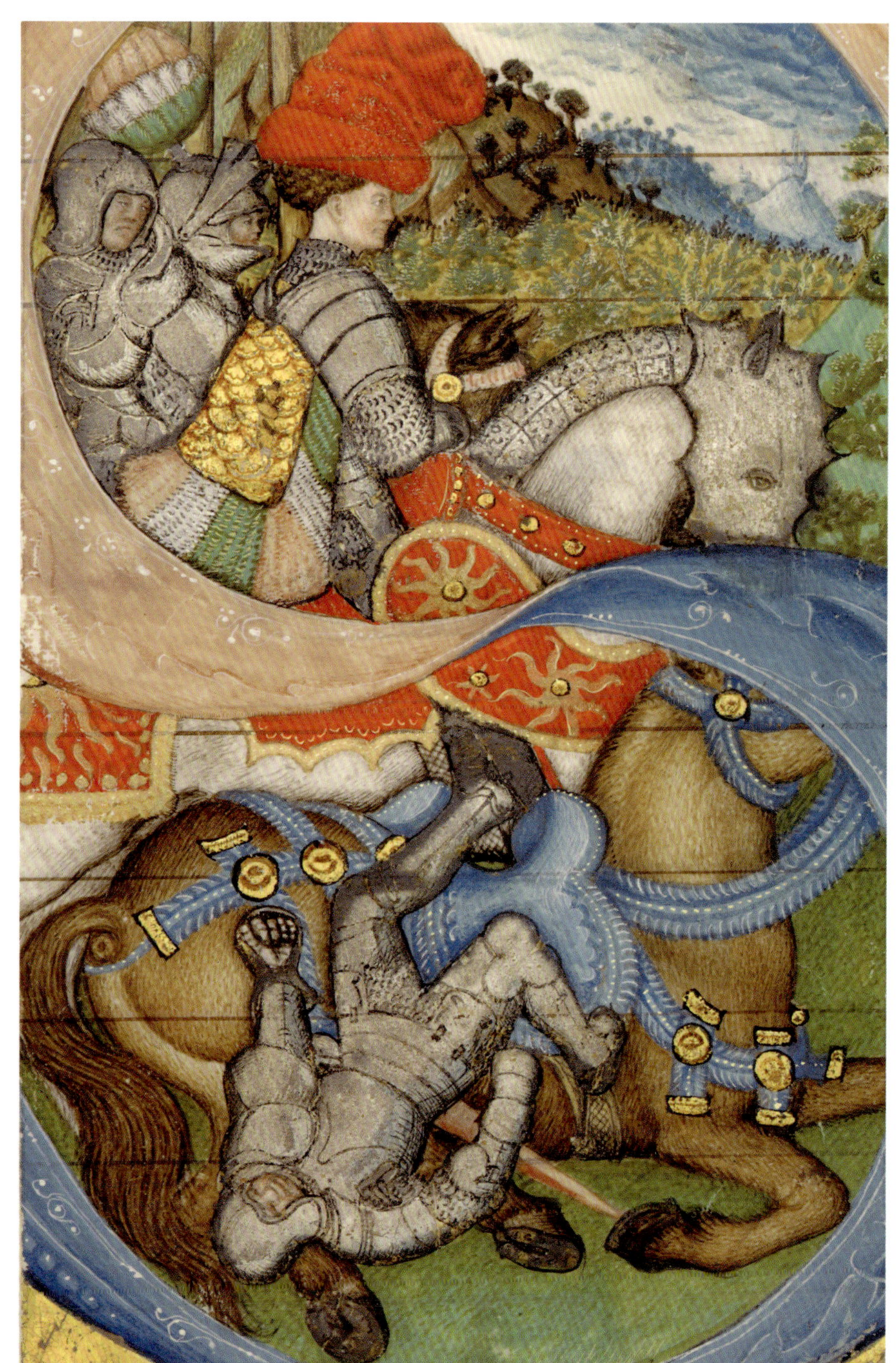

FIGURE 13 | Initial S: *The Conversion of Saint Paul*, Italian, ca. 1440–50, attributed to Pisanello and the Master of the Antiphonal *Q* of San Giorgio Maggiore, cutting from a gradual, 14.1 × 8.9 cm (5⁹⁄₁₆ × 3½ in.), Ms. 41 (91.MS.5), verso

When one returns to central Italy, one sees that artists began to conceive the painted surface mathematically and as a window onto the world—ideas put forth by the painter-theorist Piero della Francesca (ca. 1415/20–1492) and the humanist architect Leon Battista Alberti (1404–1472). Indeed, Alberti's "window" is a metaphor describing the geometric confines of a painting as an open portal onto the world. One finds this device employed by Giuliano Amadei (active ca. 1446–1490s) in a page once part of a manuscript commissioned by Pope Innocent VIII (r. 1484–92) for use during the celebration of Mass in the Sistine Chapel (fig. 14). Giuliano rendered nature's anguish through the oncoming and foreboding clouds that seem to mirror the inner turmoil of the Virgin Mary, Saint John, and Mary Magdalene in the foreground.[13] From the tiny rocks and fledgling plants at the base of the cross to the dappled light hitting the leaves of trees in the midground and the cool distant palette of the background, Giuliano achieved on a small scale a sense of depth and space that rivals the naturalism found in large altarpieces. In the late fifteenth century, the papacy celebrated this hallmark of the Florentine school of painting by commissioning Sandro Botticelli (ca. 1445–1510), Domenico Ghirlandaio (1449–1494), Perugino (1446–1524), and others to fresco the walls of the Sistine Chapel with scenes from the lives of Moses and Christ. The missal illuminated by Giuliano not only complemented the chapel's visual program but served as the object of the pope's devotion and spiritual leadership.

At about the same moment, the discovery of the enigmatic frescoes in the emperor Nero's Domus Aurea in Rome, buried since antiquity, aroused a flurry of interest among a range of artists and patrons. The so-called *grotteschi* (painted hybrid figures found in the cave-like rooms of the emperor's pleasure palace) immediately began to appear in various media, including liturgical manuscripts, and continued to be employed for the next several decades, thereby establishing a paradox between nature and artifice, the real (observation/experience) and the fantastic (invention/imagination), and *auctoritas* (authoritative precedent) and *capriccio*. Pope Alexander VI Borgia (r. 1492–1503) entrusted Antonio da Monza (active ca. 1480–1505) with illuminating a set of choir books for use at the church of Santa Maria in Aracoeli, a structure that effectively overlooked the ruined Roman fora, wherein lie the *grotteschi* (fig. 15).[14] A triumphant Christ stands above a tomb

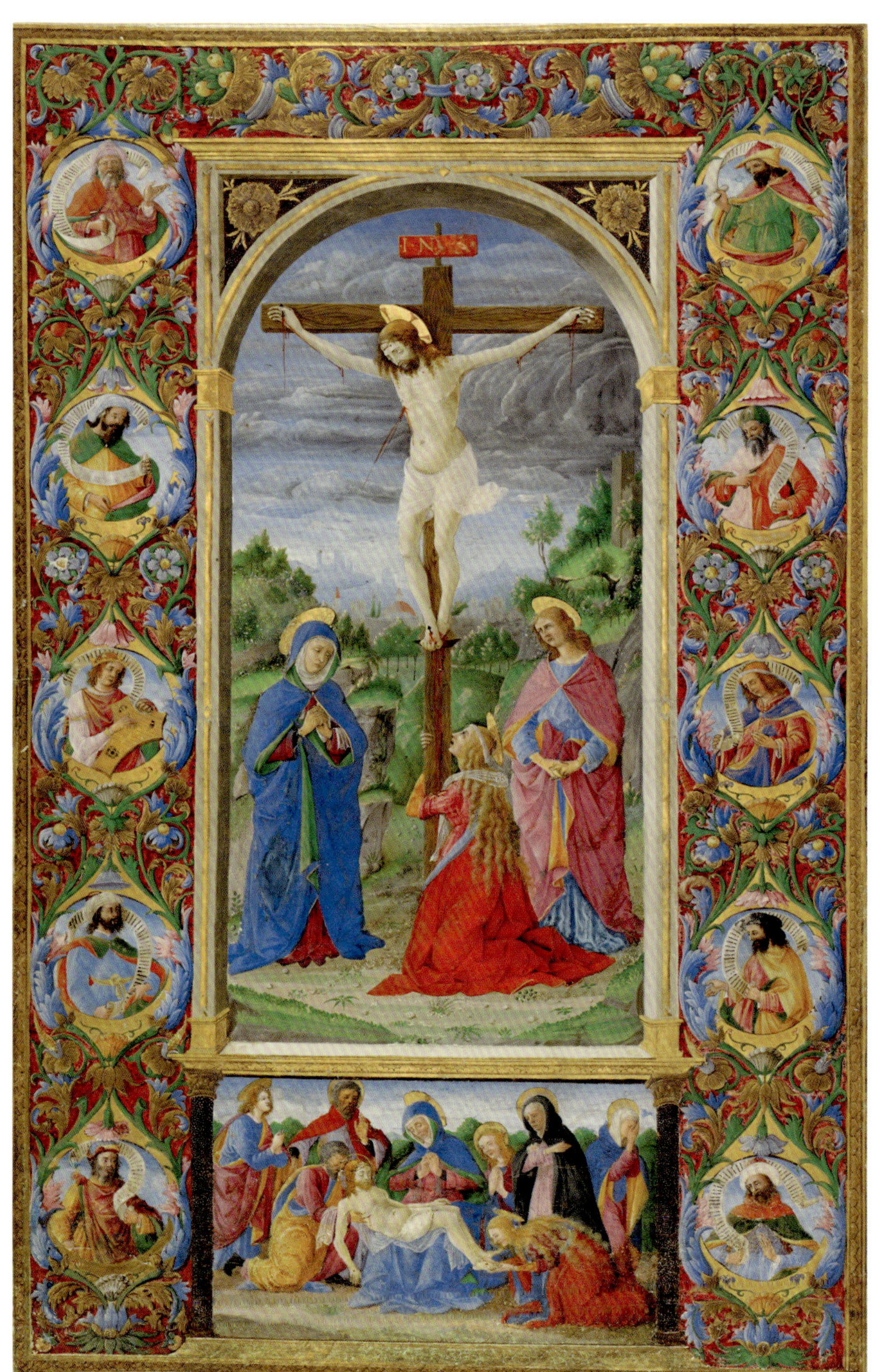

FIGURE 14 | *The Crucifixion*, Rome, 1484–92, Giuliano Amadei, leaf from the Missal of Innocent VII, 39.7 × 24.1 cm (15⅝ × 9½ in.), Ms. 110 (2012.2), recto

FIGURE 15 | Initial *R*: *The Resurrection*, Rome, late 15th or early 16th century, Antonio da Monza, gradual, 64.3 × 43.5 cm (25⁵⁄₁₆ × 17⅛ in.), Ms. Ludwig VI 3 (83.MH.86), fol. 16

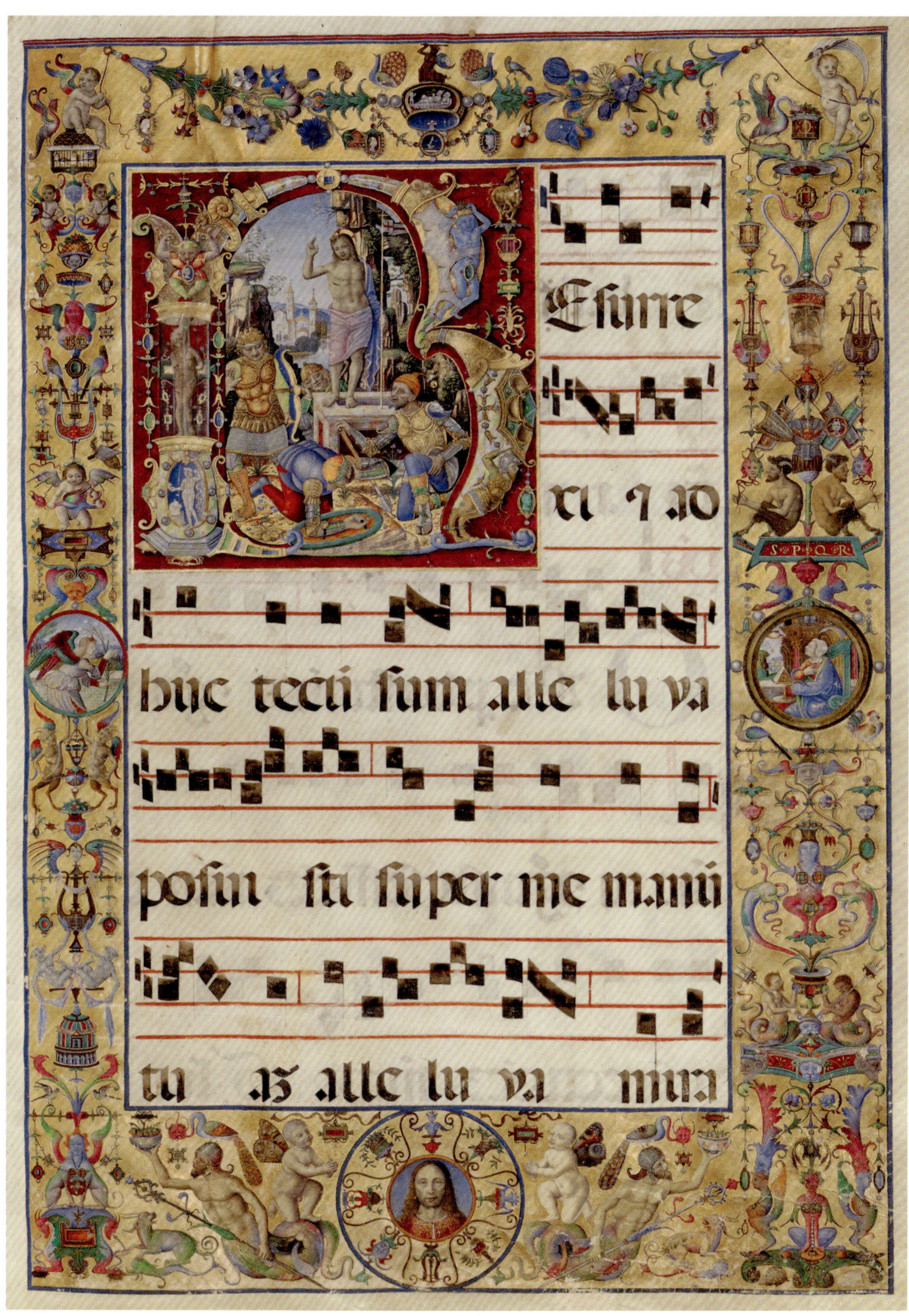

Esurre
tu i ao
huc tecu sum alle lu ya
posui sti super me manu
tu as alle lu ya mira

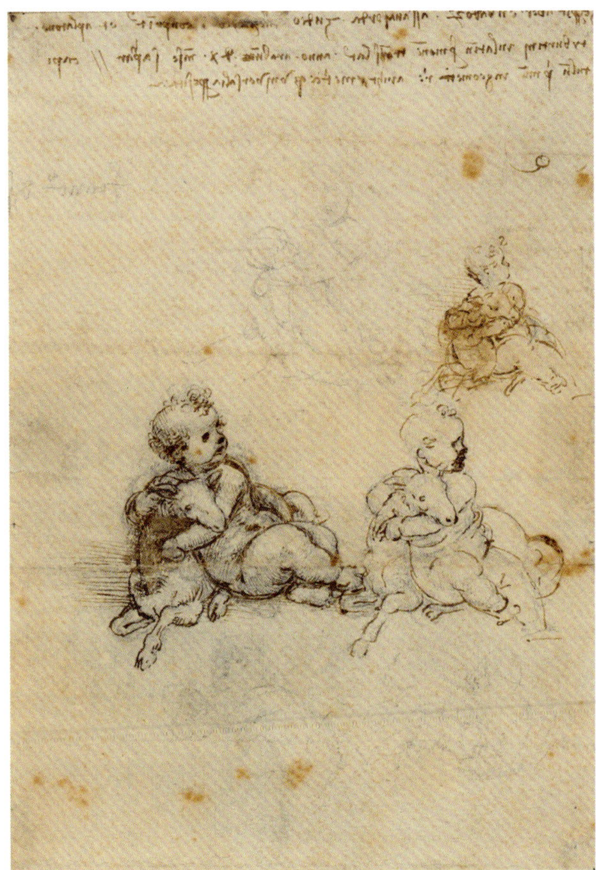

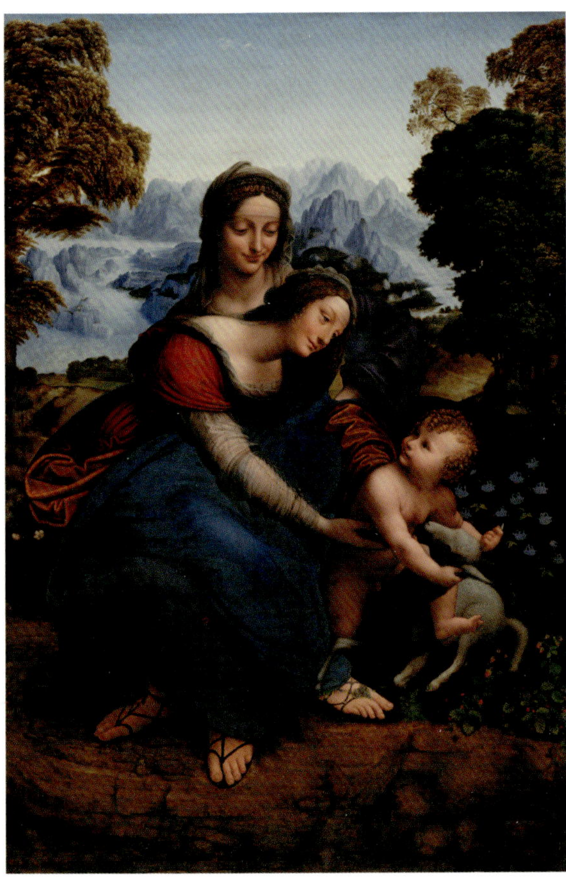

set within a large initial *R*, while soldiers jostle below, startled by the miraculous event. Beyond, the contemporaneous cityscape grounds the narrative in the physical world, while the realm of imagination abounds in the margins, where cameos with classical subjects mingle with a hodgepodge of sprites, gorgons, and indescribably odd and monstrous beasts. Yet all forms are given equal treatment and convincingly delineated.

Leonardo da Vinci (1452–1519) wrote often about nature, and the numerous works of art that he created—from drawings to paintings—reveal his respect for and debt to the natural world and direct observation of its many wonders.[15] On a single sheet of paper, Leonardo drew various studies of the Christ child embracing a lamb and made inscriptions in his characteristic mirror handwriting (fig. 16). With chalk and pen and ink, Leonardo worked out subtly different poses in order to achieve the truest effect. Studies like these were later incorporated into larger works such as *The Virgin and Child with Saint Anne*, produced by the master's workshop likely under his supervision (fig. 17). Nature abounds in this and other versions of the same composition by Leonardo. The icy blue mountains merge with the sky to establish a distant vista and contrast with the warm colors of the midground and foreground; every leaf on each tree and plant is painted with infinitesimal care, as are the petals on the columbine flowers and the curls of the lamb's wool and of Christ's hair. These were some of the painterly effects that ushered in the High Renaissance in Italy, and altarpieces and devotional manuscripts became staging grounds for demonstrating an artist's ability to rival nature (*ars simia naturae est* revived in full force).

The muscular and almost sculptural body of the crucified Christ by Vincent Raymond (see fig. 3) certainly reveals the artist's interest in a form of naturalism based on the observation of live models or sculptures, yet the hazy landscape beneath a cloudy sky suggests that nature itself posed a challenge in the simulation of believable space on a two-dimensional surface. The Renaissance is often treated as a monolithic period that saw the rebirth of an interest in classical antiquity and the reemergence of humanist philosophical texts. Italy looms large in these associations, yet artists from the Burgundian and Habsburg courts of northern Europe were integral to, if not paramount in, the history and development of landscape painting and nature studies during this period.

FLEMISH PICTORIAL INVENTION IN BIBLIOPHILE COURTS AND MERCHANT TOWNS

During the fifteenth century, Netherlandish artists, especially manuscript illuminators, revolutionized the Renaissance pictorial field.[16] Seeing the divine in the banal and earthly, they created the precursors to the landscape genre—not "pure" or empty natural spaces but environments with characters and an embedded narrative. Patronage of the Burgundian dukes and their courts set the standard for chivalric and royal magnificence, permeating Flemish visual culture and inspiring those outside noble spheres, such as merchants, members of the clergy, and wealthy citizens, to commission works for

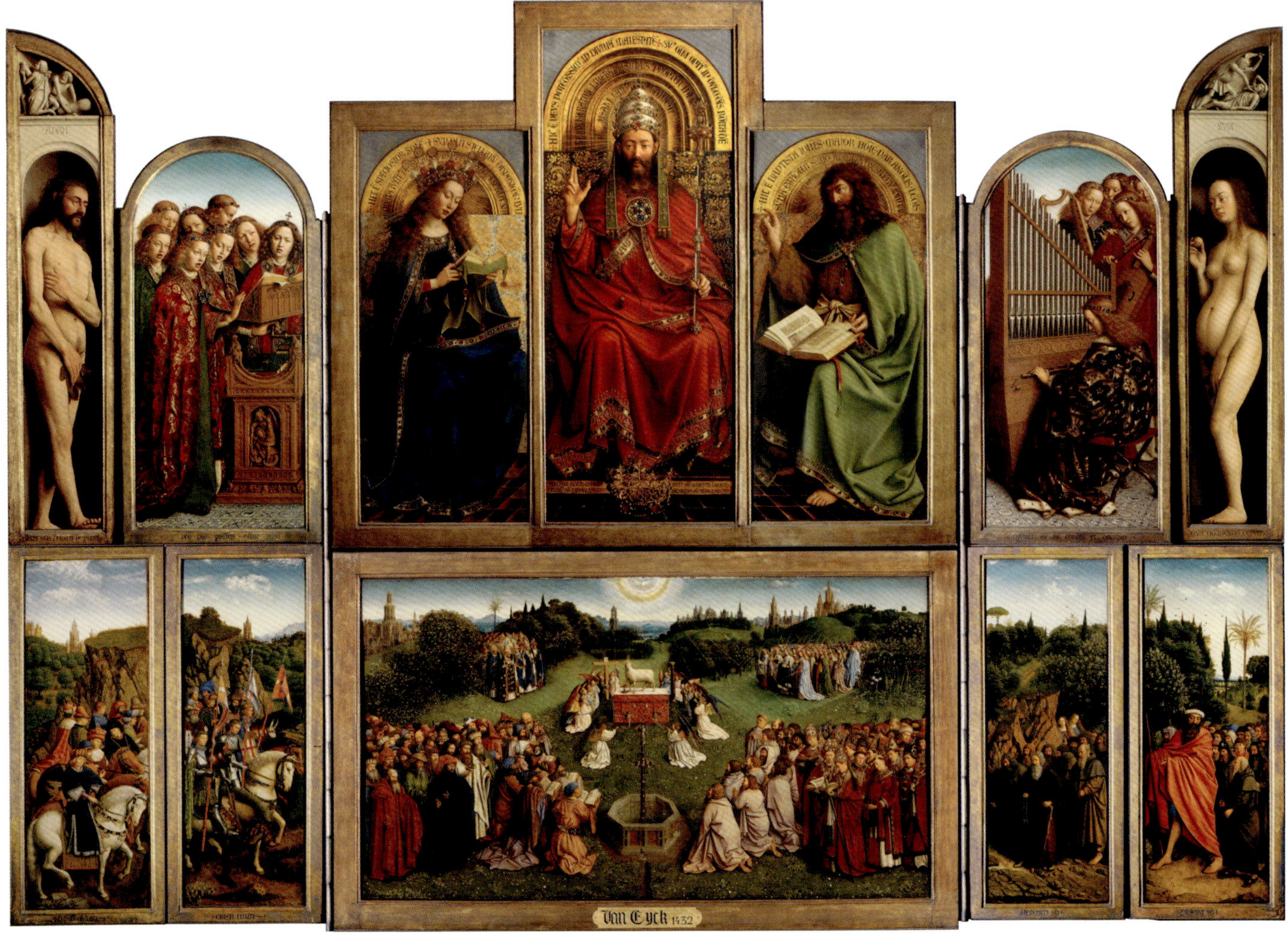

FIGURE 18 | Jan van Eyck (Flemish, ca. 1390–1441) and Hubert van Eyck (Flemish, ca. 1370–1426). *Ghent Altarpiece*, 1432. Tempera and oil on panel, opened: 340 × 440 cm (11 ft. 2 in. × 14 ft. 5 in.). Ghent, Belgium, Saint Bavo Cathedral

FIGURE 19 | Jan van Eyck (Flemish, ca. 1390–1441) and Hubert van Eyck (Flemish, ca. 1370–1426), *The Adoration of the Mystic Lamb*, detail of figure 18

private and public use. Violent iconoclastic reactions during the Protestant Reformation and various wars that plagued the European continent resulted in a lack of surviving documents and fewer extant works by Netherlandish artists compared to their Italian counterparts—phenomena that have fundamentally affected the study of Northern Renaissance art.[17]

In the *Ghent Altarpiece* (fig. 18), commissioned by the merchant Jodocus Vijd (d. 1439) for a chapel in the church of Saint John in Ghent, one continuous landscape spreads across the five lower panels depicting *The Adoration of the Mystic Lamb* (fig. 19). Lush rolling hills and sylvan groves give way to rocky precipices, medieval towns emerge from the tree line, and a flowering grass echoes the millefleur (thousand-flower) tapestries of the day, characterized by backgrounds of densely populated flowers with

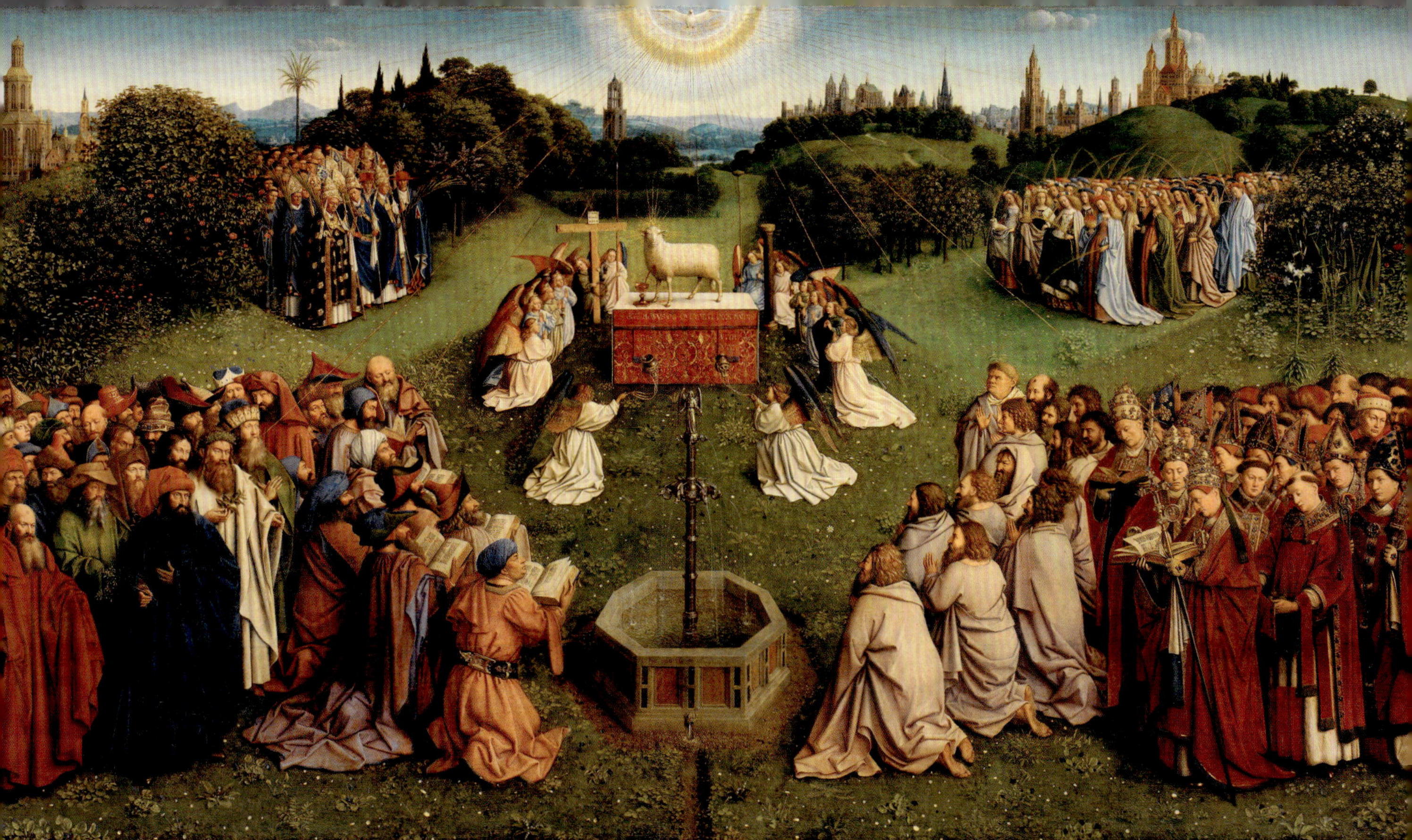

almost no negative space.[18] Jan van Eyck (ca. 1390–1441), who completed the altarpiece begun by his brother Hubert van Eyck (ca. 1370–1426), appeals to a modern viewer with his realism and detail, but at the time this exactness was seen as evidence of artistic talent and of nature as a reflection of God. Allegorical landscapes formed by weaving together built environments, observations from nature, and sacred subjects became a hallmark of Flemish Renaissance manuscript painting.

Many Netherlandish artists, including Jan van Eyck, the painter Hans Memling (ca. 1430–1494), and the illuminator Willem Vrelant (active 1454–81), lived in guild-run Bruges and catered to the local market and courtly or foreign patrons. Memling was skilled at painting from life—a talent that included rendering the natural world.[19] In a break with traditional Flemish portraits set before dark backgrounds, Memling's subjects sit with high vantage points before expansive vistas. His creativity with landscape appears in *Scenes from the Advent and Triumph of Christ* (fig. 20), which uses both architecture and geography to isolate and highlight numerous episodes simultaneously.[20]

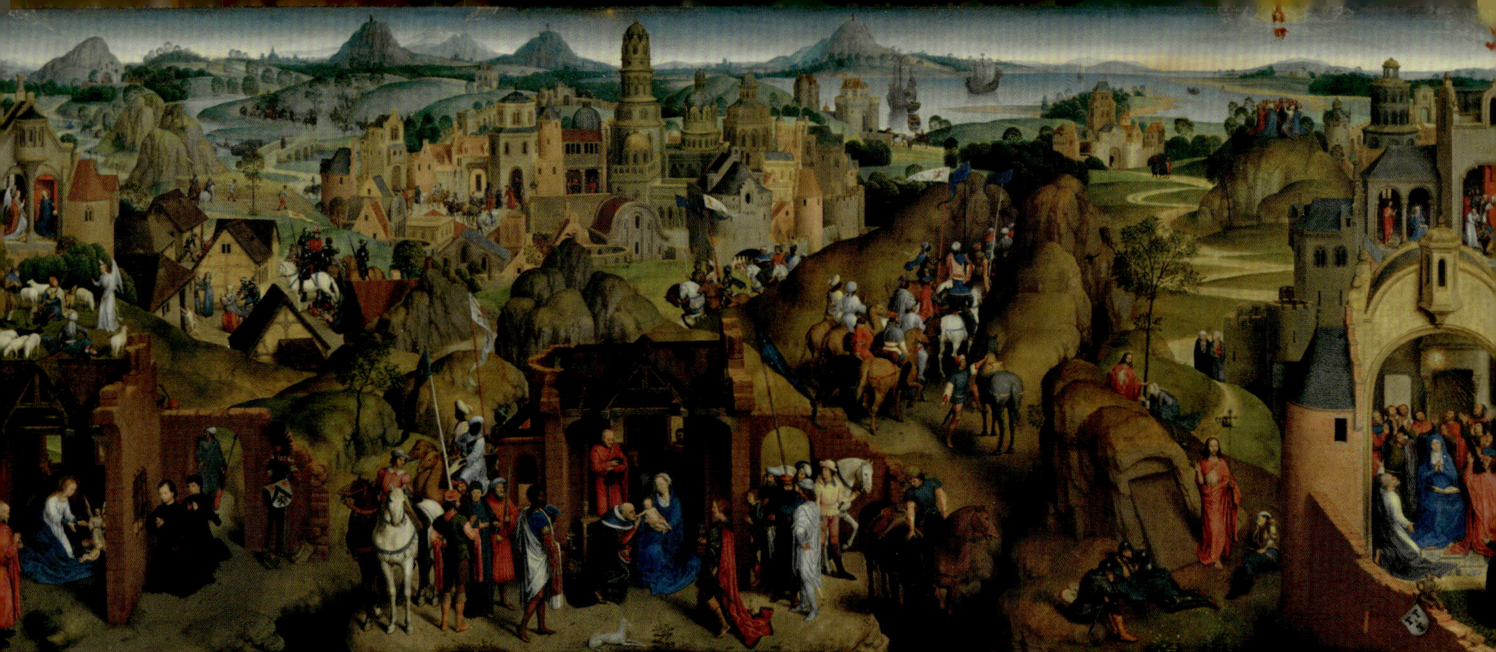

This virtual pilgrimage breaks down divisions between interior and exterior, grounding religious narrative in a contemporary setting.

Depictions of the natural world were not merely utilized within the background of miniatures; they figured predominantly in the accompanying marginalia. Traditionally in the fourteenth and well into the fifteenth century, these margins took the form of winding acanthus leaves interspersed with occasional budding blooms or grotesques. This tapestry effect is common in manuscripts, maximizing the allotted space for decoration on a page. By the late fifteenth century, innovative illuminators from the Netherlands were painting trompe l'oeil borders consisting of narrative scenes or harmoniously arranged flowers, fruits, animals, precious gems, and other objects.[21] Artists such as Simon Bening (ca. 1483–1561), Gerard Horenbout (ca. 1465–ca. 1541), the Master of Mary of Burgundy (active 1469–83), and the Master of James IV of Scotland (active before 1465–1541) all painted in this illusionistic Ghent-Bruges style. The Spinola Hours was possibly commissioned for Margaret of Austria (1480–1530), the daughter of the Holy Roman emperor Maximilian I (r. 1493–1519) and Mary of Burgundy (1457–1482). *Naturalia* are fundamental to the illumination program, beginning with seasonal activities in the calendar and continuing throughout the margins and miniatures. Characteristically Ghent-Bruges borders surround the suffrage (or prayer) to Mary Magdalene (fig. 21). Delicate red and white dianthus flowers grow from a pot, while cornflowers and an iris bloom from a faint groundline or are scattered against the

FIGURE 20 | Hans Memling (Netherlandish, ca. 1430–1494), *Scenes from the Advent and Triumph of Christ*, ca. 1480. Oil on panel, 81 × 189 cm (31⅞ × 74⅜ in.). Munich, Alte Pinakothek, inv. WAF 668

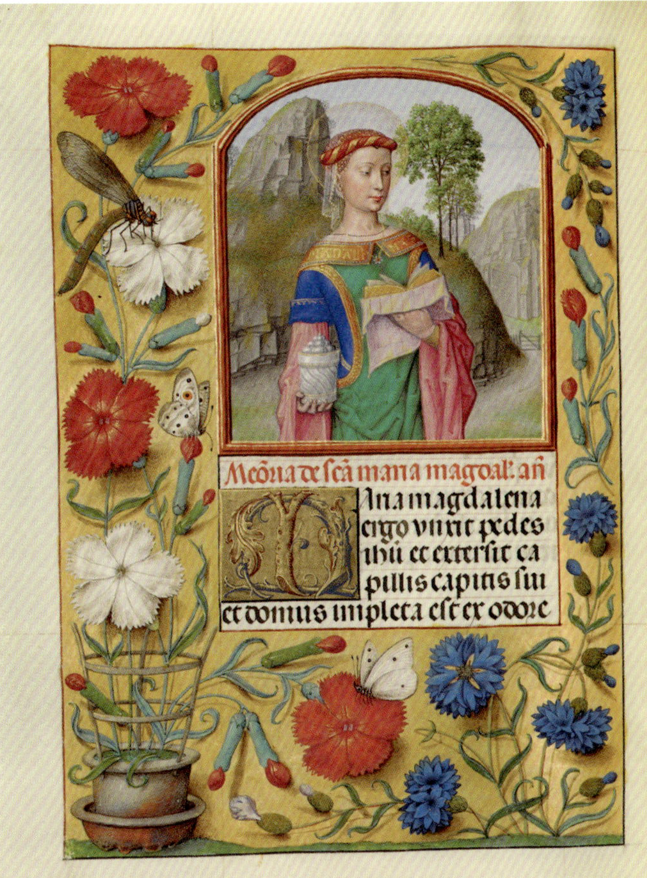
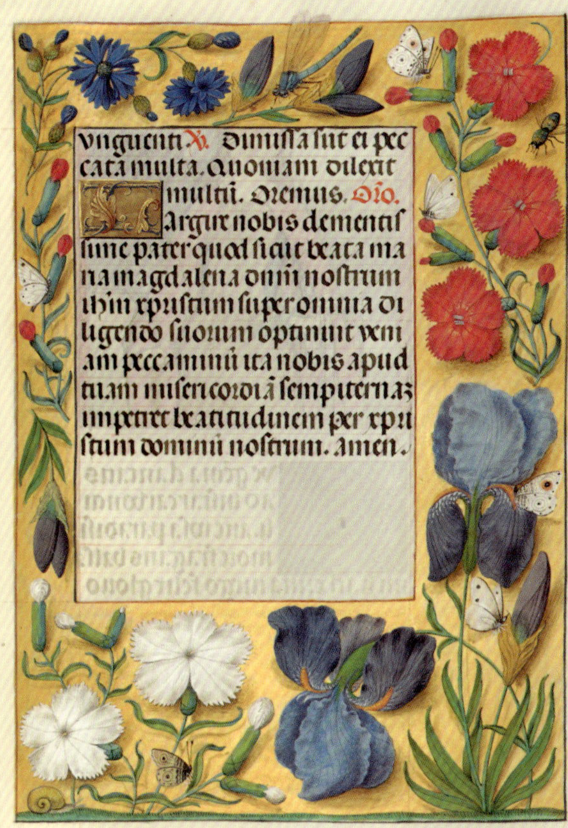

FIGURE 21 | *Mary Magdalene with a Book and an Ointment Jar; Decorated Text Page*, Bruges, Belgium, ca. 1510–20, Master of James IV of Scotland, Spinola Hours, 23.2 × 16.7 cm (9⅛ × 6⁹⁄₁₆ in.), Ms. Ludwig IX 18 (83.ML.114), fols. 264v–265

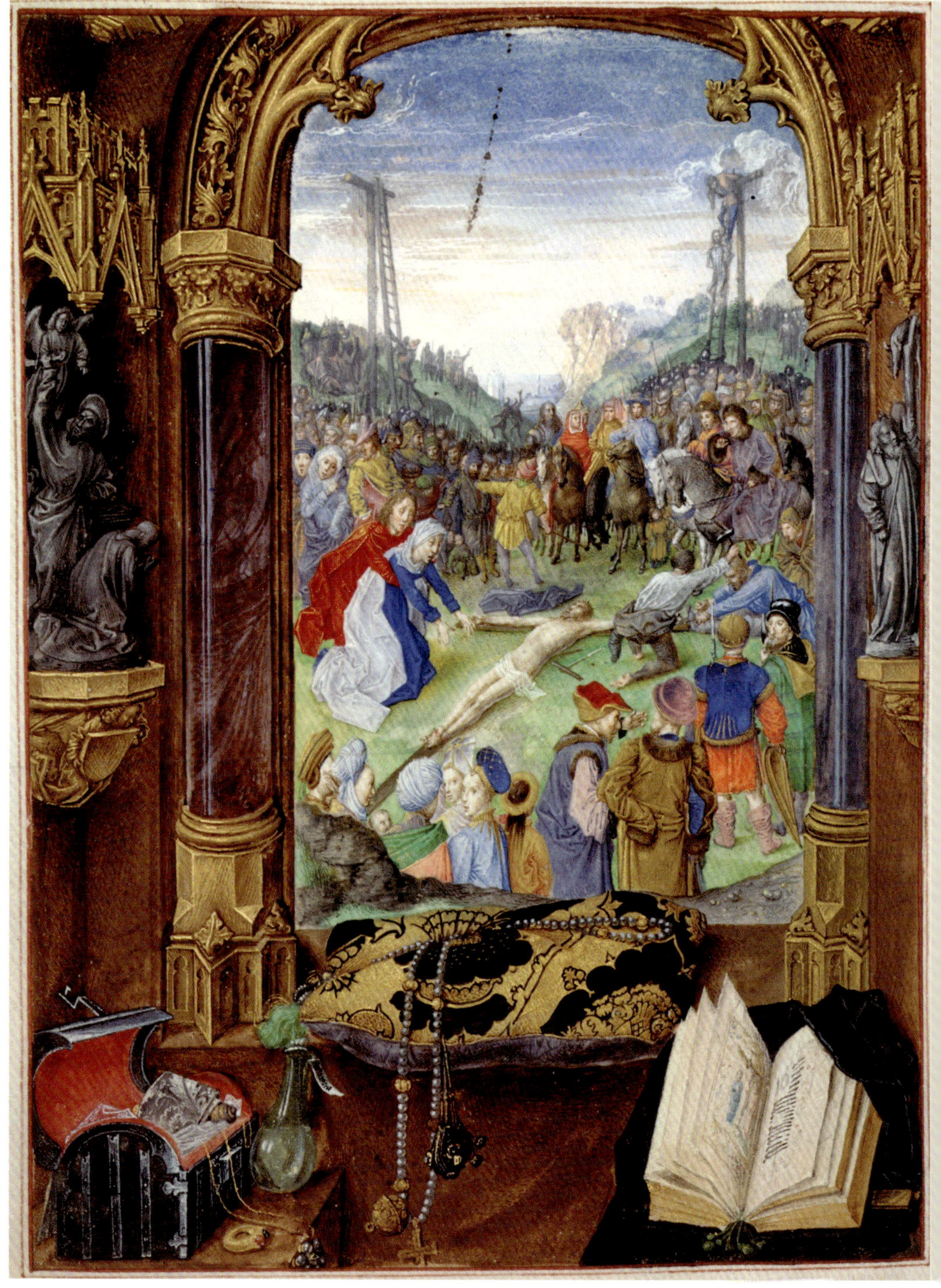

FIGURE 22 | *Christ Nailed to the Cross*, Ghent, Belgium, 1470s, Master of Mary of Burgundy, Hours of Mary of Burgundy, 22.5 × 16.3 cm (8⅞ × 6⅜ in.). Vienna, Österreichische Nationalbibliothek, cod. 1857, fol. 43v

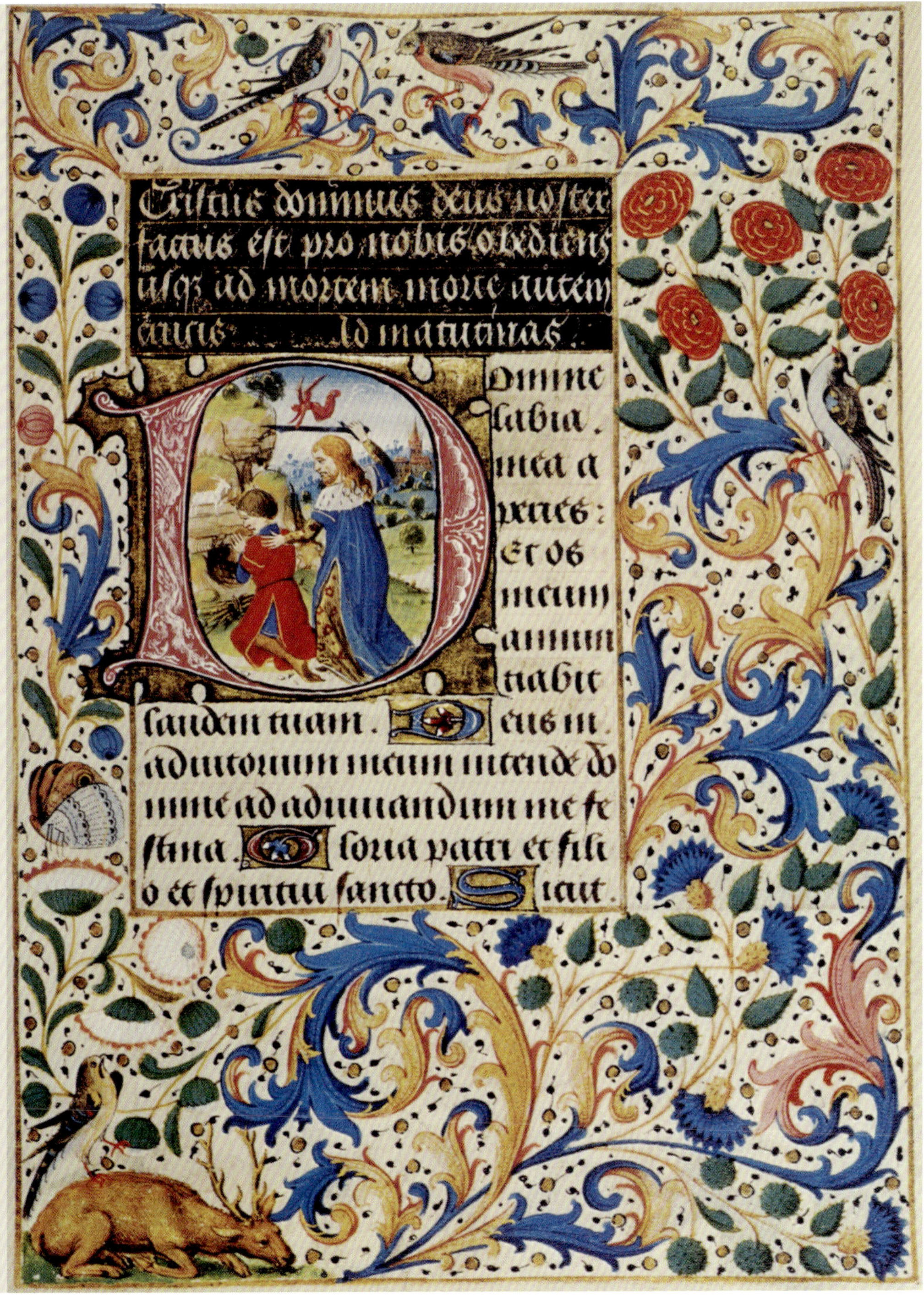

FIGURE 23 | *The Sacrifice of Isaac*, Ghent, Belgium, 1470s, Master of Mary of Burgundy, Hours of Mary of Burgundy, 22.5 × 16.3 cm (8⅞ × 6⅜ in.). Vienna, Österreichische Nationalbibliothek, cod. 1857, fol. 44

gold margin. This playful interchange between reality and floral symbolism surrounds the Magdalene holding her own prayer book in the wilderness.

In no other place is the triumph of Flemish marginalia and miniature painting so well displayed as in the Hours of Mary of Burgundy.[22] Mary of Burgundy, who inherited control of the Burgundian Netherlands from her father, Charles the Bold (r. 1467–77), was remembered as having been a great bibliophile and patron during her short life. The Hours of Mary of Burgundy mitigates the division between miniature and margin, past and present. In one miniature, a "window" opens onto *Christ Nailed to the Cross* (fig. 22). This scene is surrounded by an architectural space filled with devotional accoutrements befitting an aristocratic Christian, inviting the viewer to worship. Popular religious literature of the time emphasized *contemplatio* of the Passion, or visual meditations on it. The fourteenth-century monk Ludolph of Saxony, for example, wrote that one should imagine being "present at every single point of our Lord's Passion . . . fixing on it the eye of [one's] soul and applying to it the whole power of [one's] mind," and that "beholding" the Passion was the most effective form of worship.[23] With a deeply recessing background, turbulent sky, and groups of figures in contemporary Burgundian dress observing the Virgin's grief over Christ's sacrifice, the central scene embodies this visualization technique. In contrast to the rather avant-garde style deployed for *Christ Nailed to the Cross,* the artist decorated the facing page with traditional winding acanthus leaves interwoven with birds and butterflies, a hawk and deer at bottom left, and a small historiated initial *D* of *The Sacrifice of Isaac* (fig. 23).

Another type of framing, an illusionistic wooden tracery, encases a dark and moody Crucifixion scene from the Prayer Book of Cardinal Albrecht of Brandenburg.[24] Albrecht of Brandenburg (1490–1545) was a wealthy cleric known for his patronage of luxury arts and sales of indulgences and was a target of the Ninety-Five Theses of Martin Luther (1483–1546). The text is based on a vernacular German book of *Meditations on the Passion* printed in Augsburg in 1521. Brandenburg chose not to buy a copy but to commission Simon Bening, one of the most celebrated illuminators of the day, to sumptuously decorate the handwritten text pages. Bening was known for his emotive figures, vibrant use of color and texture, subtle plays of light, atmospheric effects, and detailed topographical vistas. Not only are scenes

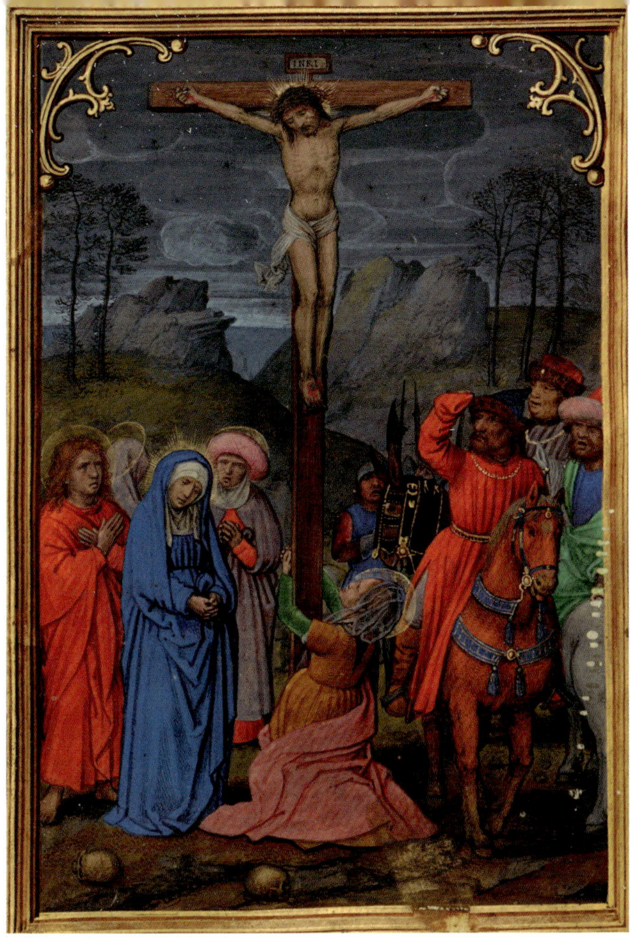

grounded in interior or exterior settings throughout the prayer book; they are anchored in time as well. In *The Crucifixion*, deep blue tones are used to create a tumultuous dark sky signifying the eclipse that occurred upon the death of Christ and the sorrow felt by the mourners below (fig. 24).

Attention to the natural environment abounds in secular as well as sacred illuminations, which is understandable, since artists across Europe produced works of both genres. Many of these so-called secular works, such as histories and chronicles, were rooted in Christian biblical traditions. Eight illuminations of God creating heaven and earth feature in a version of *Mirror of History*, an epic text by Vincent de Beauvais (1190–1264) that recounts the history of the world from the Creation until the thirteenth century. Unusually for the 1470s, when the manuscript was created, the artist also includes miniatures with "pure" landscapes—absent any human figures (fig. 25)—a particularly innovative and ahead-of-the-times approach to treating nature as an independent subject.

FIGURE 24 | *The Crucifixion,* Bruges, Belgium, 1525–30, Simon Bening, Prayer Book of Cardinal Albrecht of Brandenburg, 16.8 × 11.4 cm (6⅝ × 4½ in.), Ms. Ludwig IX 19 (83.ML.115), fol. 190v

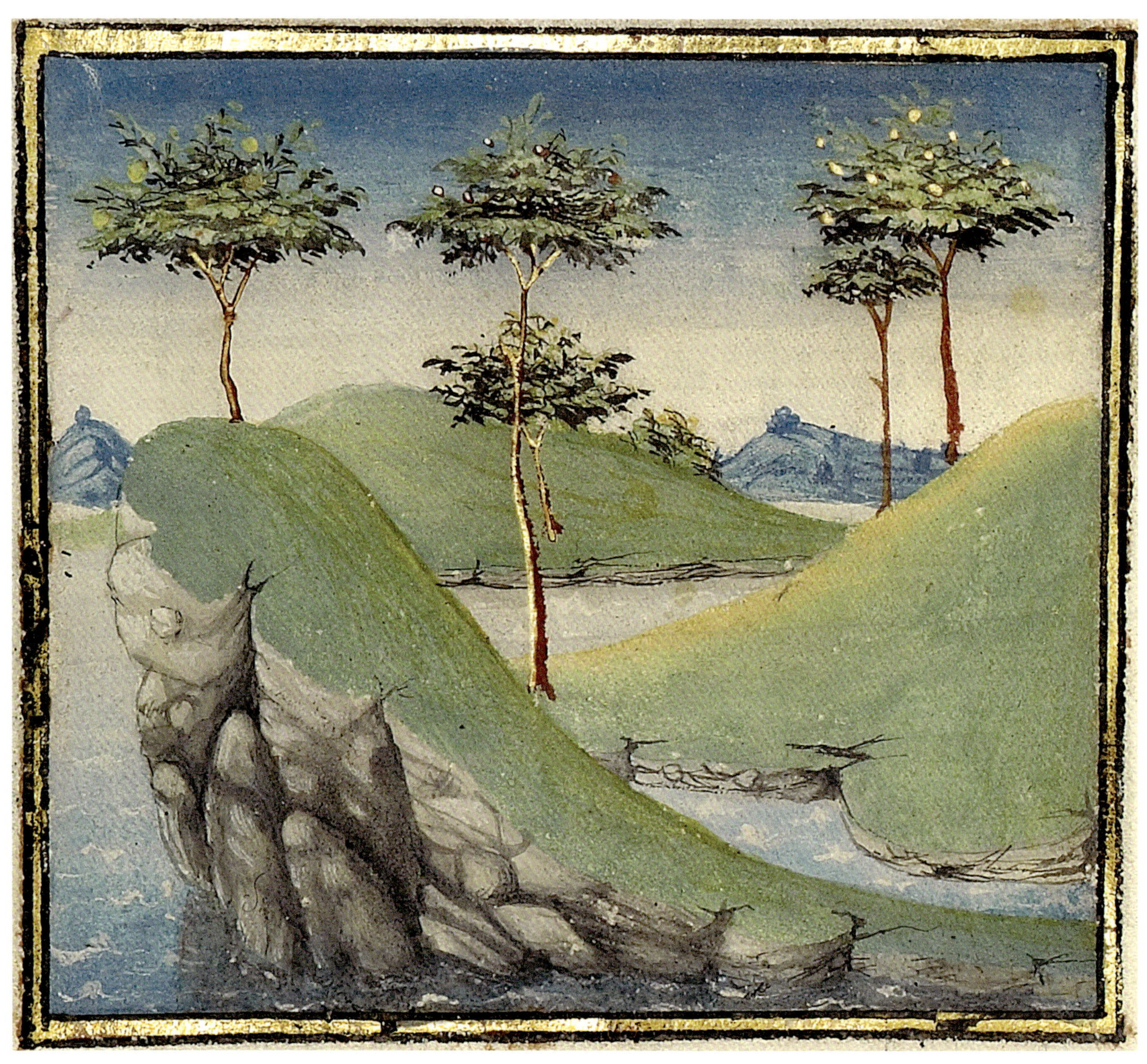

FIGURE 25 | *Islands in the Sea*, Ghent,
Belgium, ca. 1475, *Mirror of History*
by Vincent de Beauvais, 43.8 ×
30.5 cm (17¼ × 12 in.), Ms. Ludwig
XIII 5 (83.MP.148), VI, fol. 61v

By the end of the 1400s, panoramic vistas and atmospheric perspective featured prominently in painting in Germany and central Europe, including on a large parchment page that is perhaps from a missal or an independent commission that could be hung on a wall (fig. 26). The background is filled with details of a contemporaneous Franconian Renaissance city in the midst of urban development, including meticulously rendered churches, a castle, a smoking chimney, and even a construction crane. Despite this concentrated interest in representing recognizable landscapes, artists in some regions, such as Westphalia, continued to utilize carefully burnished gold backgrounds on panel and parchment. The somber mood of the foreground Crucifixion in a missal (fig. 27)—heightened by the symbolic sword piercing Mary's heart in her sorrow—contrasts with the soldiers and pilgrims milling about in the midground, just as the atmospheric perspective of the background seems to clash with the golden sky. The ensuing decades saw more than just expanding cities; the introduction of the printing press by Johannes Gutenberg in the mid-fifteenth century ushered in a new era of literacy, while the Protestant Reformation forever altered the religious landscape. Artists such as Albrecht Dürer (1471–1528) made use of this new graphic medium to express the texture and contrasts of nature.

By the mid-sixteenth century, a reverence for nature compelled artists in the so-called Danube school of southern Germany, such as Albrecht Altdorfer (ca. 1480–1538), to relinquish figural subjects in favor of pastoral and sylvan compositions. In 1563 in Florence, the Accademia del Disgeno established a corporate identity for artists and fostered drawing from nature and from life, practices that would become standard across Europe in the following centuries. Indeed, many artists began to pursue nature as theme and allegory, including Jan Brueghel the Elder (1568–1625), whose *Sermon on the Mount* (Matthew 5:13–16) features a crowd of figures gathered in the mountains to hear Christ preach, dwarfed by the surrounding forest (fig. 28). What was once a background has been transformed into an actor in the pictorial field—an incarnation of God's power, proving man's subordinacy to the divine.

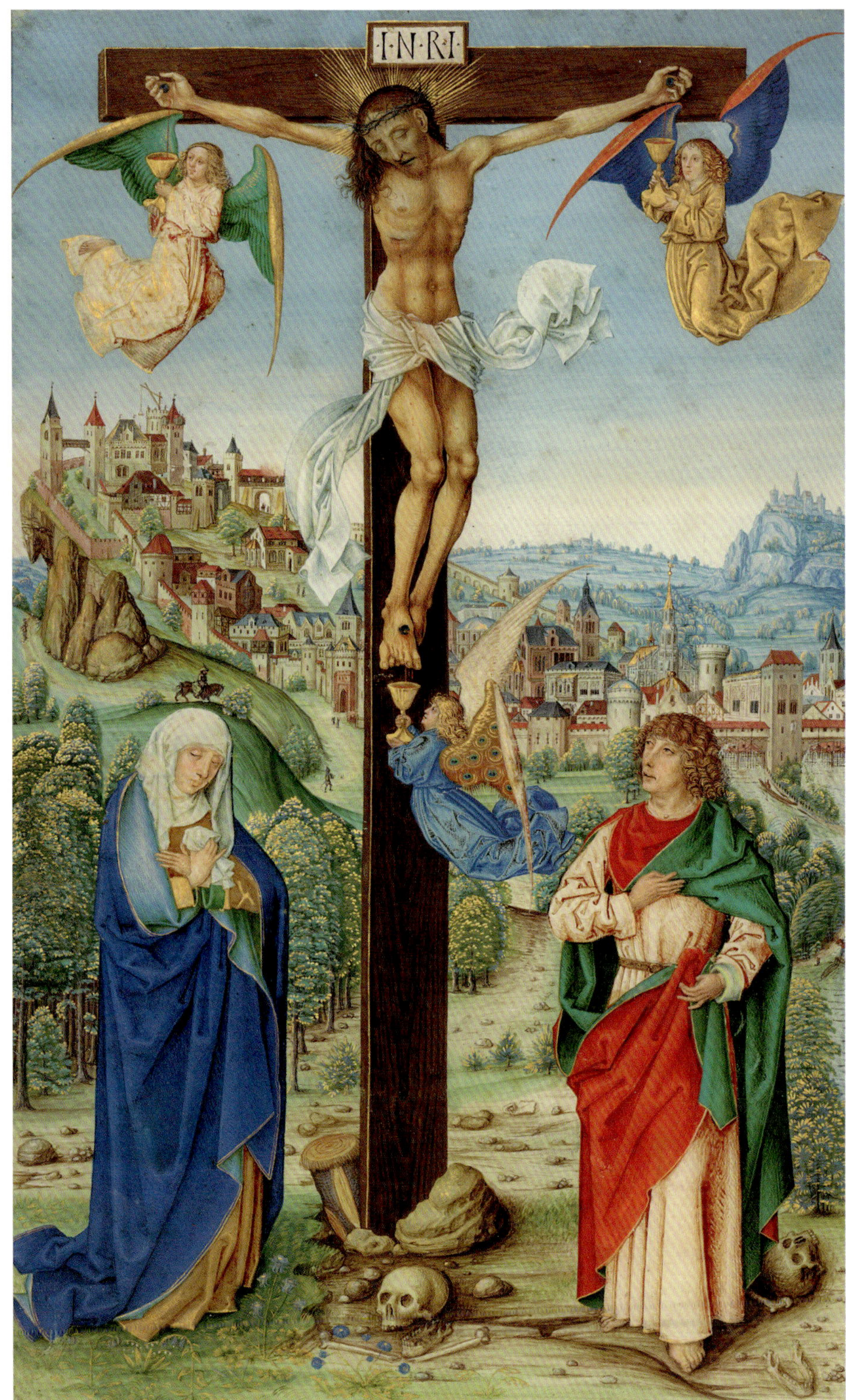

FIGURE 26 | *The Crucifixion*, Franconia, Germany, fourth quarter of 15th century, possibly from a manuscript, 38.9 × 24.3 cm (15 5/16 × 9 9/16 in.), Ms. 52 (93.MS.37), recto

FIGURE 27 | *The Crucifixion*, Westphalia, Germany, ca. 1500–1505, missal, 38.7 × 27.9 cm (15¼ × 11 in.), Ms. 18 (86.MG.480), fol. 157v

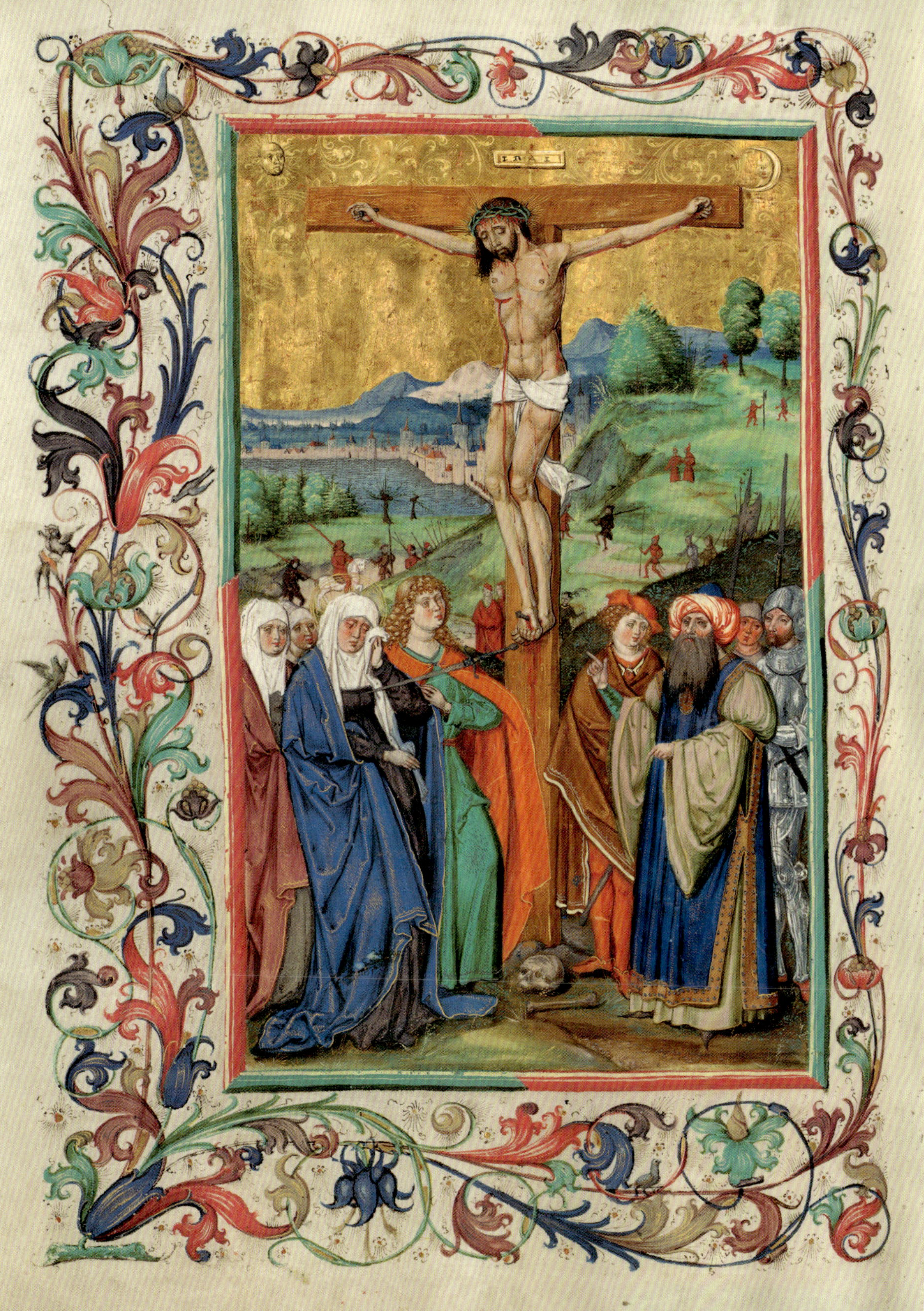

The chapters that follow present three themes pertinent to landscape painting and nature studies in the Renaissance. Particular consideration will be
given to examining the connection between text and image in devotional
manuscripts, complemented by paintings, drawings, and decorative objects.
Chapter 1 considers symbolism and the elements of the natural world used in
landscape painting, including a look at the meanings of flowers.[25] Chapter 2
centers on the garden and cultivated earth in order to reveal the positive
effects associated with viewing greenery.[26] Chapter 3 explores the wilderness
and land beyond city walls and addresses the ways in which artists adapted
the depth of field within a miniature to include expansive vistas that emphasize the isolation and potential for contemplation found in these desolate
locales.[27] Each chapter concludes with a closer look at a single book of hours,
French, Flemish, and Italian, respectively.

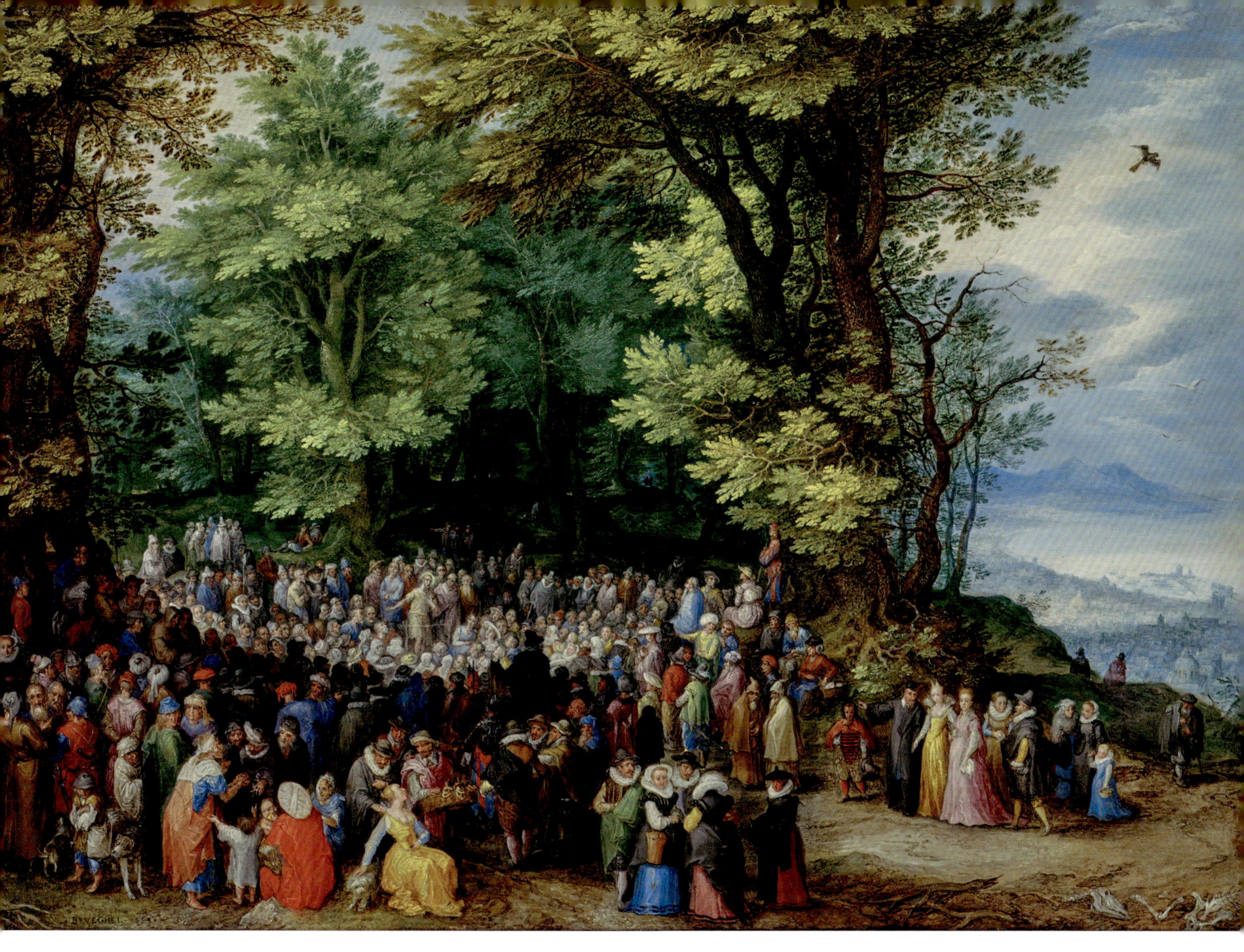

FIGURE 28 | Jan Brueghel the Elder
(Flemish, 1568–1625), *The Sermon on
the Mount*, 1598. Oil on copper, 26.7 ×
36.8 cm (10½ × 14½ in.), 84.PC.71

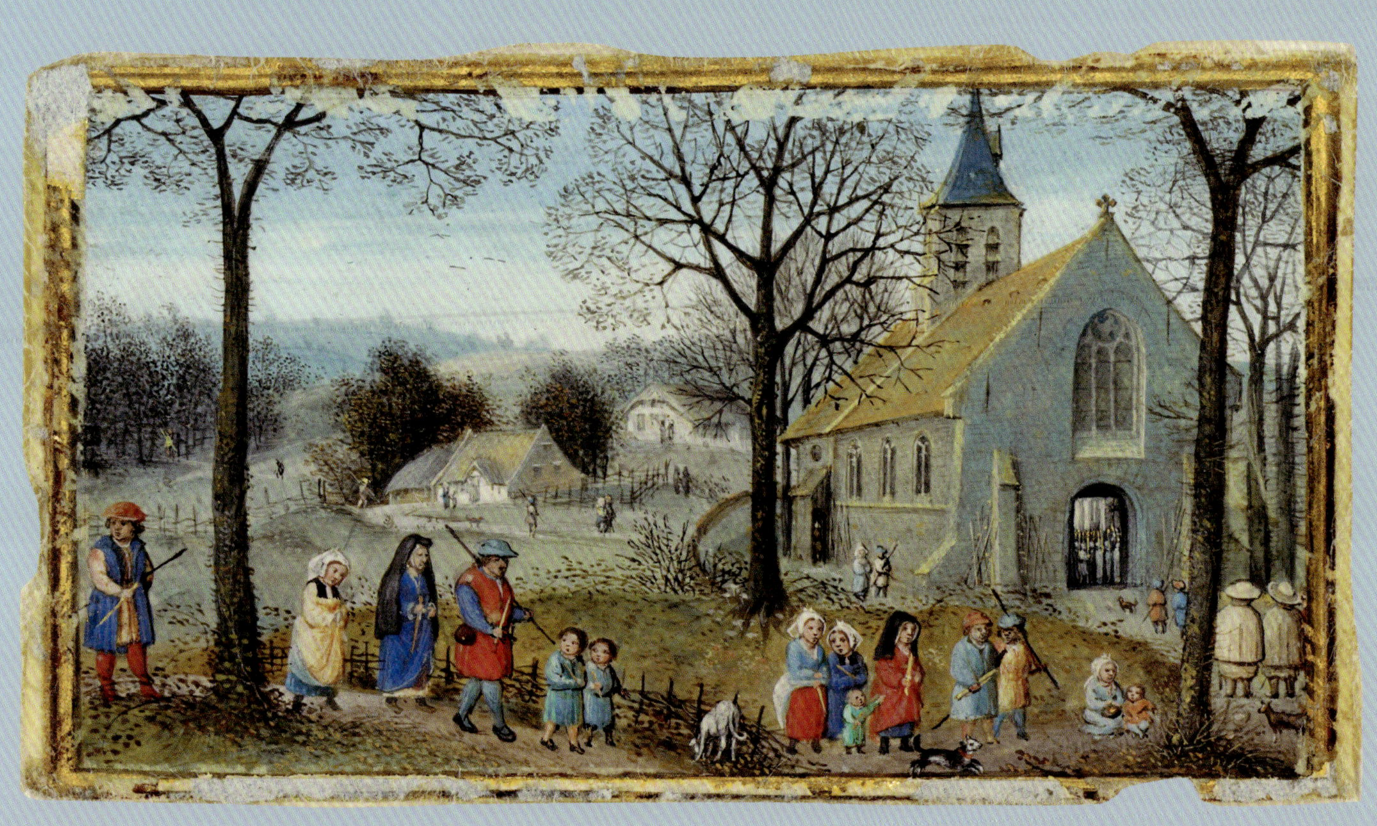

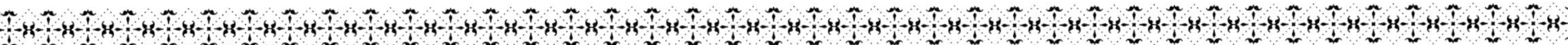

I
ELEMENTS AND SYMBOLS OF THE NATURAL WORLD

NATURE ABOUNDS WITH MEANING AND METAPHOR. IN PREINDUSTRIAL Europe, the lives of people at every level of society were governed by the seasons and the natural world. Summer, autumn, winter, and spring each radically reshape natural environments and affect the health of human bodies, and flora and fauna grow and migrate accordingly. Temporal phenomena—such as wind, rain, thunderstorms, and snowfall—combine in landscapes with living creatures and the elements earth, fire, water, and air to evoke a range of moods and engage the spectator in the wondrous experience. Even the tiniest insect or the most foreboding mountain can hold deep significance. This chapter draws attention to the artistry of and many meanings behind individual aspects of a landscape composition, from flowers and rocks to water and sky, and explores the ways in which each actively participates in the narrative and contributes to the prayers, songs, or meditations of devotees.

Calendar pages from books of hours afforded artists opportunities for mixing seasonal activities, landscapes, and even zodiacal signs. Simon Bening was renowned for his ability to capture minute details in a few brushstrokes, such as a simple country church, the locus of social and religious life, which dominates the rolling hills (fig. 29). Sparsely foliated trees and neutral earthen tones evoke winter, while warmly dressed villagers carry candles to the ceremony of Candlemas inside the church. Fanciful scenes from a sixteenth-century German book of hours juxtapose peasants hard at work with zodiacal creatures that seemingly inhabit the same space (figs. 30, 31). Throughout the calendar miniatures, architectural structures separate

FIGURE 29 | *Villagers on Their Way to Church*, Bruges, Belgium, ca. 1550, Simon Bening, calendar miniature from a book of hours, 5.6 × 9.5 cm (2 3/16 × 3 3/4 in.), Ms. 50 (93.MS.19), recto

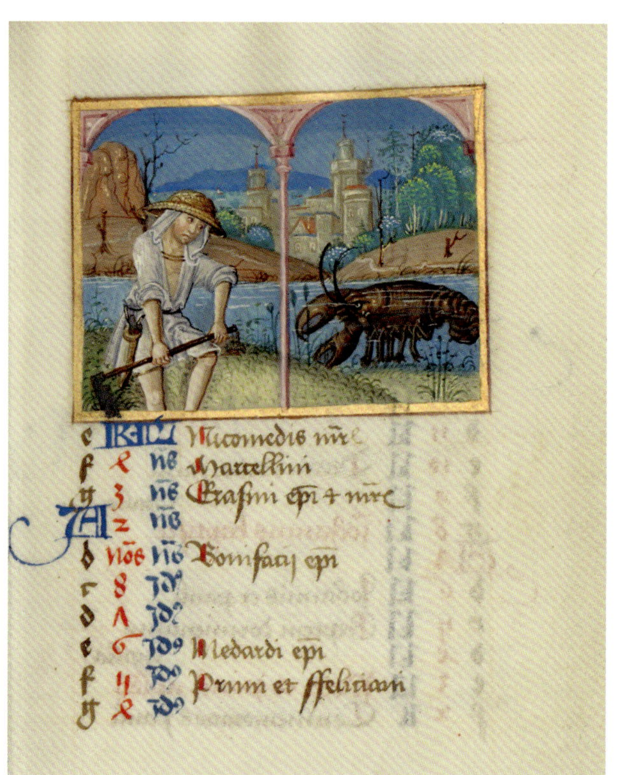

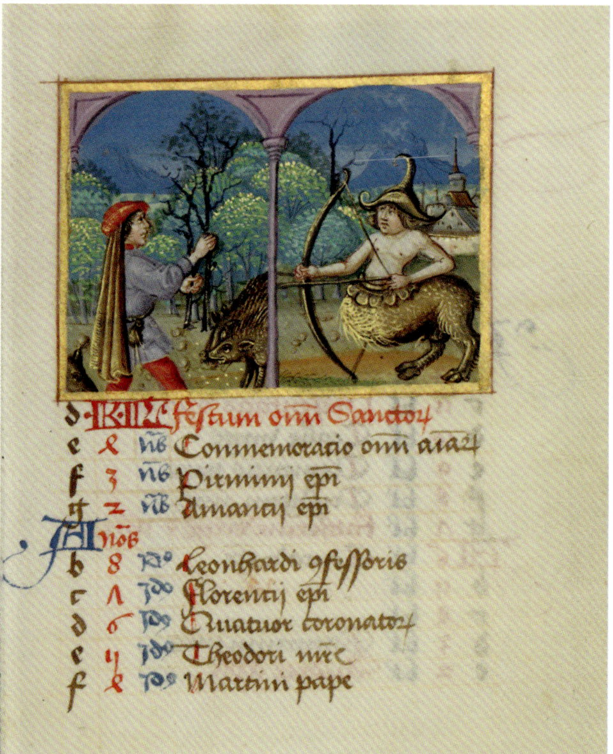

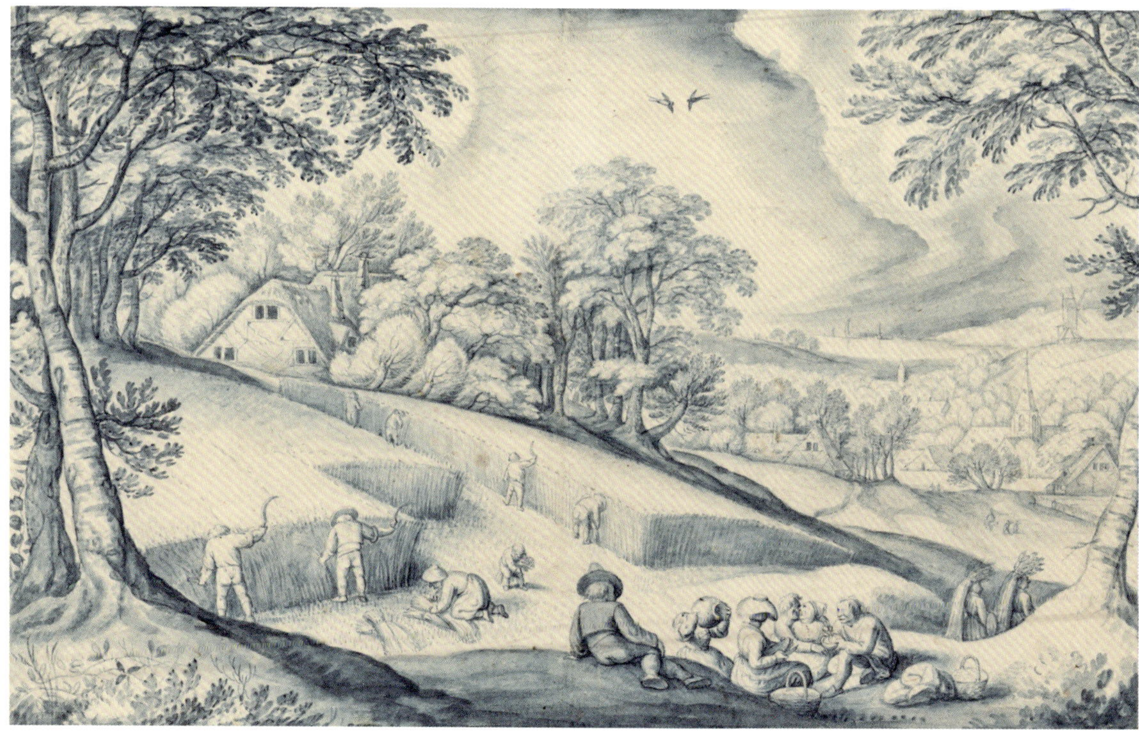

the human from the mythical, yet some scenes are united by a continuous landscape spanning compartments. Artists drew inspiration from these calendar miniatures well into the seventeenth century. *August* by Jacob I Savery (1566–1603) is a bucolic scene of men harvesting wheat and couples picnicking under the shade of trees (fig. 32), capturing changing seasons and the joyful spirit of daily life in the Netherlands.

In addition to rendering the passage of seasons in the calendar, artists also anchored their narratives in a specific time and place by expressing temporal and atmospheric changeability and by emphasizing nature's presence in a scene. Books of hours generally contain a series of prayers dedicated to the Virgin Mary, Christ, and saints. In a nocturnal scene for the Hours of the Virgin, a glowing light and cascade of angels draw attention to a stable in the distance where Christ is born (fig. 33). Atmosphere is key in recreating this biblical story, as shepherds receive news of this divine birth from the glittering angelic host. The illuminator—whose thoughtful treatment of the peasants is similar to that of the Flemish painter Hugo van der Goes (ca. 1440–1482)—selected a vantage point above the town to emphasize the Arcadian setting outside the city, while barren trees suggest the winter season.

Light and dark, salvation and sacrifice—atmosphere conveys these themes in two miniatures from another Flemish book of hours, capturing important scenes from the Passion of Christ and the Life of the Virgin (fig. 34). At left, the Virgin's body is carried through a rocky terrain toward a peaceful resting place in a glade of trees in the Valley of Jehoshaphat, on the slope of the Mount of Olives in Jerusalem, from which angels will miraculously raise Mary skyward. The landscape reflects this joyous occasion with a radiant orange sky. In contrast, at right a darkening sunset casts an ominous mood over a steep, rocky landscape, appropriate for the tense and tragic final moments of Christ's life and eventual burial. Set within illusionistic frames that are like windows onto another world, the vivacious illuminations and animated nature combine in a deeply moving spectacle. Before such an emotive vision a devotee would likely have been consumed with compassion for Christ's suffering.

Narrative scenes from the lives of saints, martyrs, and other holy figures often accompany the Suffrages of Saints in books of hours or the sanctoral cycle of chants in a choir book. Different topographies are woven throughout

FIGURE 30 | *June Calendar Page with Mowing and Zodiacal Sign of Cancer*, Strasbourg, France, early 16th century, book of hours, 13.5 × 10.5 cm (5⁵⁄₁₆ × 4⅛ in.), Ms. Ludwig IX 16 (83.ML.112), fol. 6

FIGURE 31 | *November Calendar Page with a Man Knocking Acorns from a Tree and Zodiacal Sign of Sagittarius*, Strasbourg, France, early 16th century, book of hours, 13.5 × 10.5 cm (5⁵⁄₁₆ × 4⅛ in.), Ms. Ludwig IX 16 (83.ML.112), fol. 11

FIGURE 32 | Jacob I Savery (Flemish, 1566–1603), *August*, 1595. Brush and indigo ink, indigo wash, heightened with white opaque watercolor, 21.2 × 31 cm (8⅜ × 12³⁄₁₆ in.), 2016.14.2

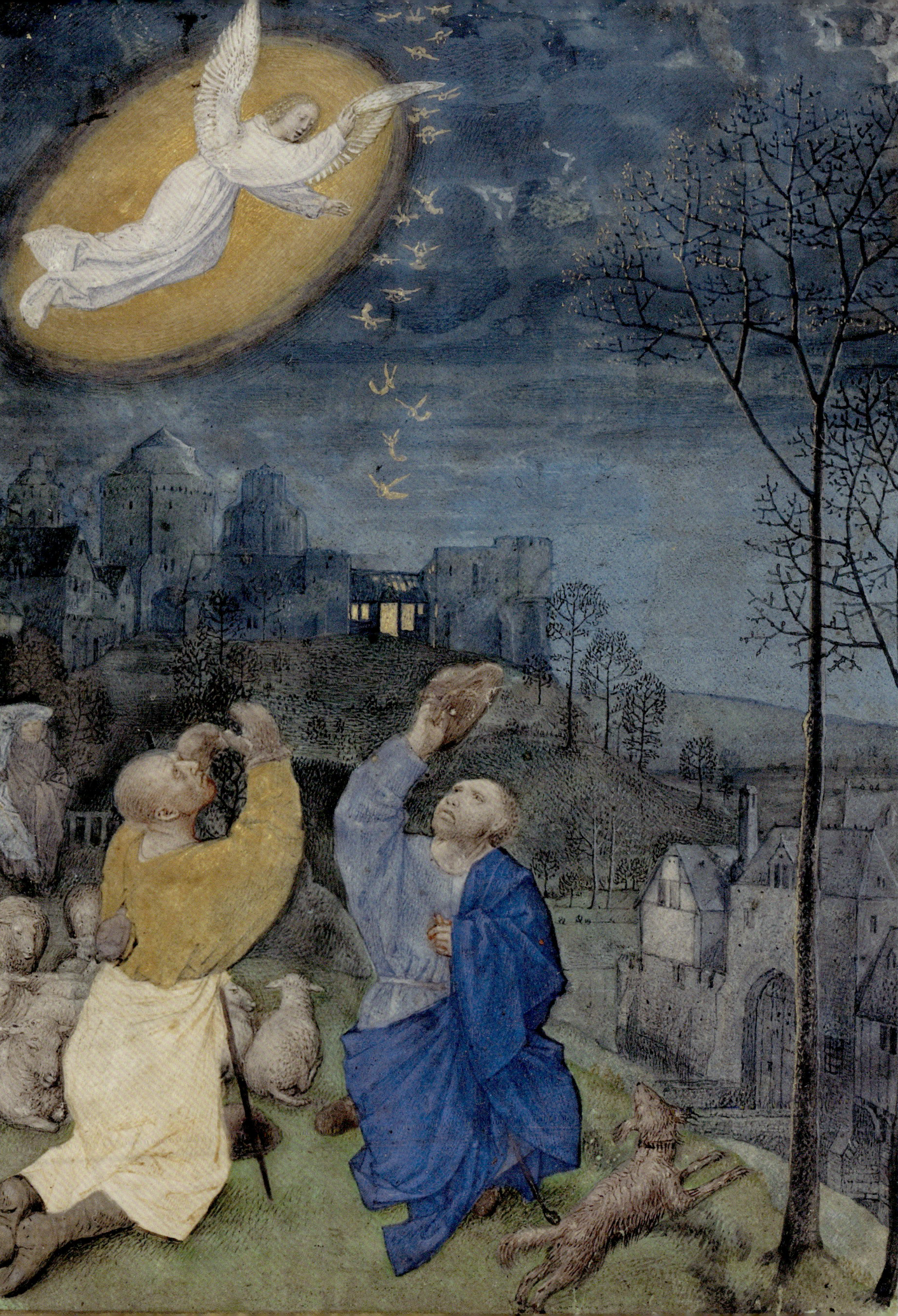

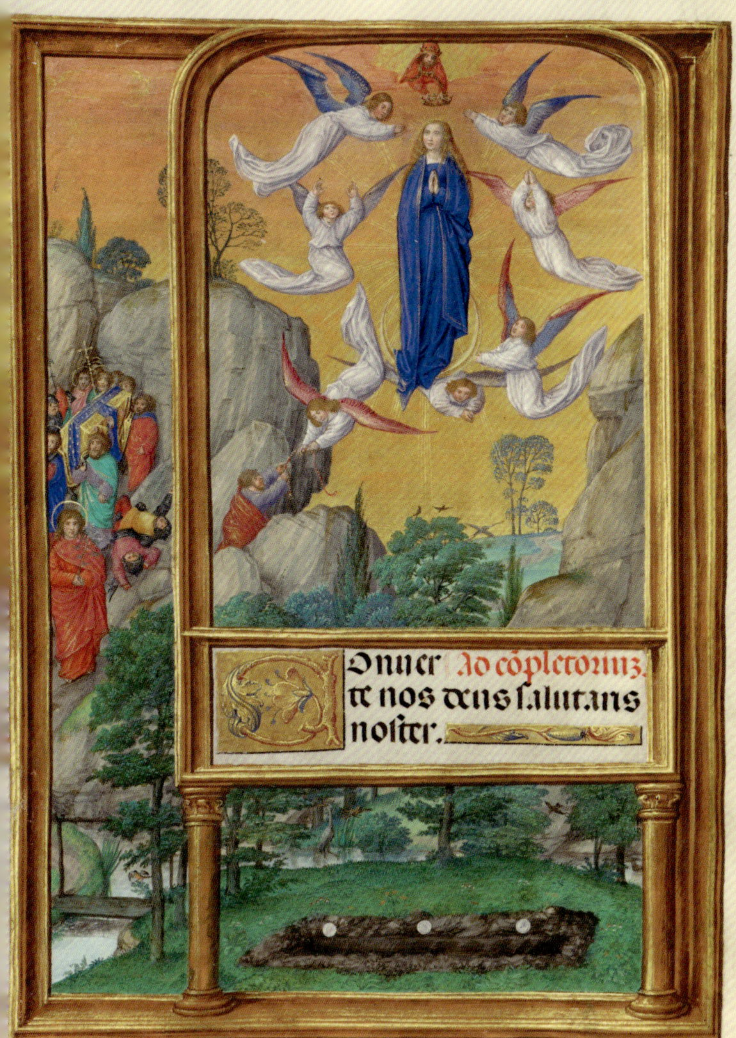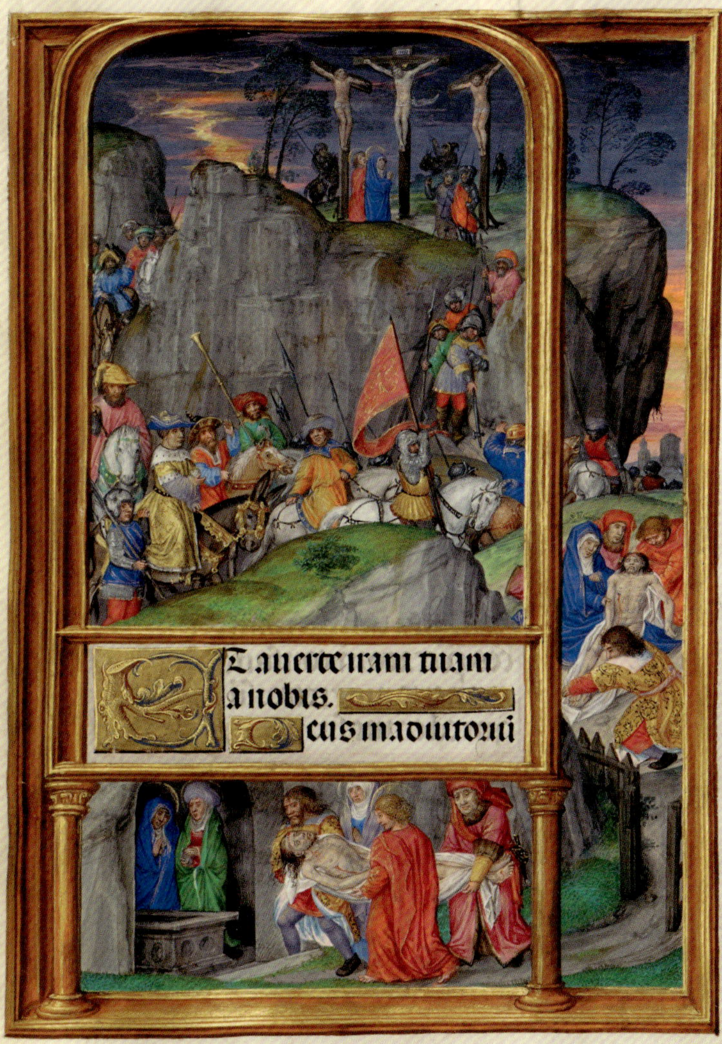

the written legends of Christopher, the patron saint of travelers, and are incorporated into the marginalia by the Spitz Master: Christopher pledges fealty to the devil beyond the Canaanite wilderness, encounters a cross, and learns about Christianity from a hermit. Taking the hermit's advice to live by a river, Christopher encounters Christ in the guise of a child. After Christopher helps him cross the river (with the Christ child's weight continually increasing), Christ praises Christopher for bearing the weight of the world and commands him to plant his staff in the earth, where it flowers and bears fruit. Here, the Spitz Master set the miraculous scene at nighttime, with the river imagined as a fifteenth-century port town with a rugged shoreline (fig. 35).

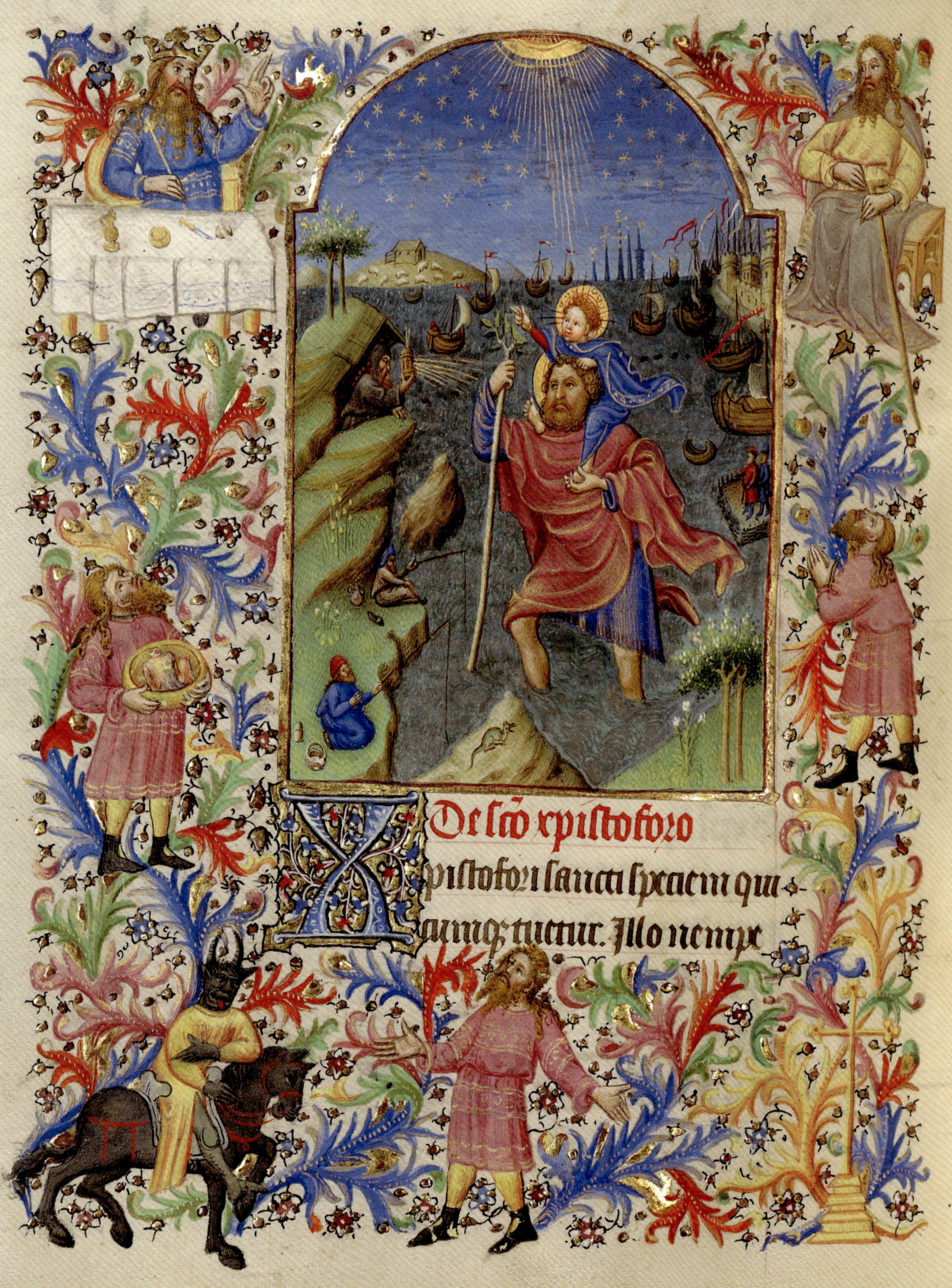
De ſcō xp̄iſtoforo
[X]p̄iſtofori ſancti ſpeciem qui-
amoꝗ tuetur. Illo nempe

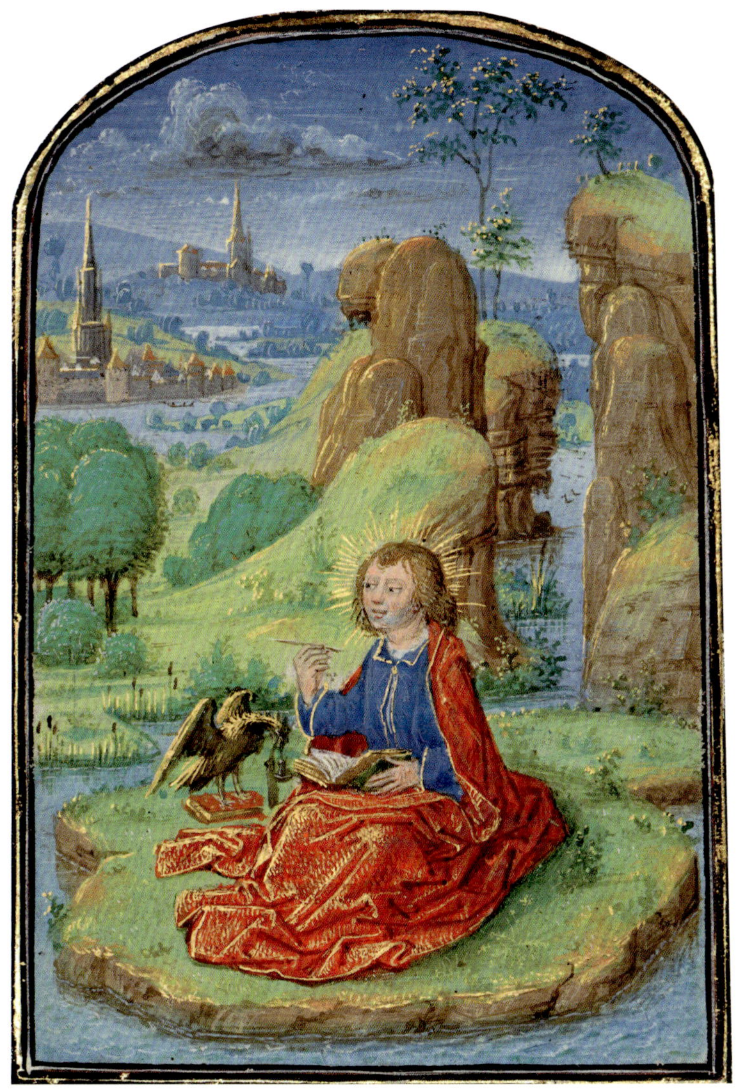

The book of Revelation in the New Testament recounts Saint John's visions of the Apocalypse, or end times. In a miniature from a book of hours illuminated by Lieven van Lathem (ca. 1430–1493) for Charles the Bold (1433–1477), the visionary sits on a tiny, flat island with book and quill in his hand (fig. 36).[28] From the hints of white to indicate cresting waves and the horizontal brushwork creating striations in the rocks to the reflections of cattails and surrounding shore in the rippling waterway that connects the foreground to the distant towns, Lathem reveals his masterful observation of the natural world in a surreal setting. A sense of verticality in the miniature is mirrored by the columnar rocks that frame the saint and the distant spires

FIGURE 35 | *Saint Christopher Carrying the Christ Child*, Paris, ca. 1420, Spitz Master, book of hours, 20.5 × 15.9 cm (8¹⁄₁₆ × 6¼ in.), Ms. 57 (94.ML.26), fol. 42v

FIGURE 36 | *Saint John on Patmos*, Ghent (written out) and Antwerp (illuminated), Belgium, 1469, Lieven van Lathem, Prayer Book of Charles the Bold, 12.4 × 9.2 cm (4⅞ × 3⅝ in.), Ms. 37 (89.ML.35), fol. 18

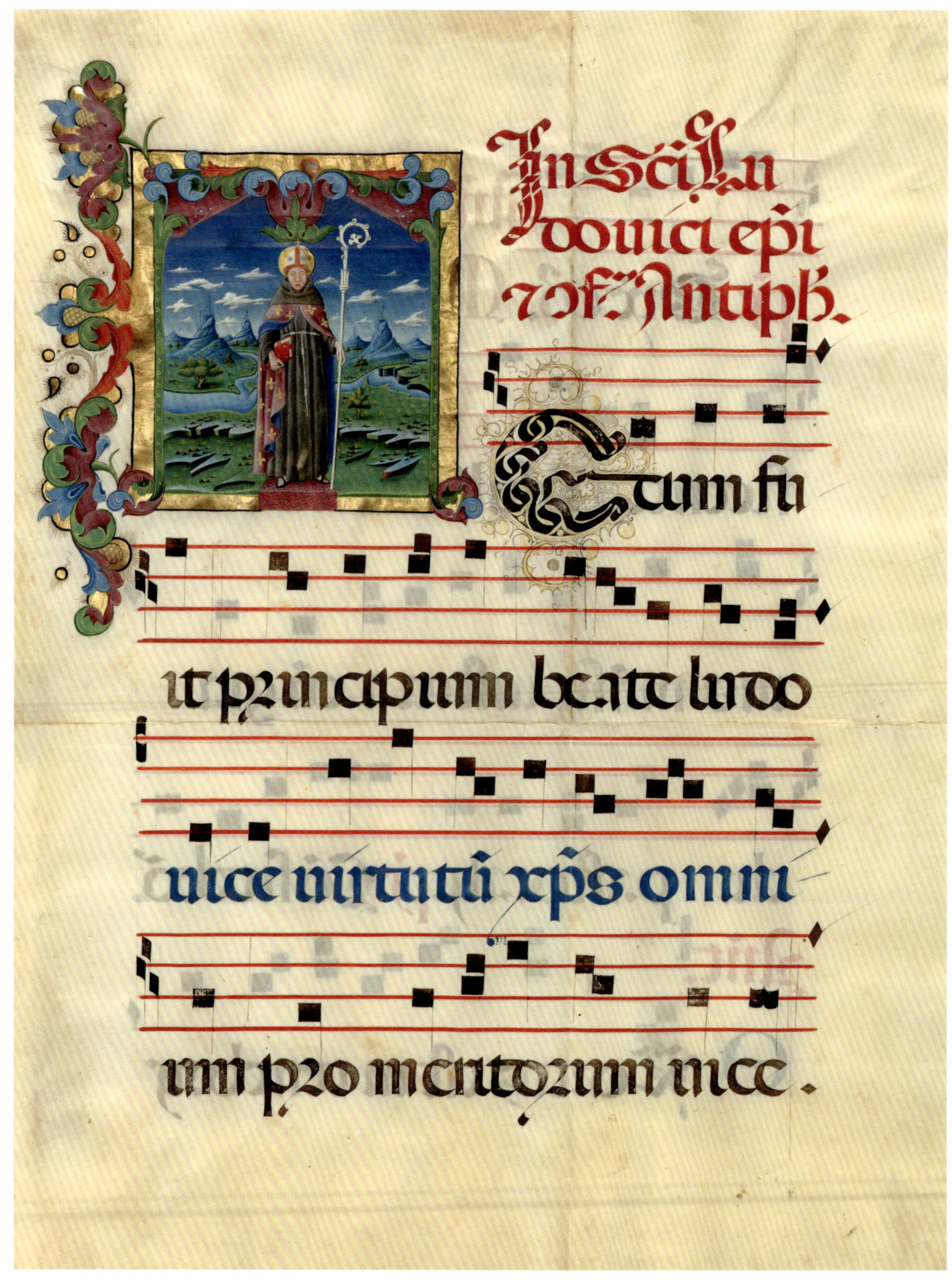
In sci Lu
douici epi
7 of Antiph.
tum fu
it principium beate lu do
uice uirtutu xps omni
um pro mentozum uice.

of the town churches, clearly showing the development in spatial construction from early Apocalypse illuminations.

An otherworldly landscape—with winding streams, high peaks topped with tall towers, wispy clouds, and gold-highlighted foliage—forms a backdrop for the imposing figure of Saint Louis of Toulouse (1274–1297), who forms the stem of a letter *T* (fig. 37). The delicate touches of fantasy and brilliant color in the desolate but lush countryside are characteristic of the artist Franco dei Russi (active ca. 1453–82) and of painting at the Ferrarese court. This page was once part of a multivolume choir book containing chants addressed to saints of the Franciscan order, who, like Louis of Toulouse, were fervently devoted to preserving the natural world. The Latin chant exhorts the listener to behold the metaphorical magnificence of virtue, which shines with outstanding brightness and whose justice covers vast fields, and to remember that light shines in the darkness and that God's might awakens out from the earth.

The mystic and visionary saint Hildegard of Bingen (1098–1179) referred to the abundance and fertility given to the created world by God as "viridity,"[29] a notion that is beautifully expressed in a miniature of the Creation of the World from the *World Chronicle* by Rudolf von Ems (ca. 1200–1254) (fig. 38). This concept of greenness is a powerful reminder that medieval Christians connected with the divine through nature, a virtue inherited by Renaissance thinkers, scientists, writers, and philosophers, as well as by authors like Rudolf whose texts blended biblical and classical history. Nature and the lived environment were often protagonists in their own right—essential components in biblical narratives—from the Song of Songs to *The Golden Legend*.

Choir books often transported singers and viewers to distant worlds through landscapes that conformed to the shape of the opening letter of a chant or hymn. Within a letter *S*, for example, luminous clouds break through blue sky while the heavens open to reveal Christ enthroned, bridging the physical landscape and the celestial realm (fig. 39). To Christ's left demons lead sinners into the rocky pit where they will be consumed by fire, while to his right the resurrected emerge from grassy tombs to be led to paradise by an angel.

Perhaps one of the most famous tales of the earth's cleansing and God's power expressed through nature (or of any natural disaster) is the

FIGURE 37 | Initial *T*: *Saint Louis of Toulouse*, Ferrara, Italy, ca. 1453–63, Franco dei Russi, leaf from the Antiphonary of Cardinal Bessarion, 73 × 53.4 cm (28¾ × 21 in.), Ms. 90 (2005.20), recto

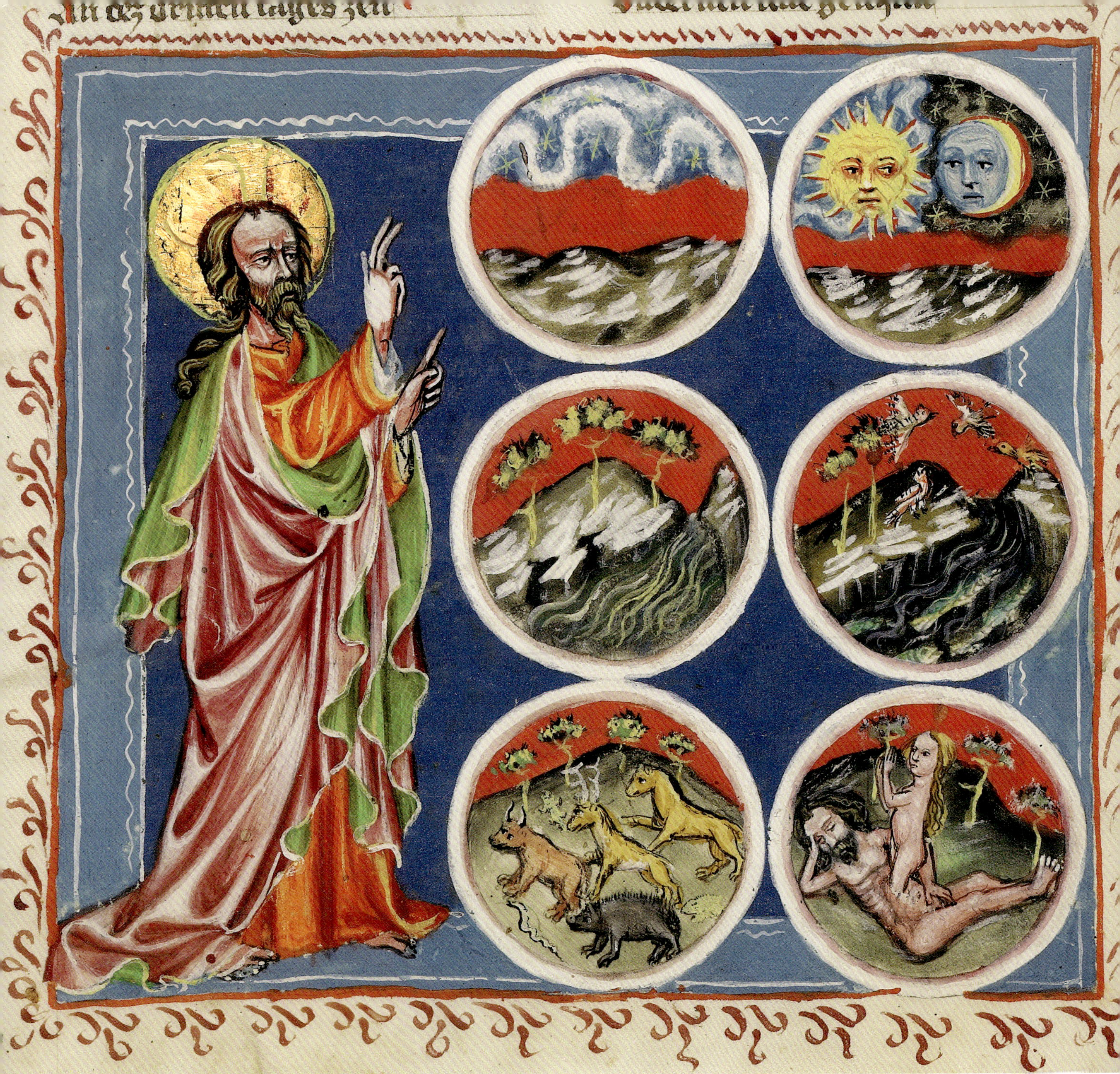

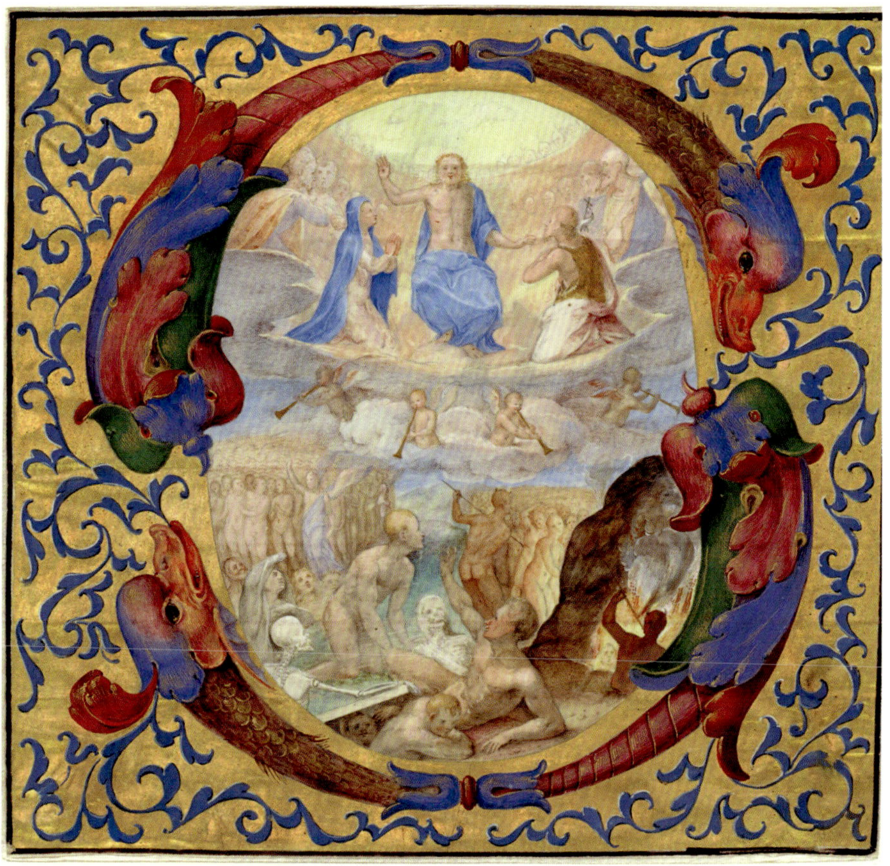

biblical story of Noah's Ark, about which a choir once sung guided by an initial *D* (fig. 40). Judging humanity to be corrupt and deciding to destroy the world with a great flood, God instructed Noah to build a large ship, or ark, ahead of the upcoming calamity, to house his family and various animals. Despite the destructive waters, Christian writers interpreted the flood as an allusion to baptism—a divine act of cleansing and salvation. In this scene, the barren landscape is executed in stark browns and pale gray-blues and greens. Felled trees fill the foreground, while the structure of the ark is echoed in the tiered shape of the mountainous outcropping in the distance, foreshadowing the destruction of the natural world so that it can be reborn.

Apart from contemplating such scenes of God's awesome power as manifested in nature, praying the rosary as an act of penance was one way

FIGURE 38 | *The Creation of Heaven and Earth; The Separation of Light and Darkness; The Separation of Water and Land; The Creation of Birds and Fishes; The Creation of Animals; The Creation of Eve*, Regensburg, Germany, ca. 1400–1410, *World Chronicle*, 33.5 × 23.5 cm (13³⁄₁₆ × 9¼ in.), Ms. 33 (88.MP.70), fol. 4v

FIGURE 39 | Initial *S*: *The Last Judgment*, Rome, ca. 1567–72, cutting from a gradual, 15.6 × 16 cm (6⅛ × 6⁵⁄₁₆ in.), Ms. 92 (2005.22), verso

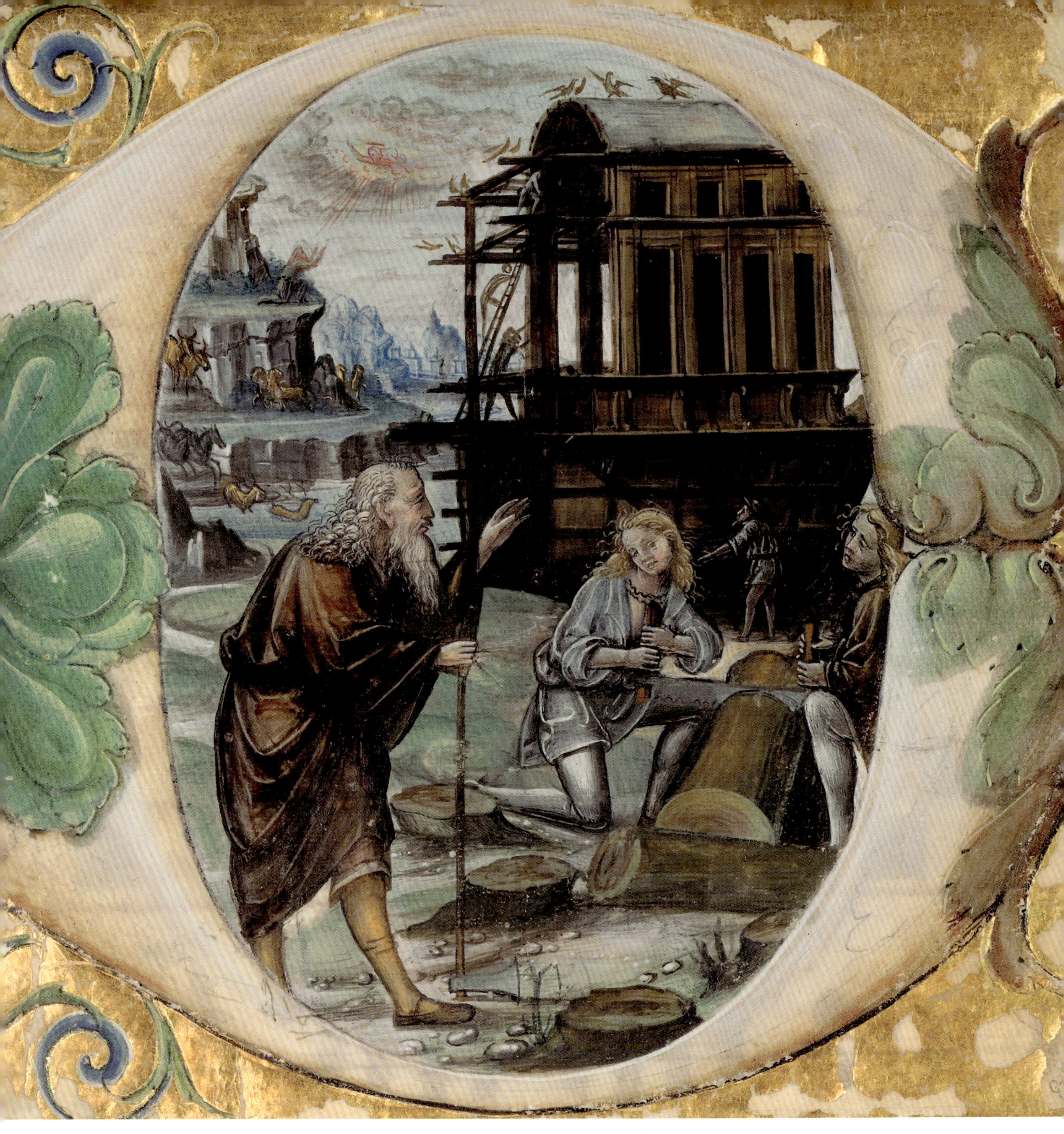

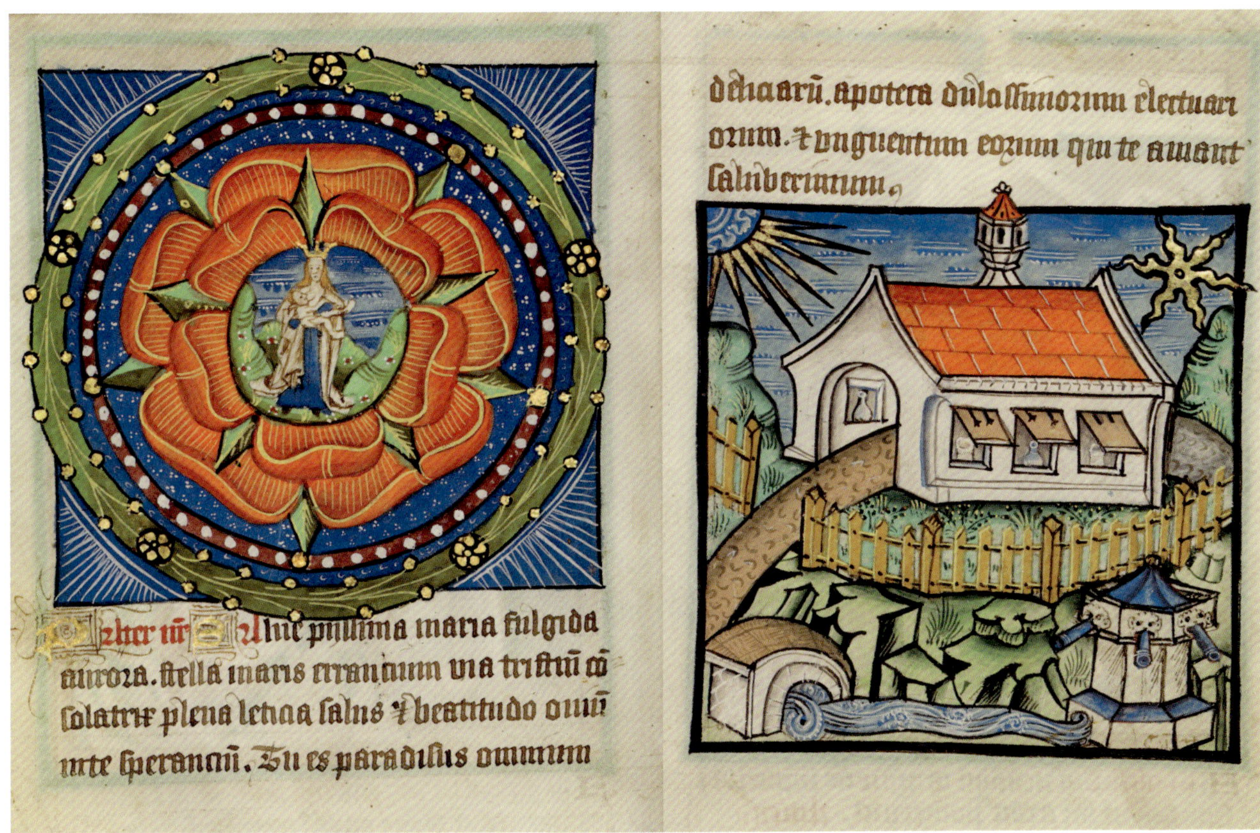

in which Catholics could achieve redemption and forgiveness for their sins. In medieval and Renaissance art, the most prevalent floral symbol for the Virgin Mary is the rose, representing her charity. Around 1490, an illustrated twelfth-century *Vita Christi* (Life of Christ) manuscript was transformed into a rosary book, with large miniatures of roses that contain the Virgin and Child and are surrounded by a string of fifty beads corresponding to a single Hail Mary prayer (fig. 41). Here, an accompanying prayer elucidates the many other symbolic associations with Mary, all drawn from nature: an enclosed garden; a sealed fountain; the *stella maris* (star of the sea), fair as the moon, bright as the sun; and sweet apothecary (an association with natural healing and medicine).

  Books of hours abounded with flower symbolism. Meandering gold and silver speech banderoles and large iris-like flowers connect two pages of

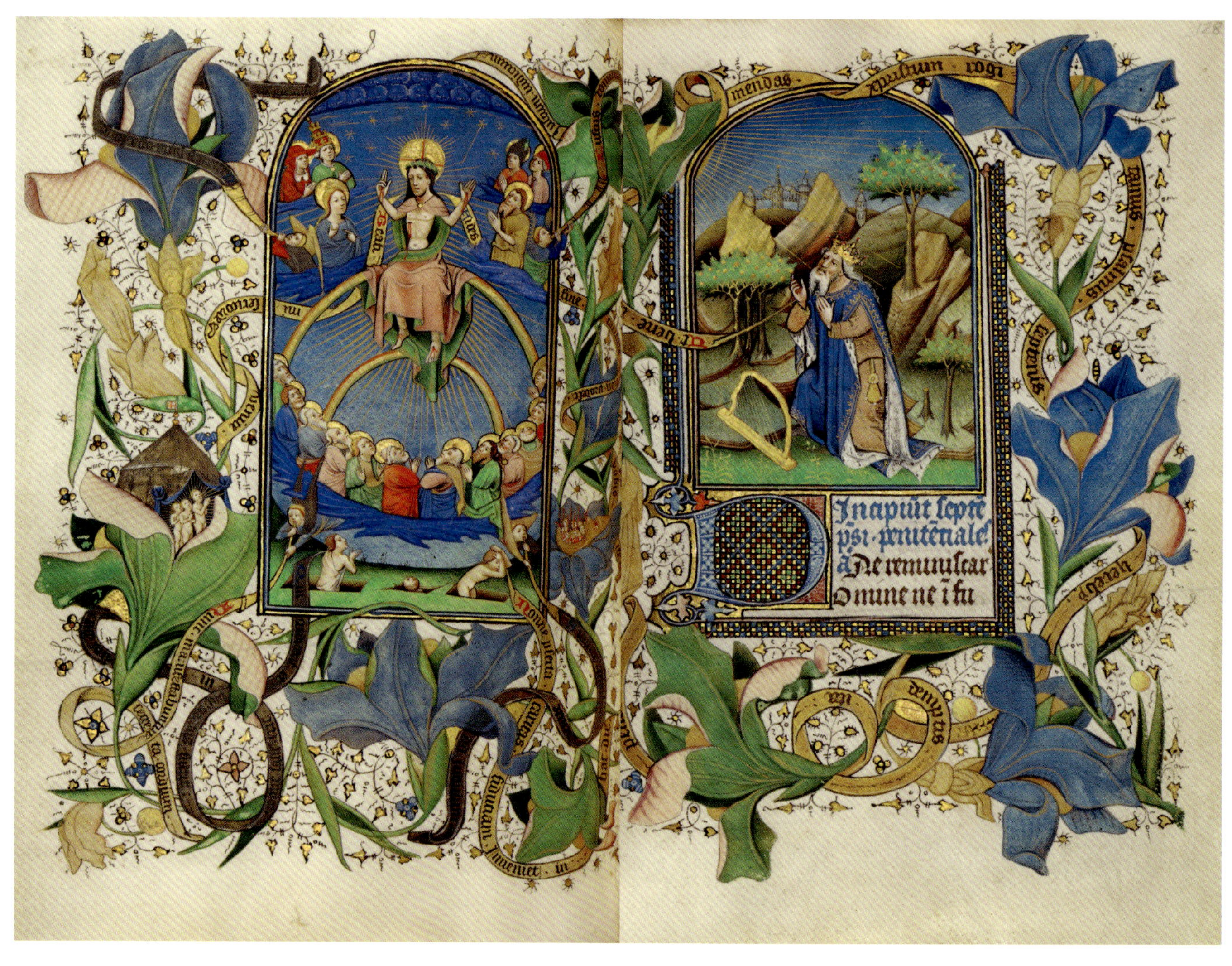

FIGURE 42 | *The Last Judgment;
David in Prayer*, Ghent, Belgium,
1450–55, Master of Guillebert de
Mets, book of hours, 19.4 × 14 cm
(7⅝ × 5½ in.), Ms. 2 (84.ML.67), fols.
127v–128

a French manuscript (fig. 42). In medieval and Renaissance art, irises sym-
bolized life and resurrection, themes that are vividly rendered here against
two very different landscapes. At left, Christ's words to the saved and the
damned—who gather amid the flowers in the margins—proclaim eternal
salvation or doom. At right, the biblical King David kneels in a rocky and
wooded place as if witnessing a vision of the Last Judgment. David's peniten-
tial prayer inscribed on the scrolls would have connected the reader to the
Psalm text in Latin below. ❧

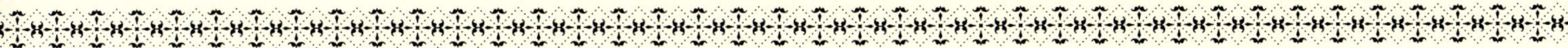

THE KATHERINE HOURS
Tours, France, ca. 1480–85
Jean Bourdichon

IN A BOOK OF HOURS ILLUMINATED BY JEAN BOURDICHON (1456/57–1521), THE initial *K* (laced together with an *I*) in many of the decorative borders and multiple prayers to Saint Catherine of Alexandria suggest the book was commissioned for a woman named Katherine. Turning the pages, Katherine and subsequent readers witnessed Bourdichon's masterful ability to fill nearly every surface of the parchment with natural elements. In *The Visitation*, for example, the growth of the potted and trellised speedwell and carnation plants—representing fidelity and love—visually echo the meeting of the two pregnant mothers, the Virgin Mary and her cousin Elizabeth (fig. 43). The two women have gathered in secret in a bucolic landscape far from the city, visible in the hazy distance atop a hillock. A border of anemones, poppies, strawberries, and thistles symbolizes Christ's eventual death.

Bourdichon's innovative use of nocturnal scenes throughout the Katherine Hours evinces a budding desire for naturalism in the French Renaissance. In *The Adoration of the Magi,* a golden beam of heavenly light shines down upon the Virgin and Child (fig. 44). Flourishing botanical specimens fill a trellised border. Some of the plants—grapes, roses, and rose campion—signify the Crucifixion, while the gromwell and speedwell blossoms connote salvation. The border decoration is mirrored on the verso, giving a sense of three-dimensionality—an ingenious illusion imitated in many of the horticultural designs throughout the manuscript.

The joyous tone of the manuscript's miniatures is halted at the Office of the Dead, a series of prayers to commemorate the souls of the

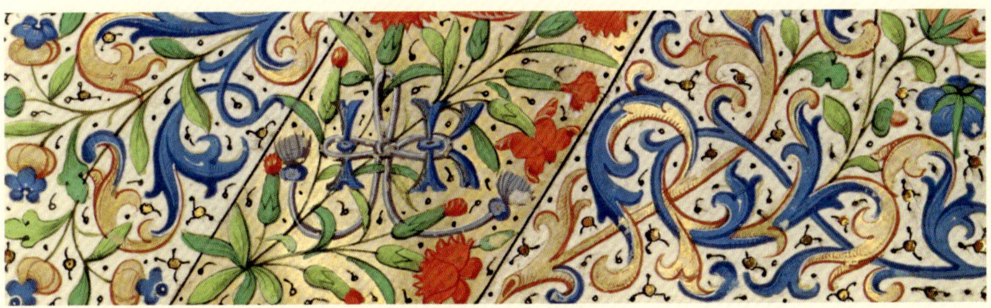

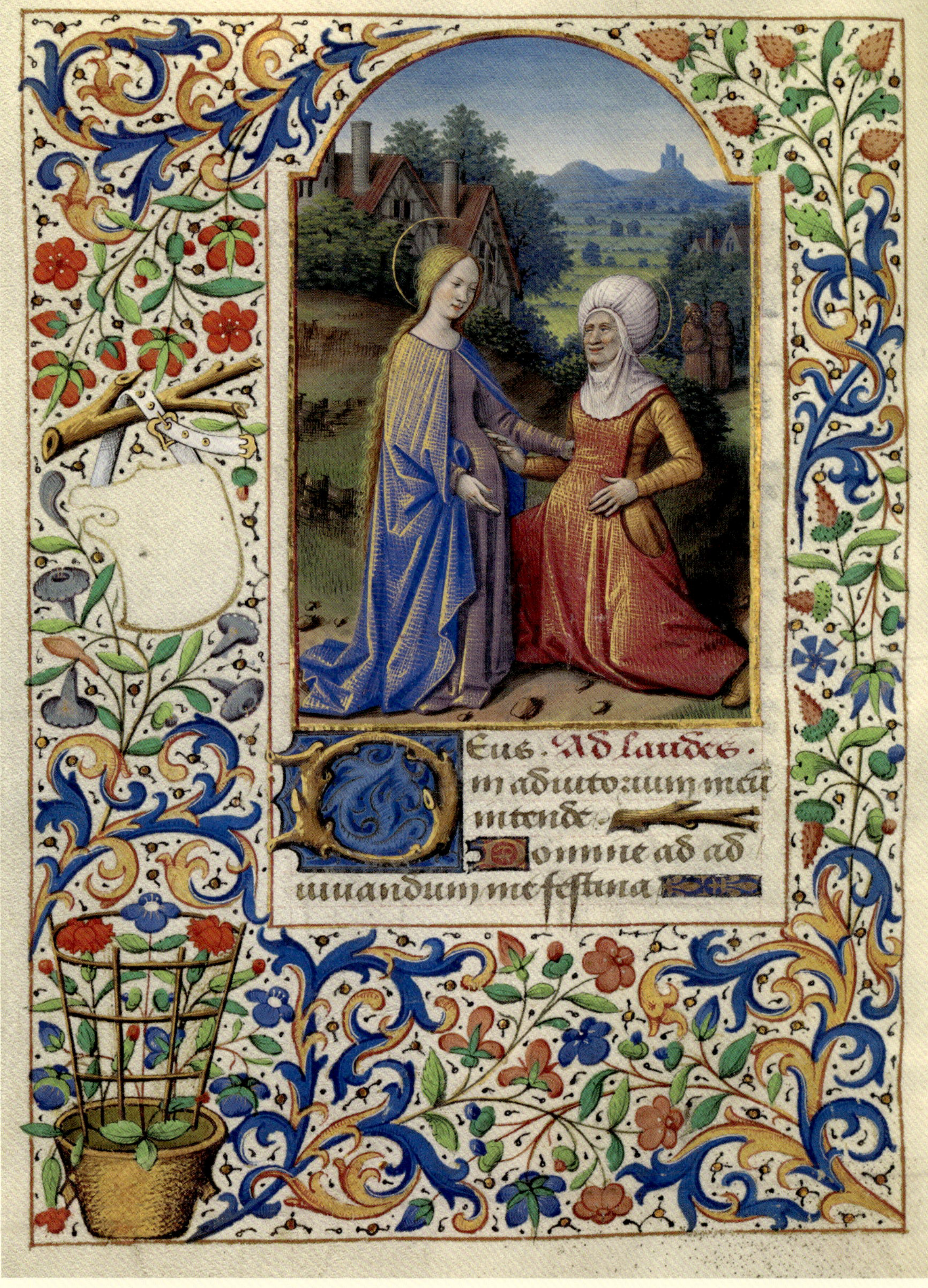
eus. AD laudes
m adiutorium meu
intende
omine ad ad
iuuandum me festina

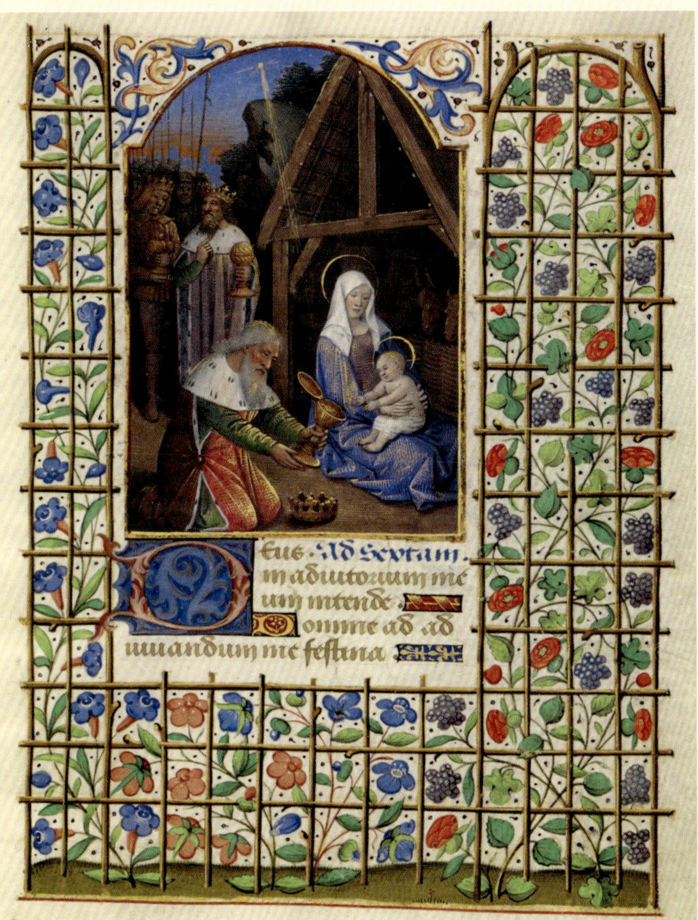

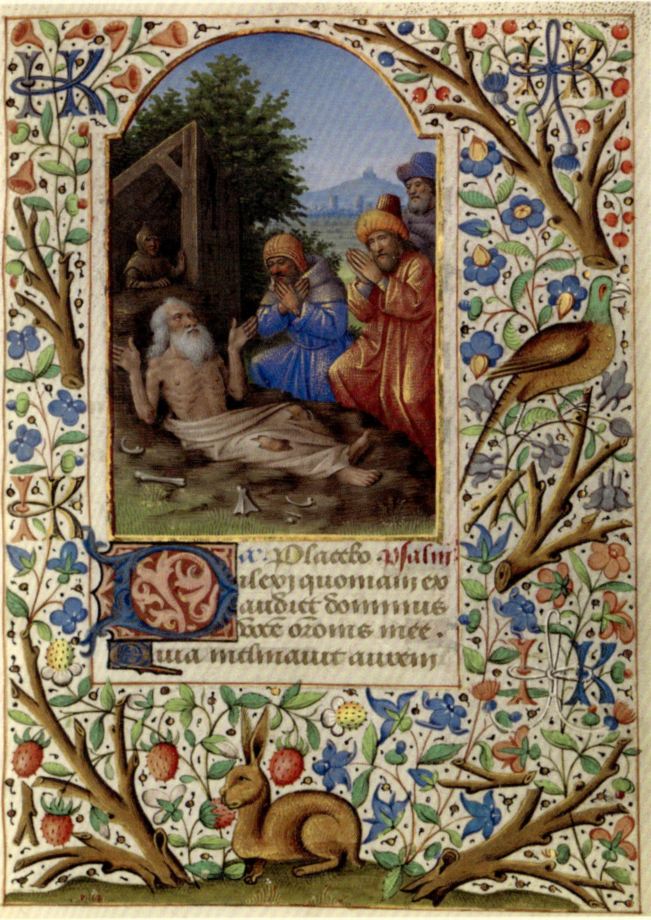

deceased and to prepare for one's own future death. Decaying filth surrounds the prophet Job, whose infirmity was just one of many hardships to befall him (fig. 45). Job's spiritual devotion, patience, and faith during tribulation—he had lost everything, including his wealth, family, and health—were models for Christians during the Middle Ages and Renaissance. Bourdichon contrasted the simple architecture of the shack, the only structural link to civilization in the distant background, with the greenery of nature in the miniature's pastoral landscape and surrounding frame. The rabbit and partridge serve as reminders of fecundity and also indicate a rustic locale. Thus Bourdichon contrasted cultivated and wild spaces across the pages of this book of hours, allowing the owner to experience different states of devotion, which will be explored in the following chapters. ❧

FIGURE 43 | *The Visitation*, Tours, France, ca. 1480–85, Jean Bourdichon, Katherine Hours, 16.4 × 11.6 cm (6⁷⁄₁₆ × 4⁹⁄₁₆ in.), Ms. 6 (84.ML.746), fol. 41v

FIGURE 44 | *The Adoration of the Magi*, Tours, France, ca. 1480–85, Jean Bourdichon, Katherine Hours, 16.4 × 11.6 cm (6⁷⁄₁₆ × 4⁹⁄₁₆ in.), Ms. 6 (84.ML.746), fol. 59

FIGURE 45 | *Job on the Dung Heap*, Tours, France, ca. 1480–85, Jean Bourdichon, Katherine Hours, 16.4 × 11.6 cm (6⁷⁄₁₆ × 4⁹⁄₁₆ in.), Ms. 6 (84.ML.746), fol. 96

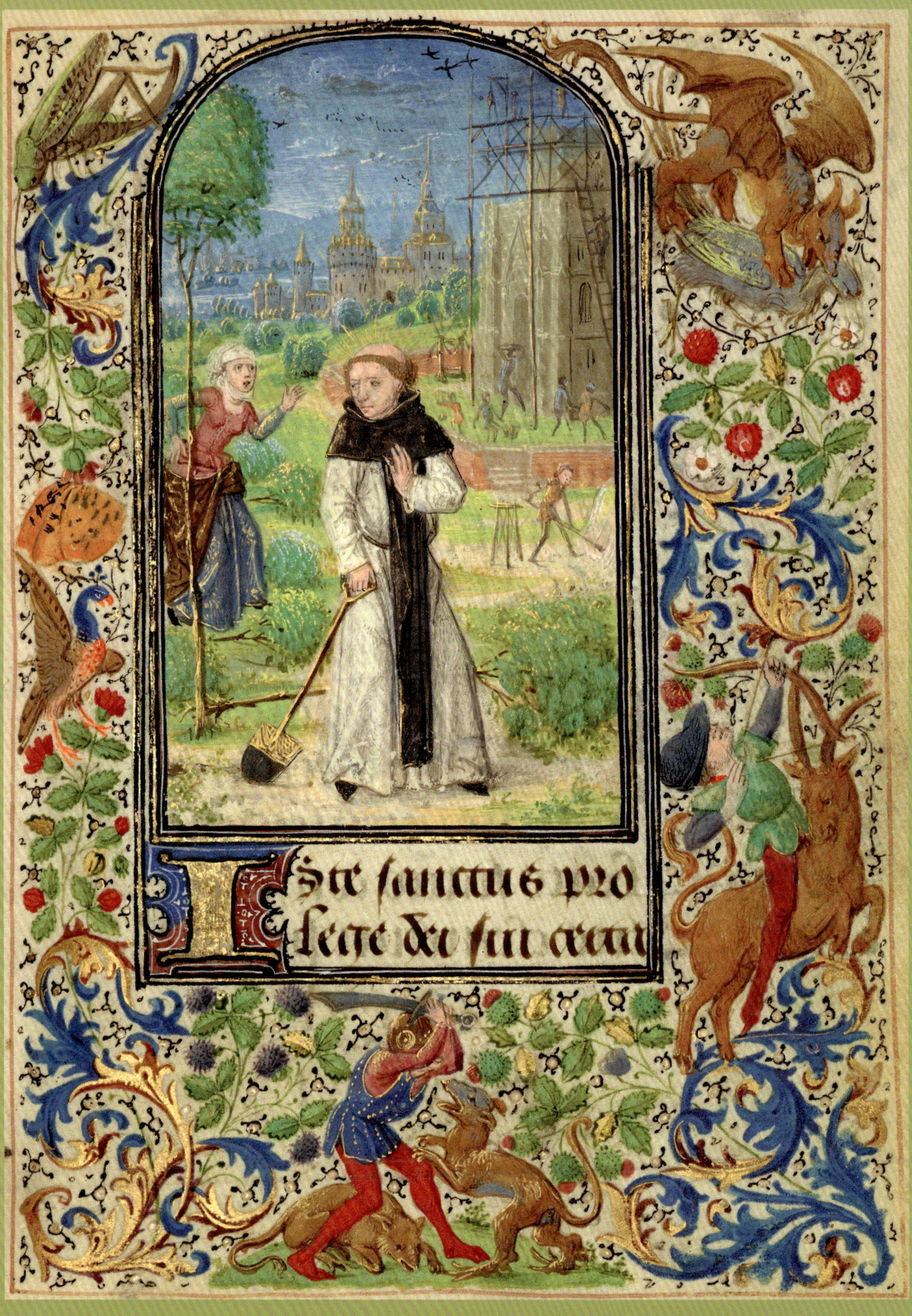
Iste sanctus pro
lege dei sui certa[vit]

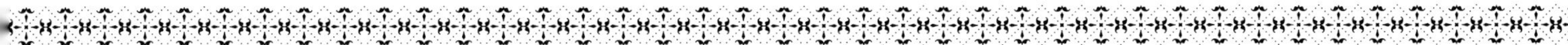

II
GARDENS AND CULTIVATED EARTH

GARDENS EMBODY HUMAN CONTROL OVER NATURE. IN THESE SPACES, flowers and plants are arranged, shaped, and cultivated in beautiful and at times marvelous ways. Renaissance villas and châteaus often featured extravagant green spaces combined with sculptures, fountains, and topiaries composed of local and exotic plants, all meant to impress visitors. In devotional manuscripts of the time, gardens, farmlands, and even harvested fields provide stunning settings or backdrops for a range of narratives centered on the theme of salvation or sanctity. From the paradisiacal Garden of Eden to the protected green spaces associated with the Virgin Mary, Christ, and certain saints, gardens were visualized either as expansive and well-planted terrains or as modest plots suitable for a kitchen or monastery. Within the tradition of landscape painting, the art of verdancy, or greenery, presents an idealized view of nature in perfect harmony, a metaphor that premodern Christians equated with heaven and that humanists associated with ideal worlds (following the philosophical writings of Plato, Aristotle, and others).

In the Middle Ages, monasteries were sites where microgreens and medicine flourished, establishing a precedent for garden culture and pharmacopoeia that lasted throughout the Renaissance.[30] The hermit-saint Fiacre (seventh century), for example, was a skilled herbalist and healer who founded an oratory that served as a hospice for travelers. One medieval legend recounts that a local bishop offered Fiacre as much land as he could work in a day. With miraculous ability, Fiacre is said to have toppled trees and cleared briars with nothing more than a shovel, a feat that attracted scorn and accusations of devilry from a local woman, as shown in Lieven van

FIGURE 46 | *Saint Fiacre and Houpdée*, Ghent (written out) and Antwerp (illuminated), Belgium, 1469, Lieven van Lathem, Prayer Book of Charles the Bold, 12.4 × 9.2 cm (4⅞ × 3⅝ in.), Ms. 37 (89.ML.35), fol. 38

Lathem's carefully composed narrative scene filled with idyllic and naturalistic details (fig. 46). This illumination also demonstrates the relationship between human agency in cultivating the natural world and the same agency in building structures that contain or encroach upon the verdant earth in an attempt to create paradise.

In Simon Bening's scene of the Garden of Eden, the earthly paradise is represented as a vast and verdant landscape (fig. 47). In the foreground, surrounding the scene of the Creation of Eve, are lilies, irises, lilies of the valley, roses, and a date palm (perhaps signifying the supposedly Eastern location of Eden, as such trees were imported from beyond Europe). Opposite a golden fountain in the midground, Adam and Eve share the forbidden fruit, and

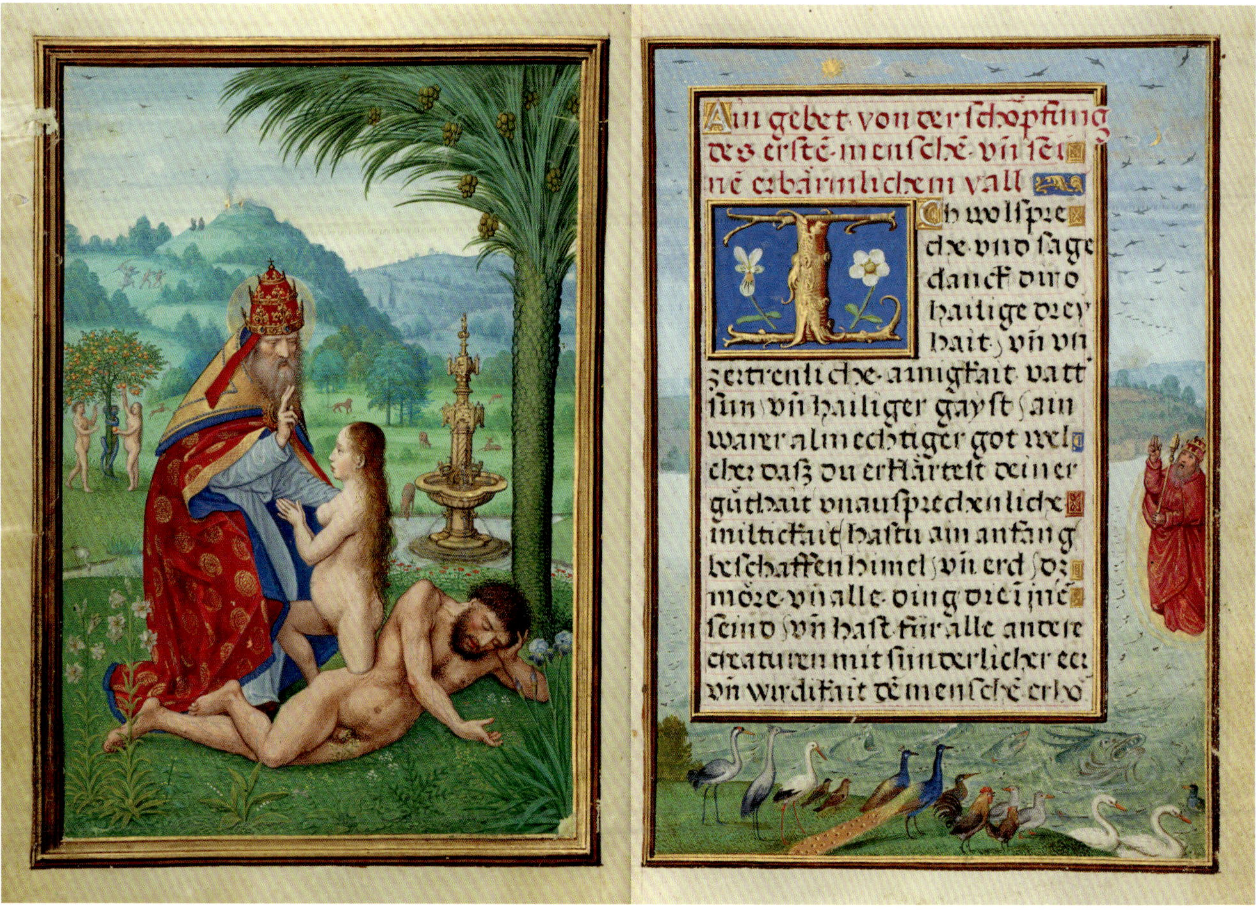

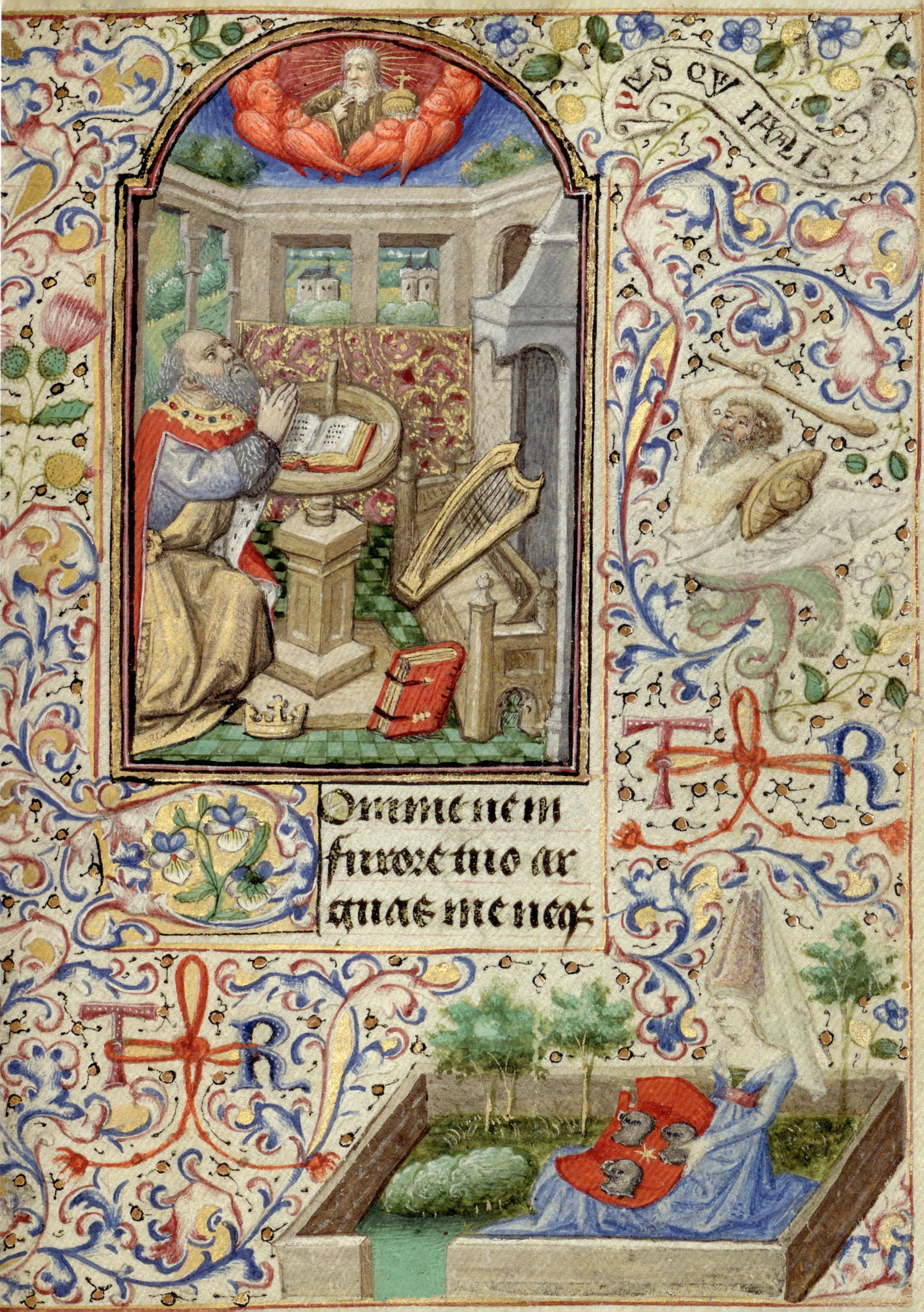
PLS QVI IHTLIS
Dñe ne in
furore tuo ar
guas me neq

farther beyond, a lion and several deer roam. In the background, the first couple are expelled from Eden, and their sons Cain and Abel offer sacrifices. Bening's landscape advances a continuous narrative by separating episodes with trees, hills, and water.

Gardens symbolize fertility, chastity, and virginity simultaneously, since nature is at once free to bloom, protected from harm, and seemingly unadulterated by the wild and untamed world beyond. These themes play out across the pages of the Hours of Simon de Varie, where an intimate study and a modest garden become spaces for acts of devotion (fig. 48). Beyond the windows of the small room, one notices a walled town and a pathway leading to King David's secluded retreat. At the bottom of the page, a fashionably dressed maiden displays the coat of arms of the manuscript's patron, the knight Simon de Varie, within the confines of an enclosed garden. Young ladies feature throughout the manuscript, and their presence bespeaks the chivalric vow of virtuous knighthood. This woman may also serve as a foil for the biblical Bathsheba, whose beauty seduced David when he spied her bathing. A page from the Hours of Louis XII (fig. 49) sets this familiar scene inside a Renaissance garden, the arrangement of which follows that of many late fifteenth-century monastic, university, and public botanical gardens. The illuminator, Jean Bourdichon, achieves perspective through the receding lines of the herb and flower parterres and fruit tree groves, which lead to the hedge of rose bushes and palace wall in the midground; beyond, atmospheric perspective reveals a mountainous kingdom and twilight sky. Humanist writers across Europe, including Marsilio Ficino (1433–1499) in Italy, advocated viewing greenery as a way to counter a melancholy temperament and in order to rejuvenate the spirit.

The late fifteenth century witnessed a renewed interest in botanical studies and the direct observation of nature. During his lifetime, Martin Schongauer (ca. 1450–1491) was known throughout Europe as both a painter and a printmaker. In an early botanical drawing, Schongauer captures flowers in differing states of bloom (fig. 50). In this preparatory study for the *Madonna of the Rose Bower* (fig. 51), the great master observed peonies (a flower that signifies Mary as "a rose without thorns") from life, rendering the veins in leaves, the pollen-filled stamen, and the arching petals. In many ways, botanical drawings mirror classical and medieval herbals, which

FIGURE 49 | *Bathsheba Bathing*, Tours, France, 1498–99, Jean Bourdichon, leaf from the Hours of Louis XII, 24.3 × 17 cm (9⁹⁄₁₆ × 6¹¹⁄₁₆ in.), Ms. 79 (2003.105), recto

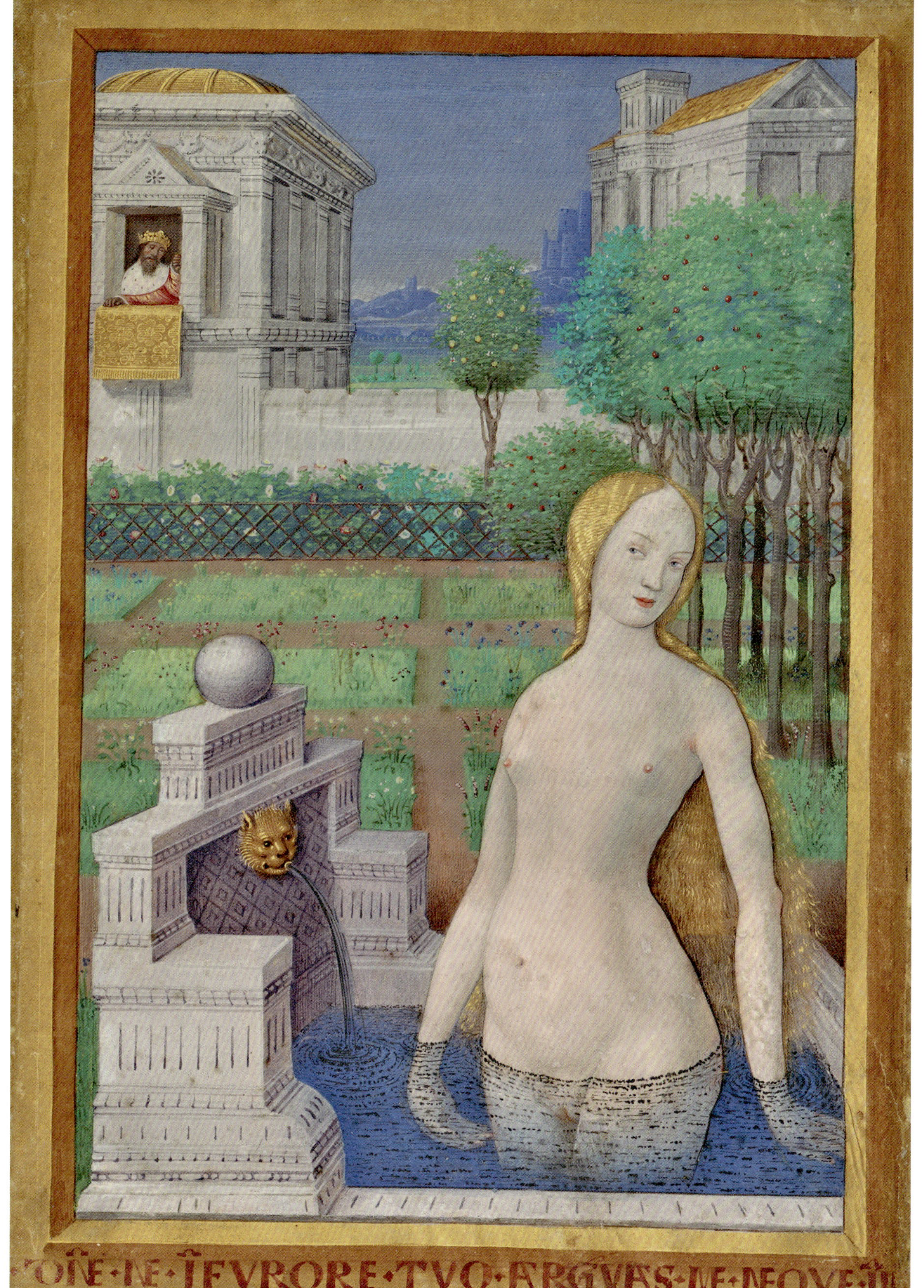

OÑE · NE · ÎFVRORE · TVO · ARGVAS · ME · NEQVE · IN

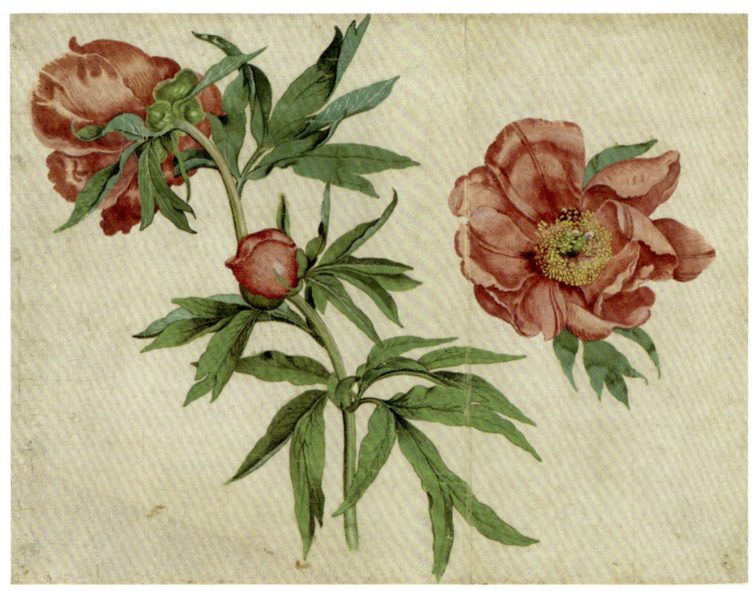

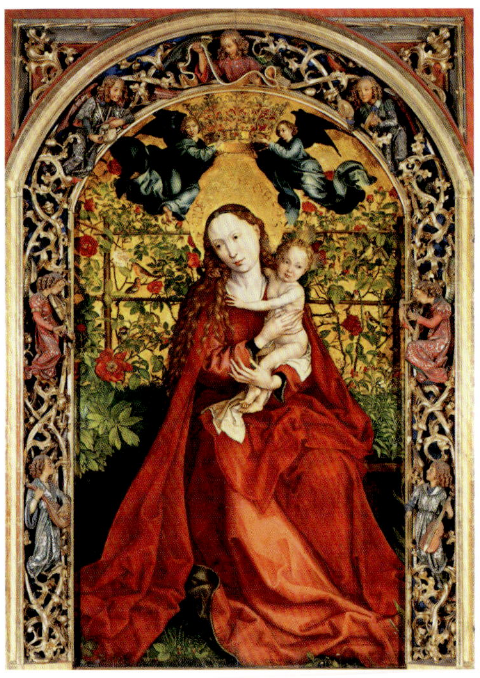

provided scientific identifications, medicinal properties, and symbolic meanings for plants. At the end of the sixteenth century, Joris Hoefnagel (1542–1600) elaborated on a model calligraphic book with magnificent illuminations of flora and fauna. The additions were produced at the request of the Holy Roman emperor Rudolph II (r. 1576–1612), known for his impressive *Kunstkammer* (cabinet of natural curiosities), menagerie, and court gardens. With a veracity of observation, Hoefnagel juxtaposes fungi and flowers, such as the cultivated four-o'clock, also called the "marvel of Peru," a plant brought to Europe from South America (fig. 52). Hoefnagel's careful studies of flora and fauna would pave the way for the development of Netherlandish still-life painting and even eighteenth- and nineteenth-century botanical drawings.

Apart from gardens, farmlands and fields provided ample inspiration for artists and thinkers in the Renaissance. In the Llangattock Hours, the Holy Family is seen passing a wheat field in their flight from King Herod's armies. According to an apocryphal legend, after the family passed a farmer sowing grain, his field grew miraculously overnight. The

IESU CORONA CELSIOR ET VE
RITAS SUBLIMIOR QUI CON
TEMENTI SÆRUULO RÆDIS
PERENNE PRÆMIUM OE SUPPLE
CENTE ATTIÆ OBTENTIÆ HUIUS
OPTIMI REMISSIONEM ARIMINU
RUMPENDO NEXUM UINAULI

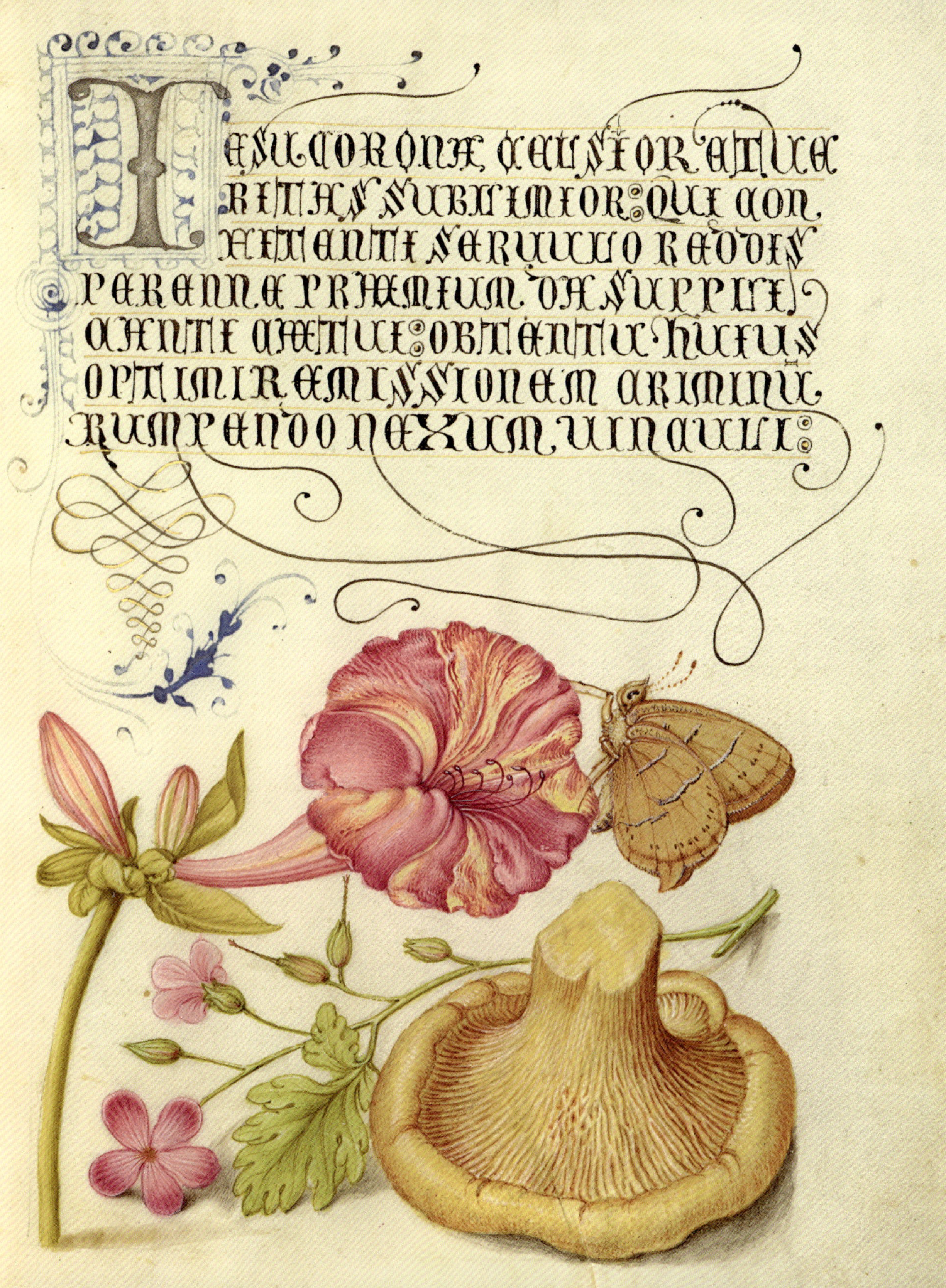

full crop fooled Herod's soldiers, who believed the family had passed the field during its planting and so could not have traveled that path for many months. Set in a familiar northern European environment instead of a more accurate Mediterranean climate, this miniature evokes rural peasant life that would have been seen (although not intimately known) by the patron of the manuscript (fig. 53). Hedges and wooden fences separate fields in various states of cultivation as villagers and even a small dog head toward town, blissfully unaware of the miracle occurring behind them.

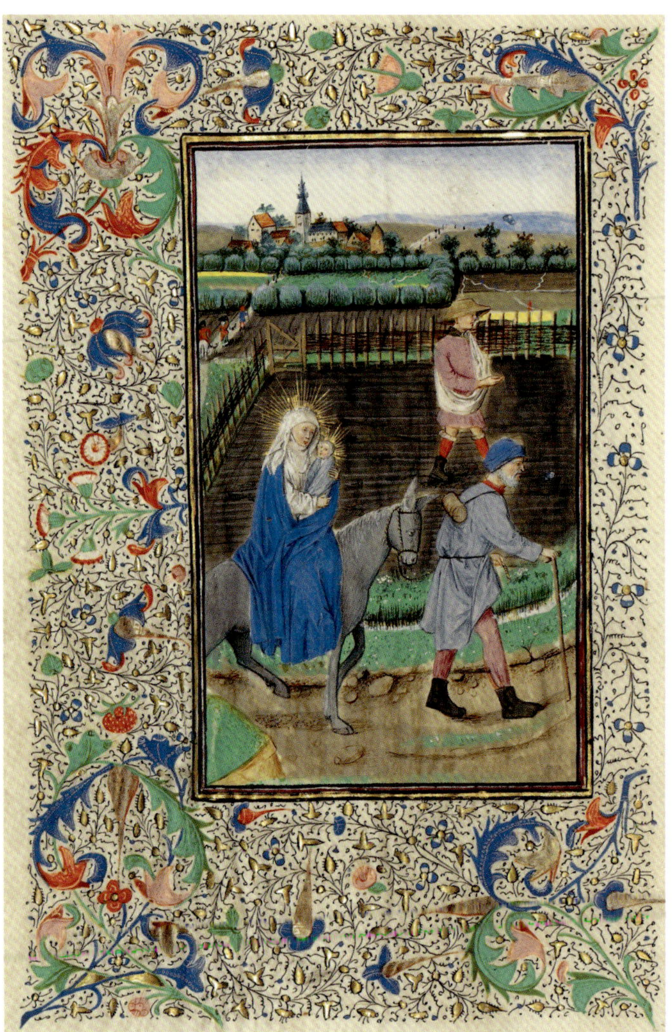

FIGURE 53 | *The Flight into Egypt*, Ghent and Bruges, Belgium, 1450s, Master of the Llangattock Hours, Llangattock Hours, 26.4 × 18.4 cm (10⅜ × 7¼ in.), Ms. Ludwig IX 7 (83.ML.103), fol. 103v

Rhythmic pen-drawn lines bring to life a scene of the Virgin Mary sitting on a raised grassy platform, tenderly holding a playful Christ child on her lap (fig. 54). Supported by a wooden fence, commonly used to enclose gardens or cultivated earth, this bench delineates a sacred space for the Holy Family. Medieval depictions of Mary often place her in a walled garden, called a *hortus conclusus,* a term derived from the Latin Bible: "My sister, my spouse, is a garden enclosed, a garden enclosed, a fountain sealed up" (Song of Songs 4:12); the walled garden was thought to allude to Mary's virginity, chastity, and fertile womb.

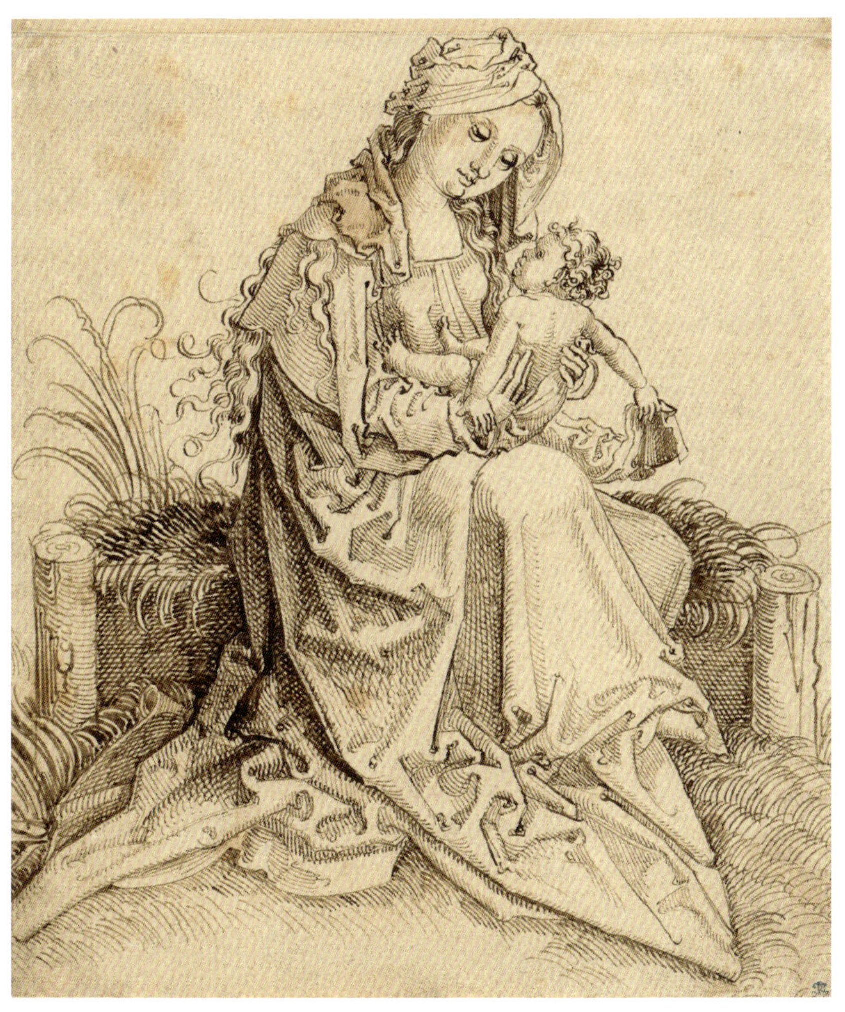

FIGURE 54 | Unknown artist, Nuremberg School, *The Virgin and Child on a Grassy Bench*, ca. 1500. Pen and brown ink; strip at the top added later, 19.2 × 15.6 cm (7⁹⁄₁₆ × 6⅛ in.), 92.GA.103

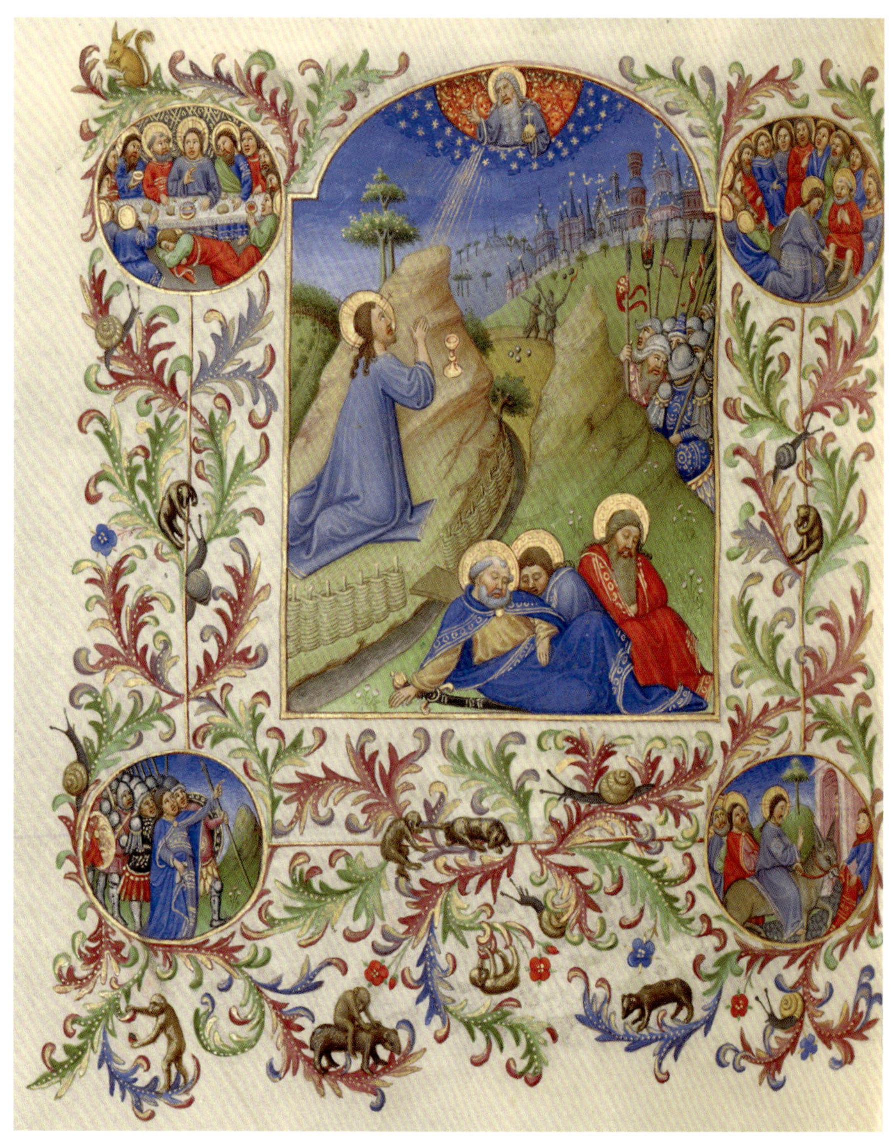

Christ, the fruit of Mary's womb, redeemed humankind from the sin introduced by Adam and Eve in the Garden of Eden. On the evening before the Crucifixion, Christ prayed with his disciples in a place beyond the walls of Jerusalem where they often went for meditation and respite. The Gospels refer to this location as the Mount of Olives, the Garden of Gethsemane, or a country place, which artists often conflated into one setting. The Garden of Gethsemane is located on the slopes of the Mount of Olives outside Jerusalem, a fact attested in numerous accounts by medieval and Renaissance pilgrims to the Holy Land. In an illumination by the Spitz Master, Christ

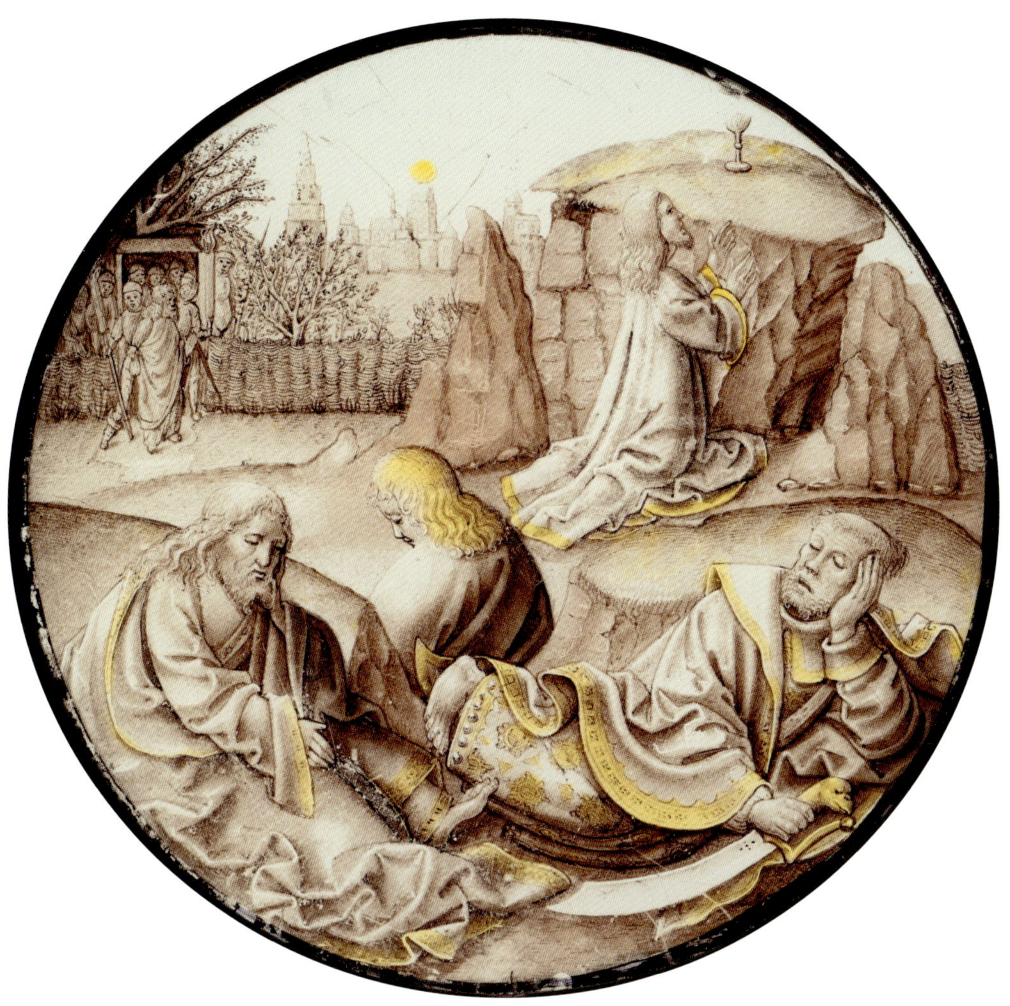

kneels at the base of the Mount of Olives, which is surrounded by a wattle
fence to represent the Garden of Gethsemane (fig. 55). The walls of Jerusalem
can be seen in the far distance. The draftsman responsible for the design
of a stained-glass window also set the episode within a fenced space and
represented a rocky outcropping at the base of which Christ prays (fig. 56).
As private green spaces, gardens are often associated with healing, since life
and beauty often repel thoughts of melancholy and gloom, yet the story of
Christ's prayer is interrupted by a band of soldiers led by Judas Iscariot; in the
foreground of both images, the disciples sleep unaware.

FIGURE 56 | Unknown Netherland-
ish artist, *Christ on the Mount of
Olives*, ca. 1480–1500. Colorless
glass, vitreous paint, and silver stain,
Diam 27.2 cm (10¹¹⁄₁₆ in.), 2003.50

The Resurrected Christ Appearing to the Marys aptly fills the historiated initial *N* of an Easter chant in an antiphonal (fig. 57). Having come to mourn at Christ's tomb, the women discover it empty. The scene is an elaboration on the *Noli me tangere* subject (John 20:14–18; see fig. 2), in which Mary Magdalene visits the garden of Joseph of Arimathea and mistakes the resurrected Christ for a gardener. A wattle fence defines the perimeter of the private garden, while pale yellow highlights indicate leafy foliage and cast a golden light on the hills beyond. Across Europe, walls and wattle fences were commonly used to evoke green spaces. The illuminator, Bartolomeo Rigossi da Gallarate (ca. 1460–1480), was known for his palette of bright colors and for creating richly painted surfaces with an imaginative play of light. ❧

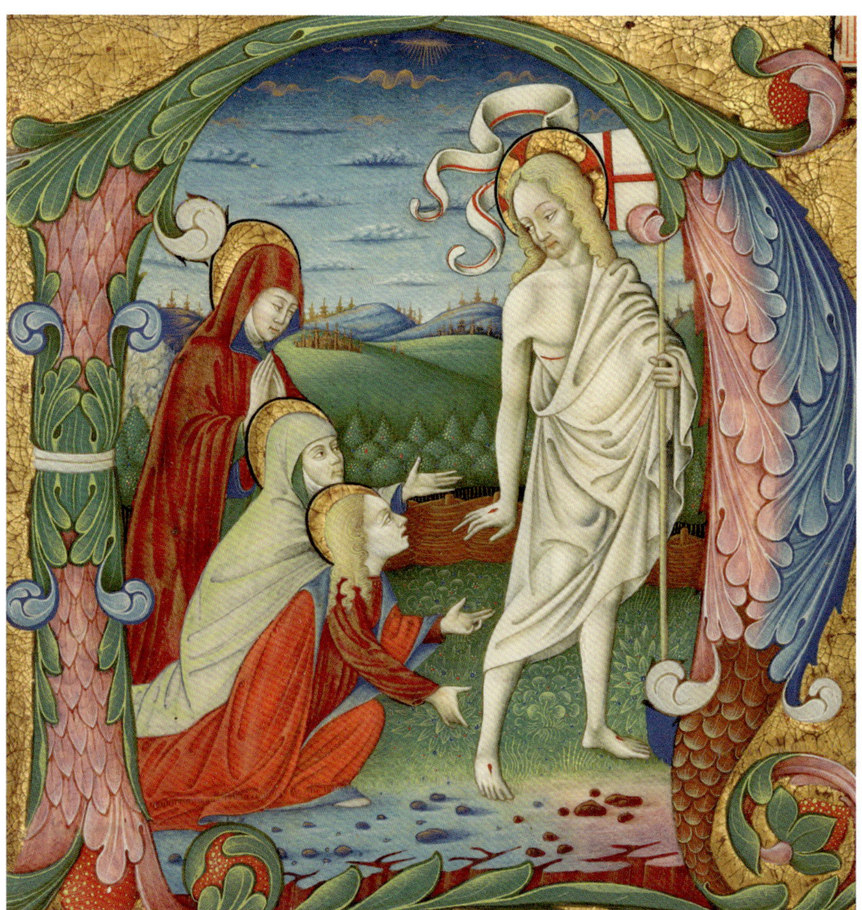

FIGURE 57 | Initial N: *The Resurrected Christ Appearing to the Marys*, Lombardy, ca. 1465, Bartolomeo Rigossi da Gallarate, cutting from an antiphonal, 15.1 × 14.6 cm (5¹⁵⁄₁₆ × 5¾ in.), Ms. 49 (93.MS.8), recto

THE CROHIN–LA FONTAINE HOURS

Bruges, Belgium, ca. 1480–85(?)
Master of the Dresden Prayer Book

FOLLOWING THE RELATIVELY NEW STYLE OF BORDER PAINTING IN GHENT AND Bruges, the Master of the Dresden Prayer Book (active ca. 1480–1515) filled the space surrounding the devotional text of this book of hours with scattered flowers (fig. 58), thereby effectively transforming the manuscript into a garden and reminding the reader-viewer of the fleeting nature of life. Flowers and insects appear very much alive, an effect achieved through cast shadows. But there is a certain degree of whimsy, detectable especially when one

FIGURE 58 | *The Visitation*, Bruges, Belgium, ca. 1480–85(?), Master of the Dresden Prayer Book or workshop, Crohin–La Fontaine Hours, 13.3 × 9.4 cm (5¼ × 3¹¹⁄₁₆ in.), Ms. 23 (86.ML.606), fols. 71v–72

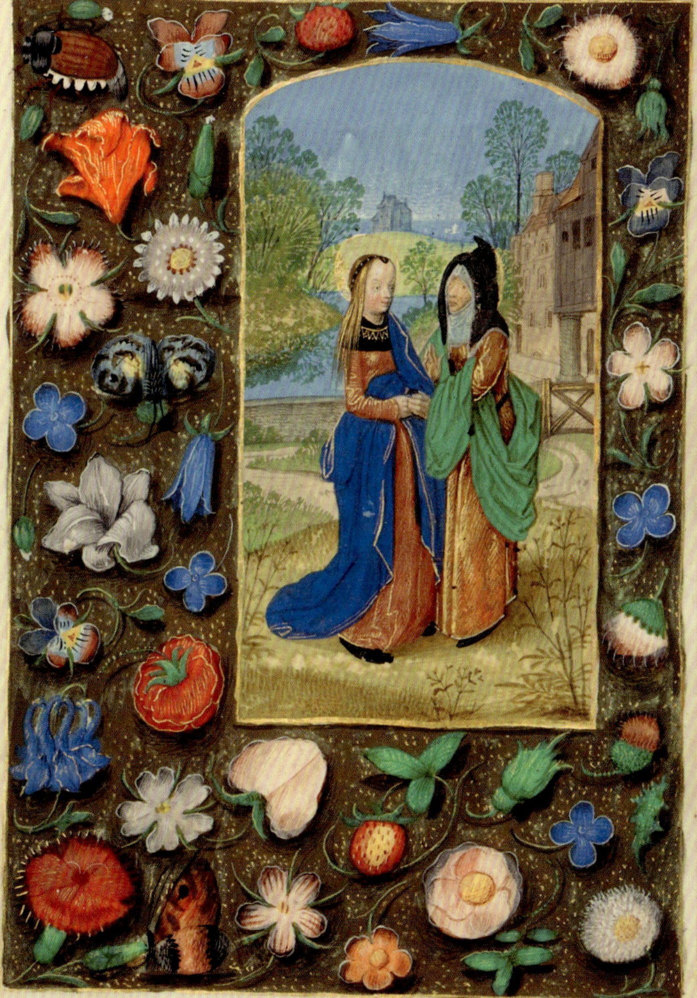

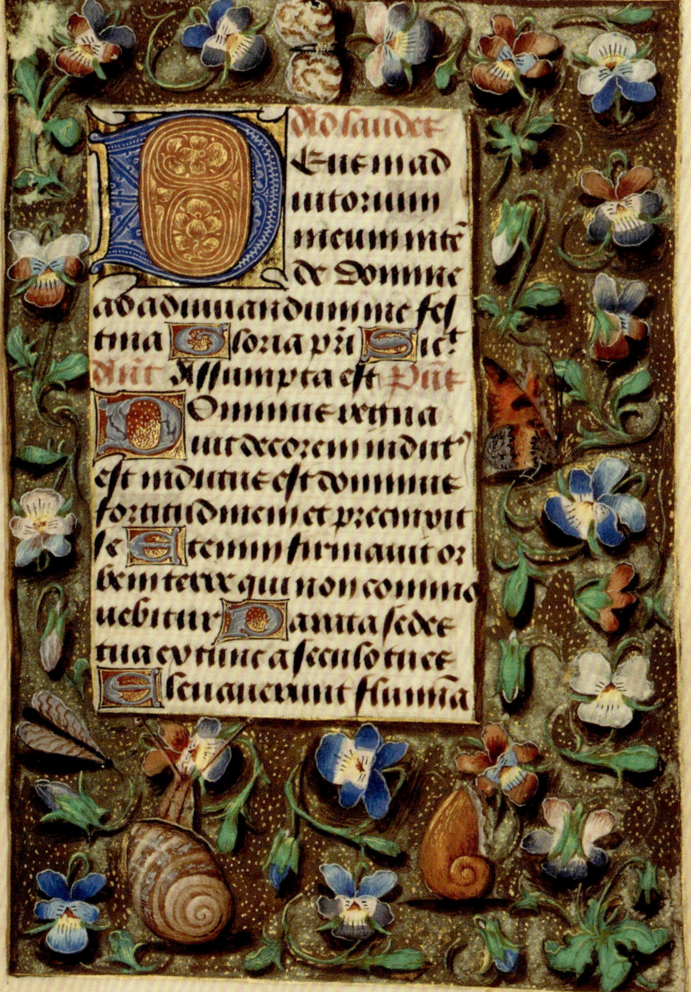

scrutinizes the living matter for botanical or entomological precision: carnations, pansies, daisies, and sweet-pea flowers appear to grow from a leafy acanthus stem, for example (fig. 59). These living paintings recall the practice of pressing flowers into manuscripts and the long tradition of illuminated herbals based on Greco-Roman and medieval medicinal texts.

Artists often depicted Mary and Elizabeth meeting to share the news of their pregnancies in a garden at the edge of a town, since the womb

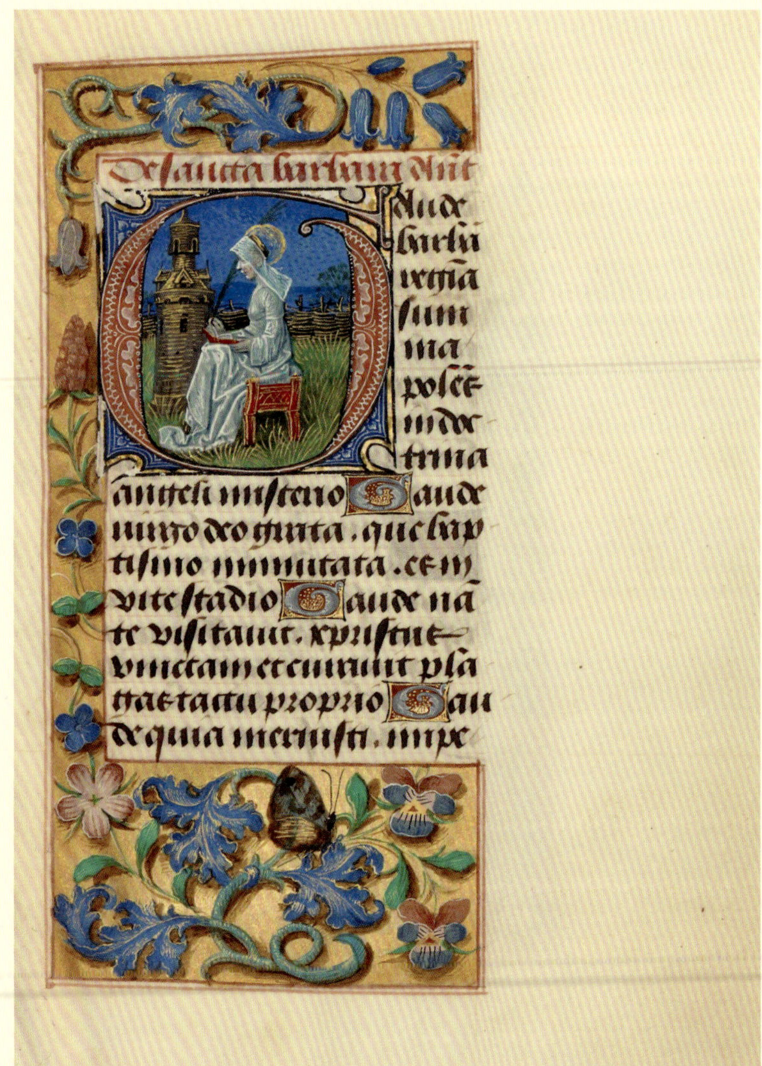

FIGURE 59 | Initial *G: Saint Barbara*, Bruges, Belgium, ca. 1480–85, Master of the Dresden Prayer Book or workshop, Crohin–La Fontaine Hours, 13.3 × 9.4 cm (5¼ × 3¹¹⁄₁₆ in.), Ms. 23 (86.ML.606), fol. 207

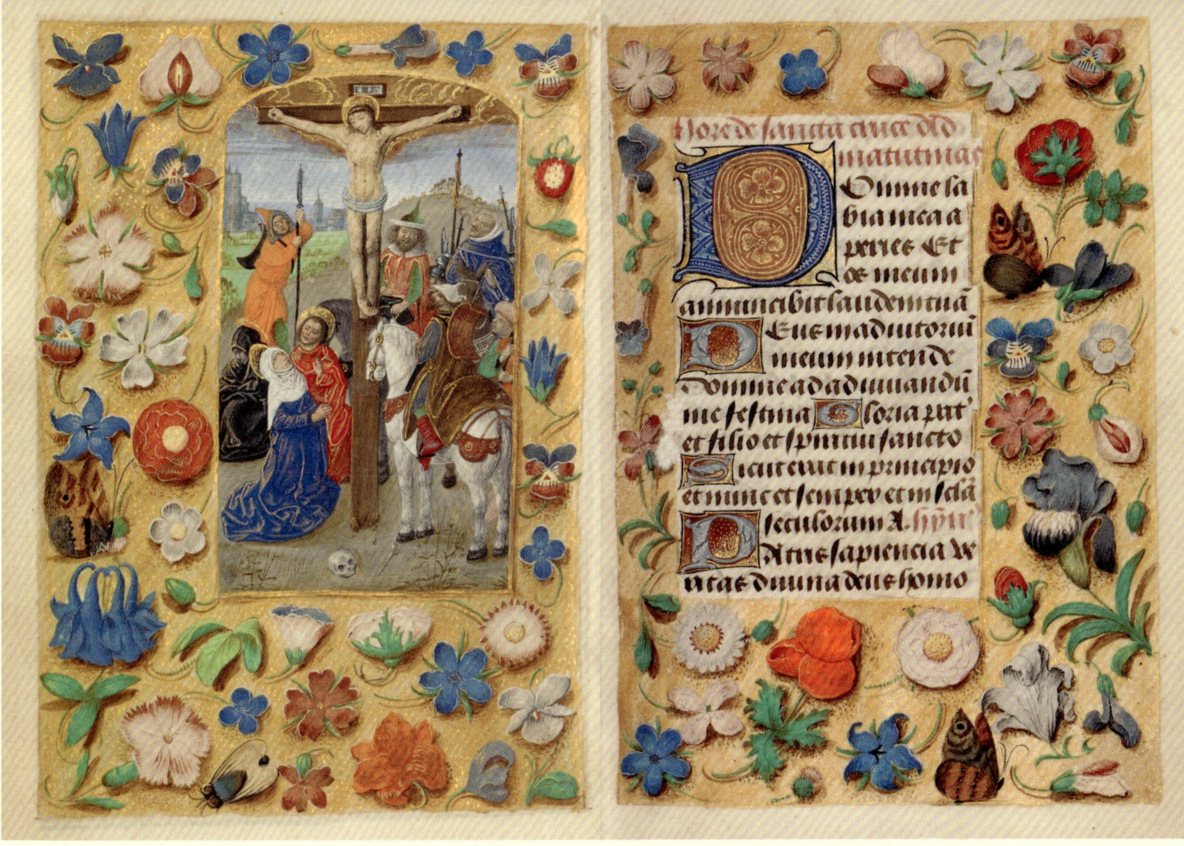

was often referred to metaphorically as a protected garden with the potential
to nurture life and produce all manner of beauty (see fig. 58). This garden is
set apart from its surroundings by a wall and a gate; inside, pathways wend
and flowers bloom. The verdancy within the small miniature is outdone by
the myriad strewn flowers that fill the borders of the two pages, imitating a
millefleur tapestry. A discerning eye will notice a vibrant palette composed
of roses, lilies, pinks, flowering strawberries, columbines, pansies, and forget-
me-nots, among others. Many of these plants were used medicinally to treat
pains associated with childbirth.

A Renaissance reader would have inherently understood the divine
presence manifested by these painted pages, an experience heightened by
flower symbolism in the borders. A bouquet or meadow of blossoms fills the
golden background surrounding *The Crucifixion* and text for the Hours of the
Cross (fig. 60). A prism of colors and panoply of textures indicate speedwell,
borage, dianthus (red), cranesbill, sweet pea, strawberry fruit and flower,
primrose, heartsease, columbine, daisy, wild rose (white, pink, and red),
wood sorrel, white lily, blue bells, tiger lily, poppy, thistle, and iris. ❧

FIGURE 60 | *The Crucifixion*; Deco-
rated Initial *D*, Bruges, Belgium,
ca. 1480–85, Master of the Dresden
Prayer Book or workshop, Crohin–
La Fontaine Hours, 13.3 × 9.4 cm
(5¼ × 3¹¹⁄₁₆ in.), Ms. 23 (86.ML.606),
fols. 13v–14

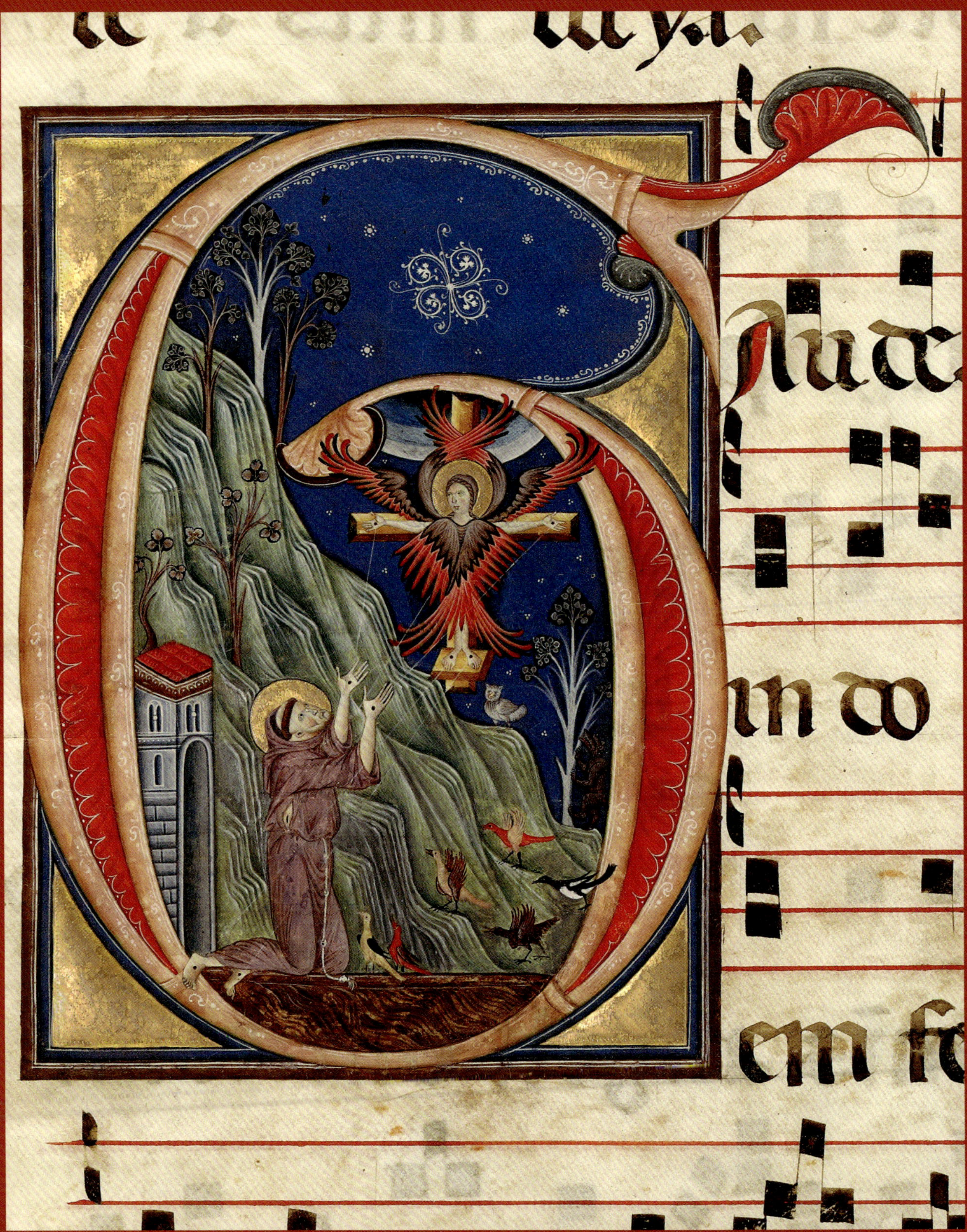
alla
aude
m co
em fe

III
WILDERNESS AND THE LAND BEYOND THE CITY

MANY PEOPLE EXPERIENCE A SENSE OF PEACE AND CALM OR EVEN WONDER when out in nature. During the Renaissance, people looked to nature to heighten their religious experiences. Historically, monasteries fostered separation from society and the singular focus on a lifestyle dedicated to prayer and contemplation, but for certain devotees this solitude was often not enough. Sometimes an individual chose to pursue life as a hermit or recluse, living apart from civilization, or as an ascetic, relinquishing worldly goods and the pleasures of the body, often fasting and practicing abstinence in isolation. By journeying out into the wilderness, these Christians hoped to achieve a more authentic and pure relationship with God, free from all distraction. Artists at the time also chose to depict these harsh rocky terrains or woodland spaces in religious artworks as environmental features that highlight humankind's inability to master the wilds of nature and that express the wondrous richness of God's creation. By gazing upon images of these desolate locations, members of the laity engaged in mindfulness experiences centered on meditation and the divesting of distractions.[31]

While kneeling in meditation on Mount La Verna, Saint Francis of Assisi (ca. 1181–1226) witnessed a stunning vision of the crucified Christ surrounded by the flaming wings of a seraph. In that moment, Christ's wounds (stigmata) were imprinted on Francis's body (fig. 61). The proto-Renaissance illuminator Rinaldo da Siena (active 1270s) included birds of various plumages and a terrifying wolf in the scene as references to stories of the saint's dedication to preaching to every part of creation. In contrast to this large page, a small folding altarpiece (called a diptych) for private

FIGURE 61 | Initial *G*: *The Stigmatization of Saint Francis*, Siena, Italy, ca. 1275, attributed to Rinaldo da Siena, leaf from a gradual, 52.9 × 37.2 cm (20 13/16 × 14⅝ in.), Ms. 71 (2003.15), verso

devotion presents Francis's stigmatization in a context that emphasizes Christlikeness and chastity (fig. 62). At right, an angel bestows wreaths of virtue on Saints Cecilia and Valerian for their vows of celibacy. The original owners of this devotional painting—perhaps the Blessed Delphine de Signe (1284–1360) and her husband, Saint Elzéar, Count of Sabran (1286–1323)— likely understood a deeper spiritual connection between these two scenes in relation to their marriage and Christian piety. Poverty, chastity, and religious obedience are vows of the Franciscan order, to which Delphine and Elzéar belonged as lay devotees.

Mount La Verna attracted the attention of artists, pilgrims, and religious ascetics for centuries. The Florentine artist Jacopo Ligozzi (1547– 1626) traveled to this spiritually rich site in central Italy to create preparatory

FIGURE 62 | Unknown artist, Avignon or Neapolitan School, *Saint Francis Receiving the Stigmata and An Angel Crowning Saints Cecilia and Valerian*, 1330s. Tempera and gold leaf on panel, with engaged frame: 31.3 × 45.7 cm (12⁵⁄₁₆ × 18 in.), 86.PB.490

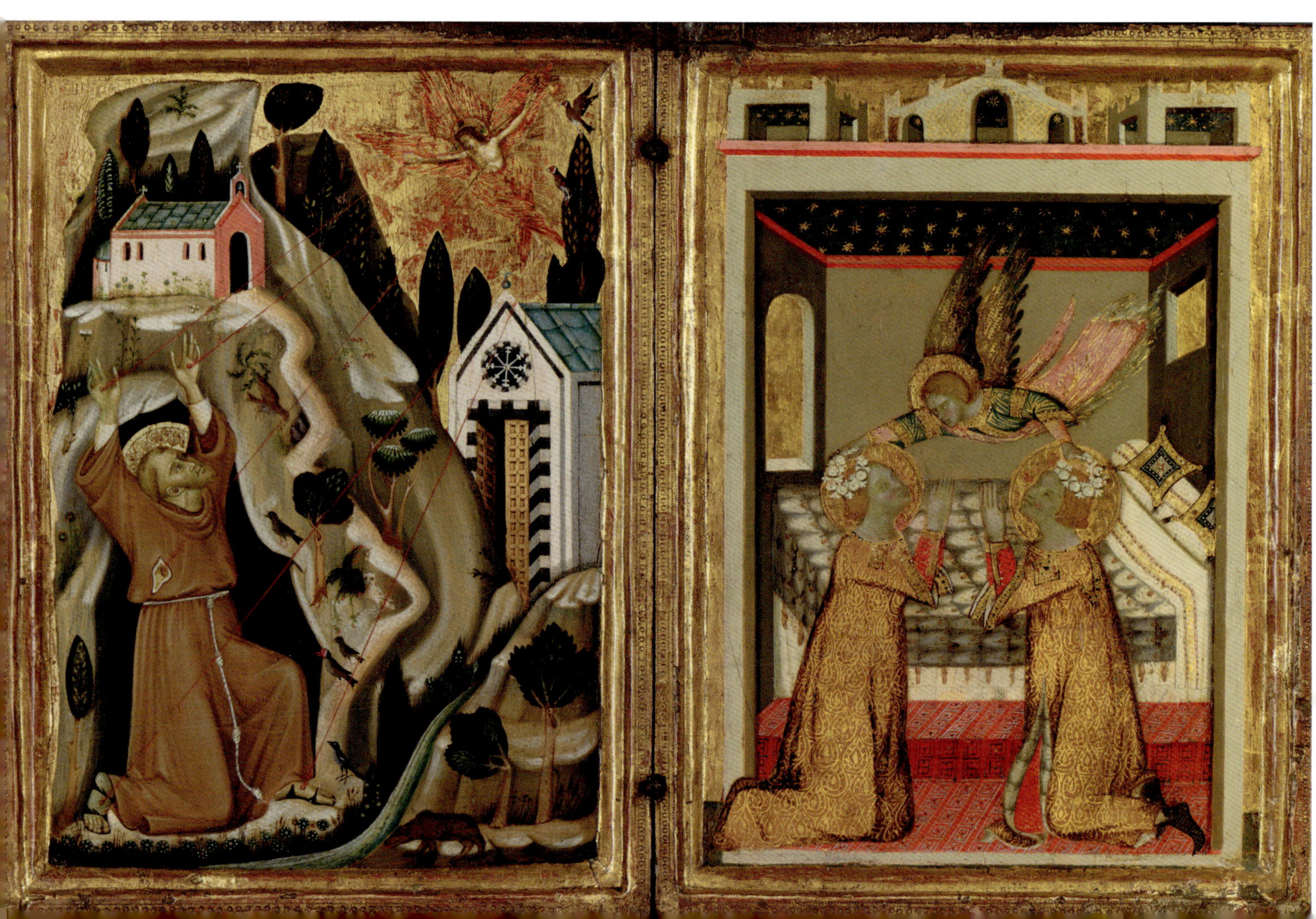

drawings for what would ultimately become highly finished etchings and engravings. In one drawing, Ligozzi depicts the miraculous encounter of the Blessed Giovanni della Verna (1259–1322) with Christ at La Verna (fig. 63). Giovanni spent years in solitude on the mountain before embarking throughout the Italian peninsula as a preacher. Each of the aforementioned artists captures a sense of isolation despite the fact that all the landscapes are filled with trees and rocky outcroppings.

The precedent for drawing directly in nature was established and brought to fruition during the fifteenth century. On a large sheet of paper once part of an album, Fra Bartolommeo (Baccio della Porta; 1472–1517) drew studies of trees in black chalk and brown ink (fig. 64). The artist may have sought inspiration in the hills surrounding his native Florence or along the

FIGURE 63 | Jacopo Ligozzi (Italian, 1547–1626), *La Verna: The Chapel of the Blessed Giovanni della Verna*, 1607. Pen, brown ink, and brown wash, 39.1 × 25.1 cm (15⅜ × 9⅞ in.), 97.GA.69

FIGURE 64 | Fra Bartolommeo (Baccio della Porta; Italian, 1472–1517), *Three Studies of Trees*, ca. 1508. Black chalk, point of brush and brown ink, 40.8 × 27.5 cm (16¹⁄₁₆ × 10¹³⁄₁₆ in.), 2001.9

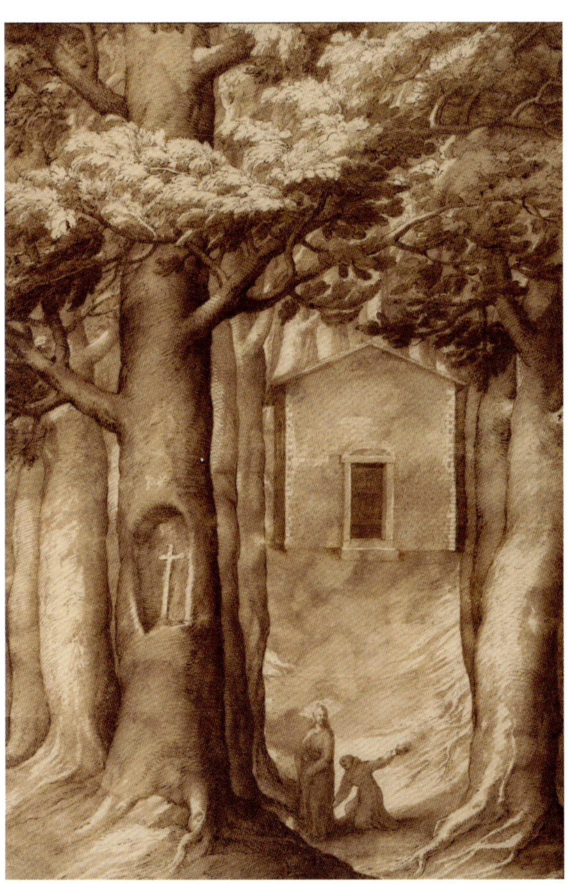

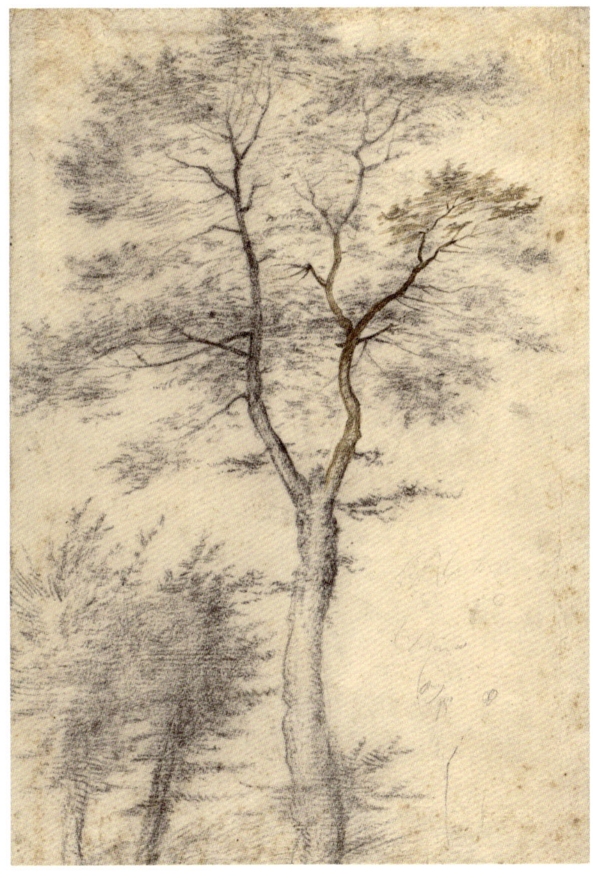

roadways to Venice, where he learned to paint in oils. Fra Bartolommeo triumphed as a master of artistry, observation, and storytelling. The date palm symbolizes the foreign land of Egypt and recalls a legend in which the same tree provides nourishment to the Holy Family during their journey and recognizes Christ as God. The pomegranate tree and broken fruit refer simultaneously to the Crucifixion and the Resurrection (based on the crimson color of the juice and inspired by the role of pomegranate seeds in the classical myth of Persephone, who every year returned to earth from Hades). In order to emphasize the theme of a strenuous and perilous journey, Fra Bartolommeo unfolds the story as a continuous narrative, which begins in the home in the background, continues in the midground episode showing Joseph leading Mary on a donkey, and culminates in the foreground (fig. 65).

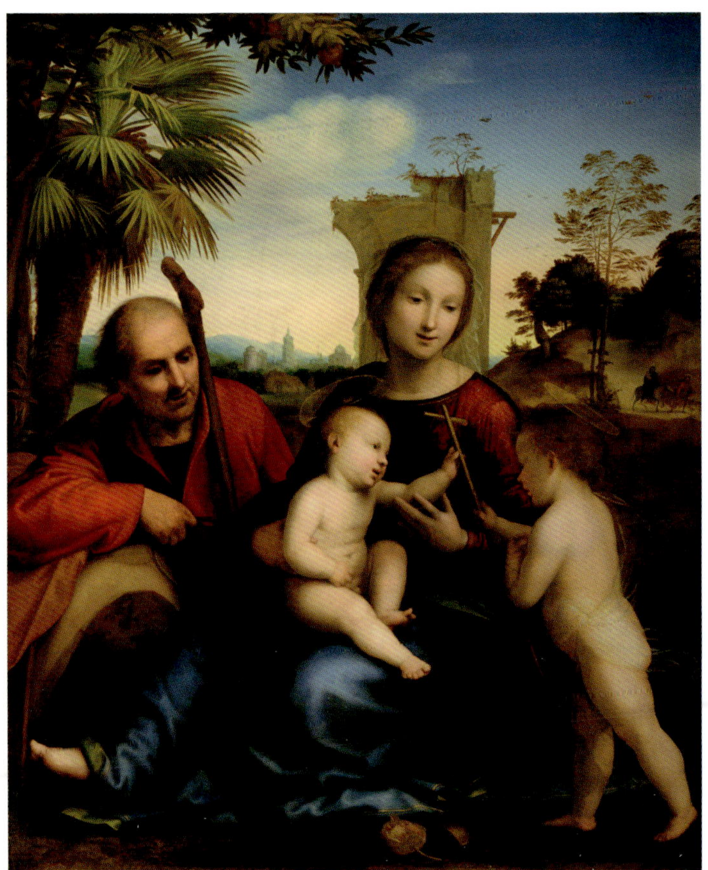

FIGURE 65 | Fra Bartolommeo (Baccio della Porta; Italian, 1472–1517), *The Rest on the Flight into Egypt with Saint John the Baptist*, ca. 1509. Oil on panel, 130.8 × 105.7 cm (51½ × 41⅝ in.), 96.PB.15

The wilderness and desert were seen as pure or untouched environments, reflective of God's savage and beautiful creation, able to test the religious conviction of those who entered. By relinquishing the comforts of city life and inhabiting these wild spaces, ascetics and hermits believed they could overcome bodily and worldly desire and achieve a more authentic connection with God. In a miniature opening a Mass to Saint John the Baptist, the ascetic saint sits holding the Lamb of God, surrounded by tamed wild beasts who recognize the presence of the divine (fig. 66). As recounted in the Gospels, Saint John dons a shirt of camel's hair and performs his ministry in the wilderness, subsisting off wild honey and locusts. The juxtaposition of the naturalistic scene in the foreground with a diapering pattern in the background expresses a tension between Gothic and Renaissance painting.

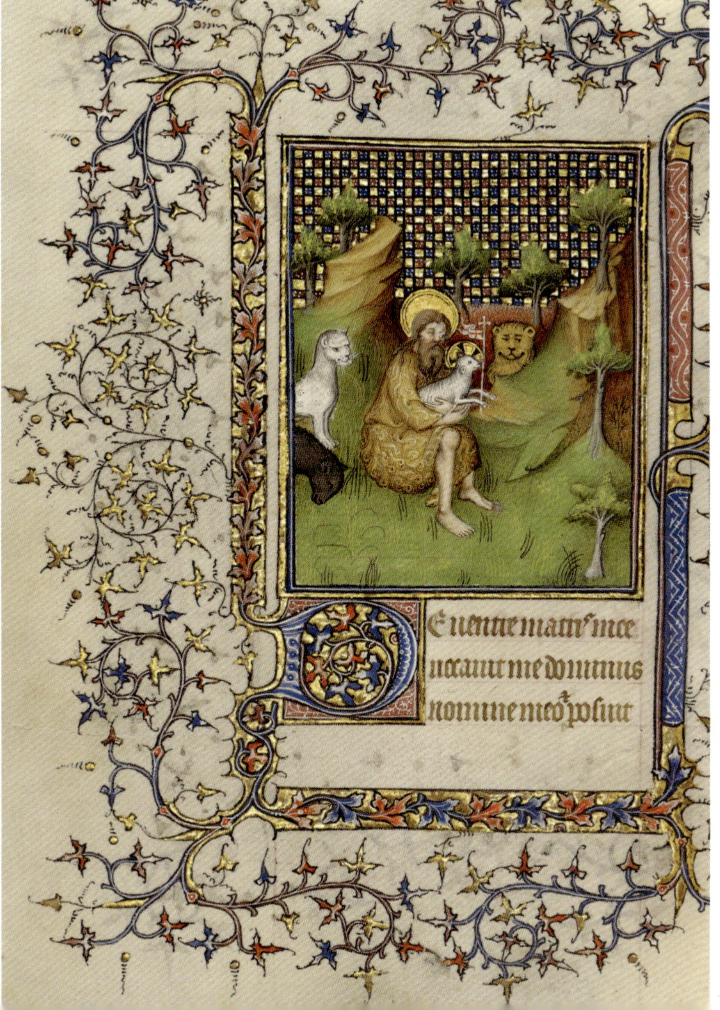

FIGURE 66 | *Saint John the Baptist in the Wilderness*, France, ca. 1410, book of hours, 17.9 × 13.3 cm (7¹⁄₁₆ × 5¼ in.), Ms. 36 (89.ML.3), fol. 59v

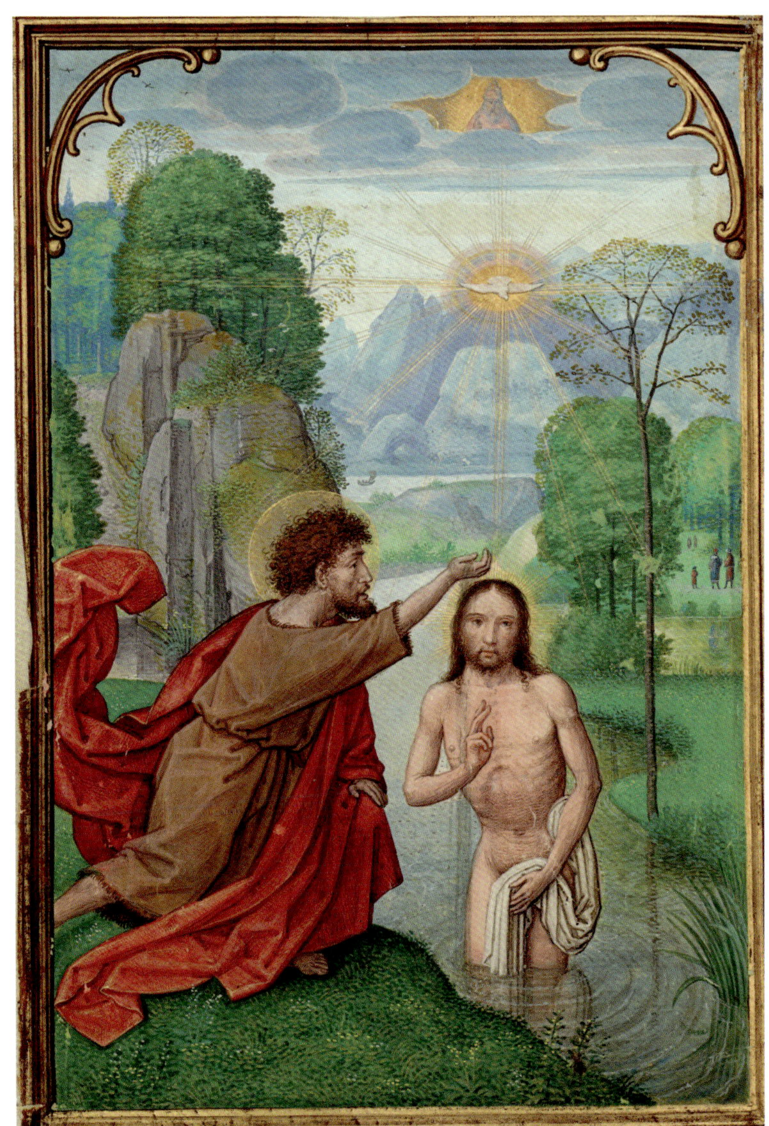

The Baptism of Christ afforded artists infinite possibilities for imagining a scene in a lush river valley (fig. 67). On the bank of the Jordan River, John the Baptist cleansed the souls of sinners. After Christ was baptized, the Holy Spirit descended upon him in the form of a dove and inspired him to journey forth into the wilderness, where he fasted for forty days and forty nights, resisting the devil's attempts to test his fortitude. The episode is rendered with meticulous detail in a scene just pages away (fig. 68). In the foreground, Christ faces off against an almost human-looking devil, who strides into the frame on avian talons. In both illuminations, Simon Bening

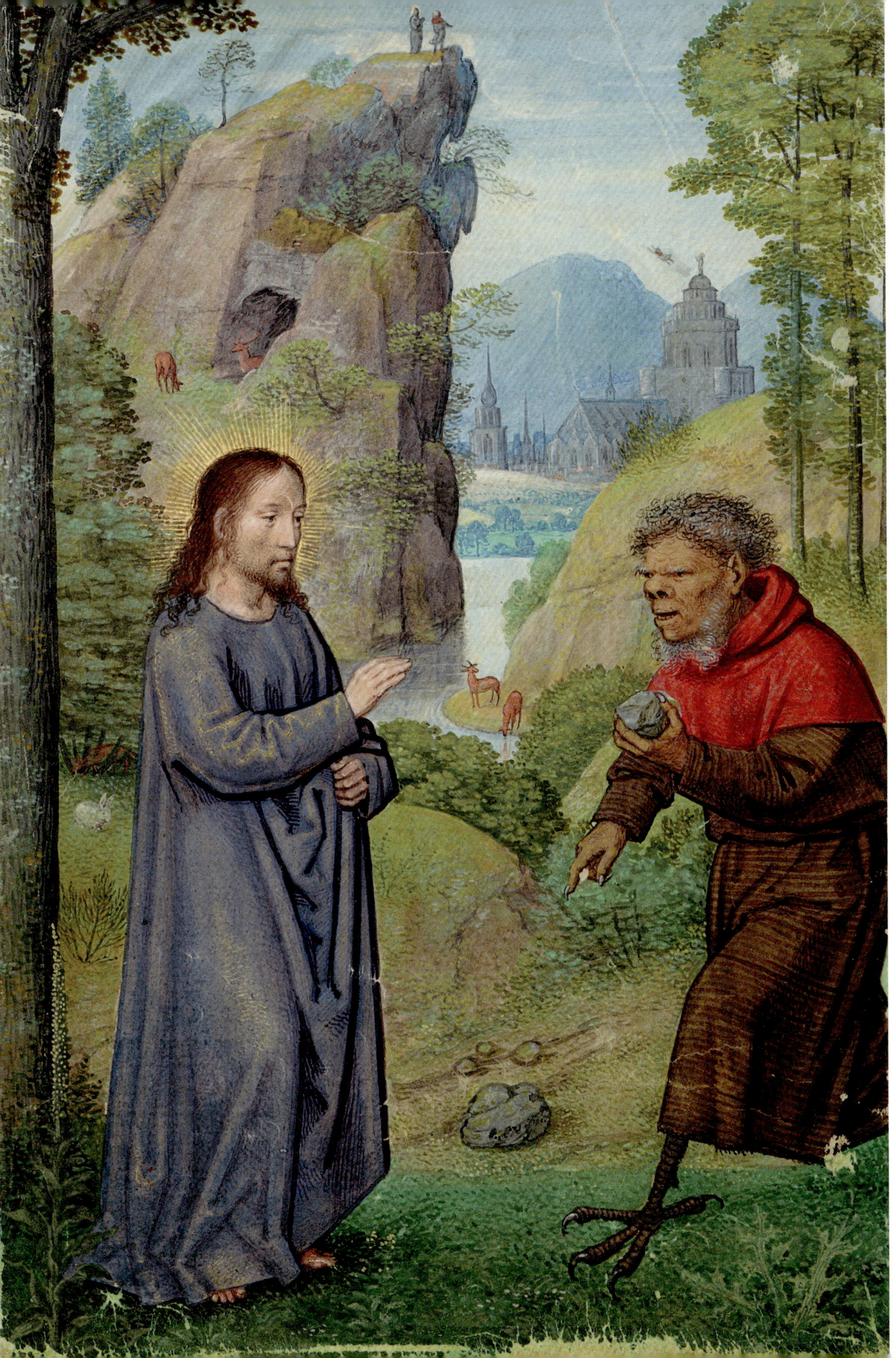

composed a verdant and bucolic wilderness. The compositions of the two miniatures mirror each other: a large cliff with exposed rock looms over a winding body of water leading back to a central blue mountain in the distance. Various types of vegetation; low, mossy grasses giving way to dirt and rocks; and ripples, reflections, and transparency in the water are all natural features that Bening masterfully crafted.

Many saints, like Francis of Assisi, experienced divine encounters while in the wilds. During a forest hunt, the Roman soldier Placidus (second century) received a vision of Christ speaking to him from the mouth of a stag with a cross between its antlers. Placidus converted to Christianity and took the name Eustace. Albrecht Dürer transposed this ancient story to a contemporaneous northern European landscape, with meticulous attention paid to rendering textures in the terrain (fig. 69). Not only does this engraving capture a spiritually charged moment; it also displays Dürer's technical mastery of landscape and visual depth. The invention of prints—lightweight, reproducible, and affordable objects—made religious imagery accessible to people of varying classes and spread artistic fame. The story of Bishop-Saint Hubert (ca. 656–727/28) borrows directly from Eustace's vision in the forest. After the death of his wife, Hubert gives himself up to the delights of hunting and also encounters a stag with a cross between its antlers that commands him to turn toward a holy life. Hubert complies, giving up his worldly possessions and joining the church. In the Prayer Book of Charles the Bold, Saint Hubert kneels between his horse and dogs with hands raised in prayer before the stag with a castle and water in the distance, an unintentional echo of Dürer's composition (fig. 70).

Christian monasticism arose in the desert of the Thebaid, a Roman division along the upper Nile River. In fact, the Latin word for "wilderness" is *solitudinem*, whereas *desertus* means "waste" or "wasteland." A pen-and-ink drawing by Lorenzo Costa (1459/60–1535) features a tightly composed scene of monks, hermits, and even some saints (Paul of Thebes, Anthony of Egypt, and Mary Magdalene) finding solace in the desolate oasis away from city life, suggested by faint structures in the distance (fig. 71). Two figures receive food from a bird, others gather near a hermitage built of stone; some watch as boaters pass on the flowing river, and still others kneel beneath a mature tree. This range of activities—reliance on the divine for spiritual nourishment,

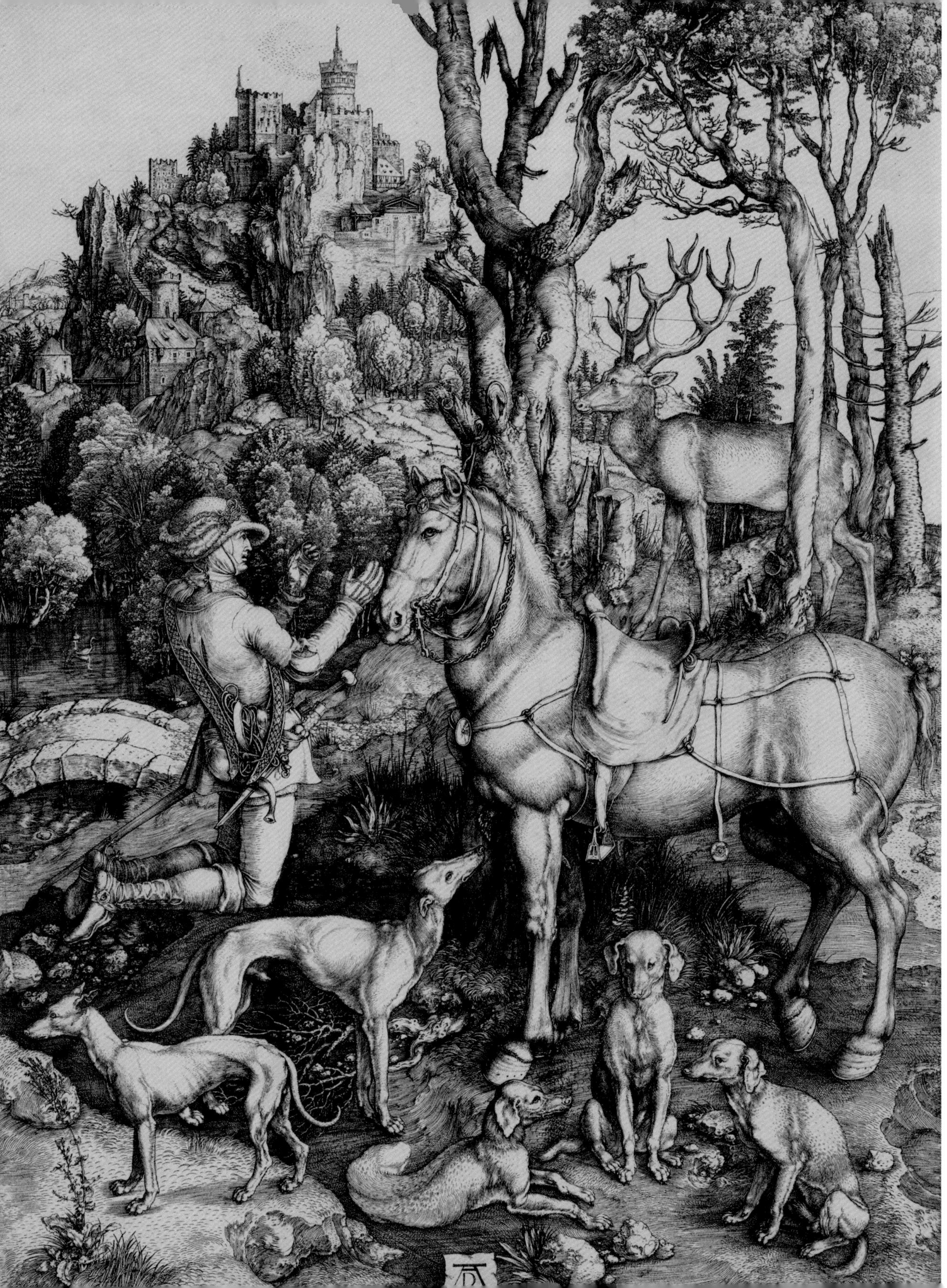

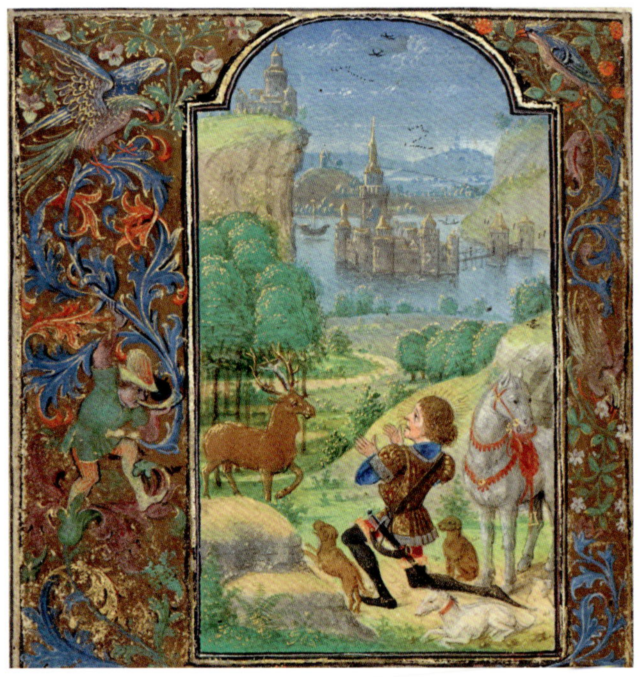

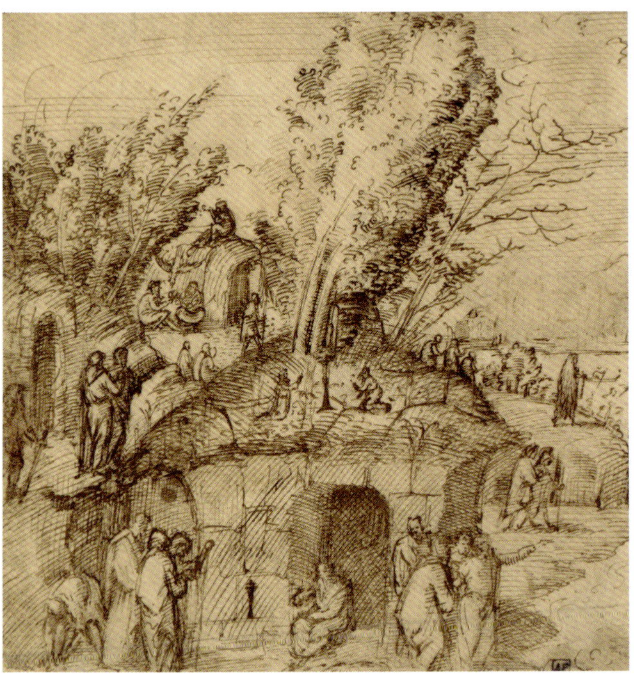

finding a quiet spot for meditation, and slowing the pace of life—could be emulated by the laity through contemplative readings and vibrant images in manuscripts.

A scholar and cardinal, Saint Jerome (ca. 347–420) had an affinity for nature and animals, including a lion from whose paw the saint removed a thorn.[32] Although Jerome was a young man when he set out into the Syrian desert, searching for a space of solitary reflection, he was often depicted as an old man (fig. 72). Having stripped off his cardinal's robes, he kneels at a grotto, grasping a bloody stone used for self-mortification. The rocky cave, dead tree stump, and broken branch separate this barren setting from the wealthy town in a traditionally pastoral vista, which Jerome has abandoned.

Legend recalls that Saint Honofrius (or Onuphrius; fourth or fifth century), desiring to properly embrace an ascetic lifestyle, abandoned his monastery and journeyed into the desert (fig. 73). For the next sixty years, he lived in a barren cave, subsisting on dates from a nearby palm tree, while an angel appeared every Sunday to offer Communion. Honofrius's body hair, like Mary Magdalene's (see fig. 76), grew to shield him from the elements and

FIGURE 70 | *Saint Hubert*, Ghent (written out) and Antwerp (illuminated), Belgium, 1469, Lieven van Lathem, Prayer Book of Charles the Bold, 12.4 × 9.2 cm (4⅞ × 3⅝ in.), Ms. 37 (89.ML.35), fol. 39v

FIGURE 71 | Lorenzo Costa (Italian, 1459/60–1535), *A Thebaid: Monks and Hermits in a Landscape*, ca. 1505. Pen and brown ink, 20.3 × 20.6 cm (8 × 8⅛ in.), 87.GA.11

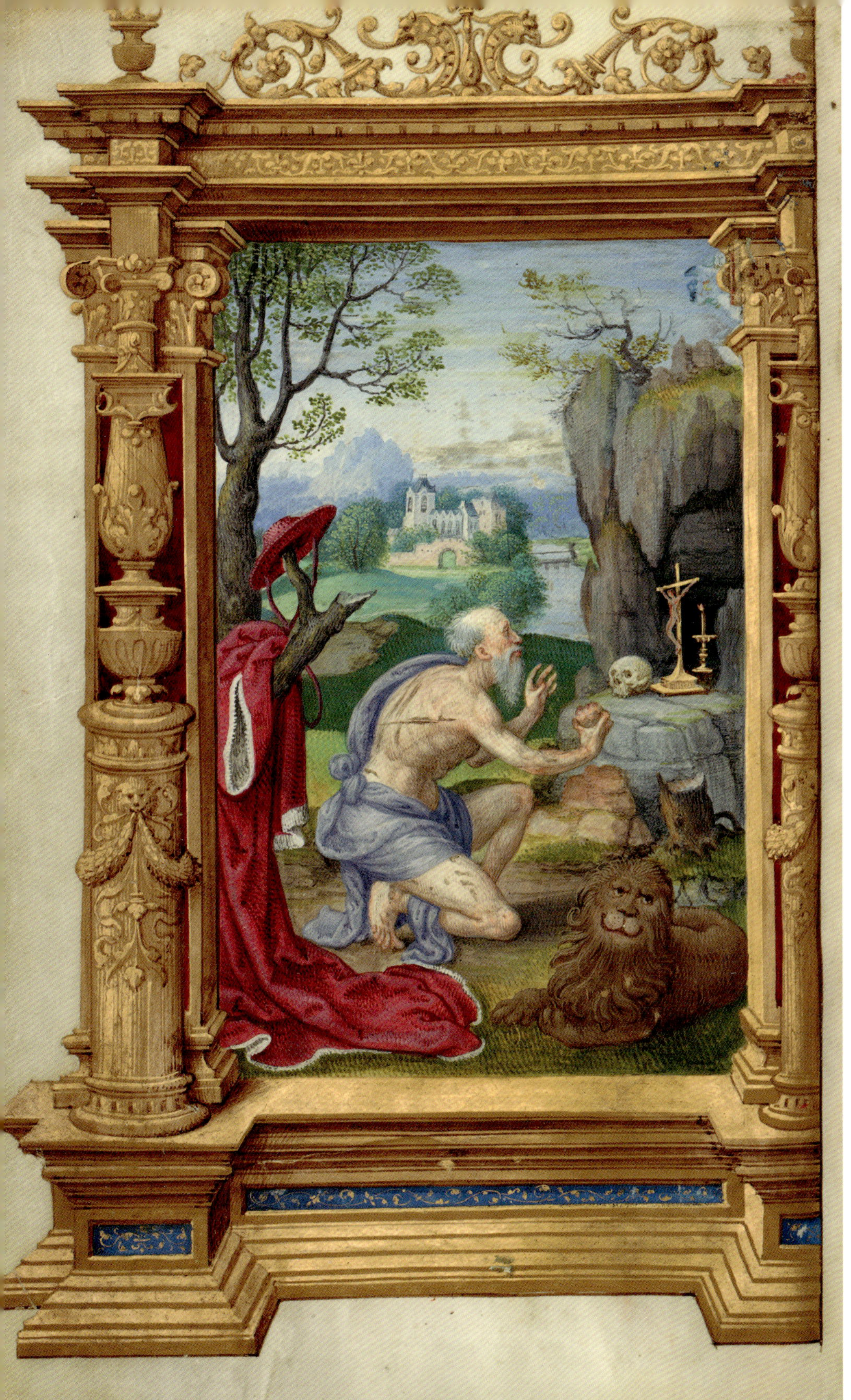

FIGURE 72 | *Saint Jerome*, Paris or Tours, ca. 1528–30, Master of the Getty Epistles, Getty Epistles, 16.5 × 10.3 cm (6½ × 4¹⁄₁₆ in.), Ms. Ludwig I 15 (83.MA.64), fol. 1v

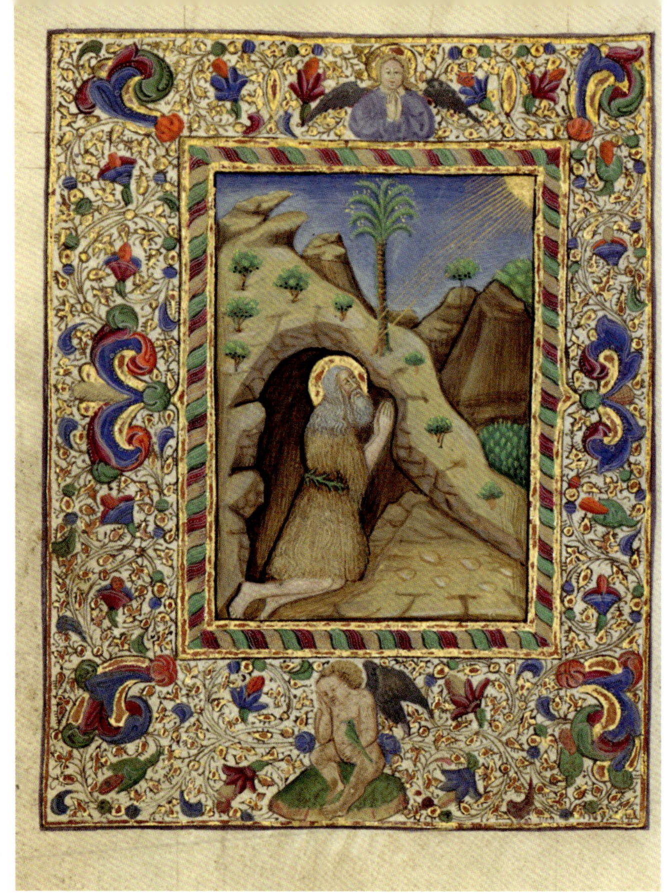

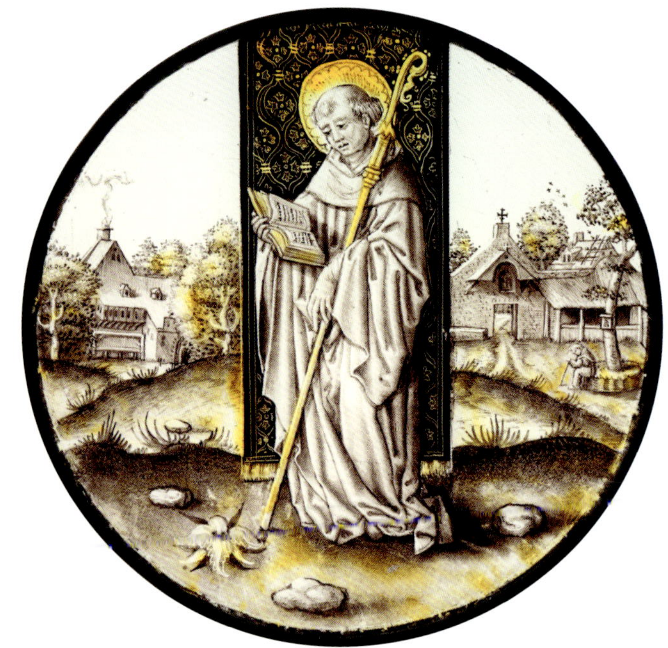

FIGURE 73 | *The Hermit Honofrius in Prayer*, Naples, ca. 1460, book of hours, 17.1 × 12.1 cm (6¾ × 4¾ in.), Ms. Ludwig IX 12 (83.ML.108), fol. 329v

FIGURE 74 | Unknown German artist, *Saint Bernard*, ca. 1500. Colorless glass, vitreous paint, silver stain, Diam 23.2 cm (9⅛ in.), 2003.55

protect his modesty. Here, the saint prays at the entrance to his cave, set in a dry, rocky terrain with only a few small shrubs populating the landscape. The miraculous palm is placed at the center of the composition, and heavenly beams rain down upon the praying hermit to suggest divine blessing.

Saints who did not embrace a hermetic path nonetheless advocated for a spiritual relationship with the natural world. Born to Burgundian nobles, Saint Bernard of Clairvaux (1090–1153) went on to join the Cistercian monastery of Cîteaux and to found an abbey at Clairvaux. He was known for his austerity and love of nature, having once famously written, "Believe me, you will find more lessons in the woods than in books. Trees and stones will teach you what you cannot learn from masters."[33] A German glass window renders the saint before a cloth of honor on a plain outside a typical northern European town (fig. 74). A brick church and houses with thatched roofs give

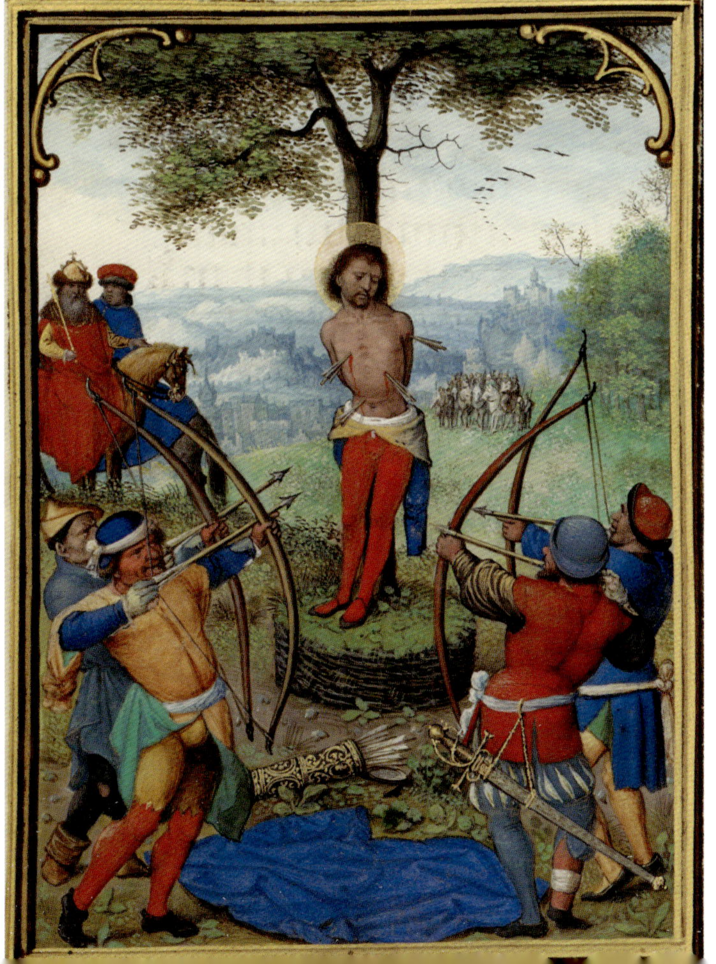

FIGURE 75 | *The Martyrdom of Saint Sebastian*, Bruges, Belgium, ca. 1535–40, Simon Bening, Munich-Montserrat Hours, 13.7 × 10 cm (5⅜ × 3¹⁵⁄₁₆ in.), Ms. 3 (84.ML.83), leaf 2v

way to low, grassy hills, while a smaller image of the abbot can be spotted sitting on a raised platform around a tree, perhaps in contemplation. Northern Renaissance artists often incorporated scenes of everyday life into religious sequences in order to locate the figure in history, make the scenes accessible to contemporaneous viewers, and suggest the sacred can be found in the quotidian.

The structure that Saint Bernard sits upon also appears in a leaf from the Munich-Montserrat Hours (fig. 75). Atop it stands Saint Sebastian (third century), a Roman soldier of great regard who was executed for being a Christian. During one attempt to slay him, Sebastian was tied to a tree and brutally shot with arrows. In the miniature, the muscular youth is stripped to the waist and arrows begin to pierce his body. On their way to sainthood, Christian martyrs often miraculously overcame bodily harm (which evoked Christ's suffering and resurrection). A Renaissance viewer would see Sebastian tied to a column-like tree as a parallel to the Flagellation of Christ. Simon Bening's command of landscape is obvious in this scene at the edge of a forest, a wild setting that the artist has infused with a sense of order. The raised grassy platform encased by a wattle fence separates Sebastian from the physical world and relegates him to a sacred space of reverie, which is violated by his oppressors. Here, tension between sanctity and sin is manifest in the setting—the divine defined by the cultivated, civilized, and organized, encasing and protecting a wild tree. ❧

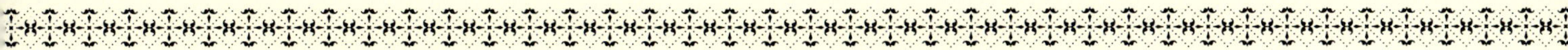

THE GUALENGHI-D'ESTE HOURS
Ferrara, Italy, ca. 1469
Taddeo Crivelli and Guglielmo Giraldi

ACCORDING TO MEDIEVAL ACCOUNTS OF SAINTS' LIVES, AFTER CHRIST ASCENDED into heaven, Mary Magdalene traveled to a desert or wilderness (often identified as Aix-en-Provence or Marseilles, in the South of France) where she spent the next thirty years as a hermit (fig. 76). As she lived in quiet contemplation, her hair miraculously grew to cover her body, and at each of the eight canonical hours of the day she ascended to heaven and was nourished by heavenly

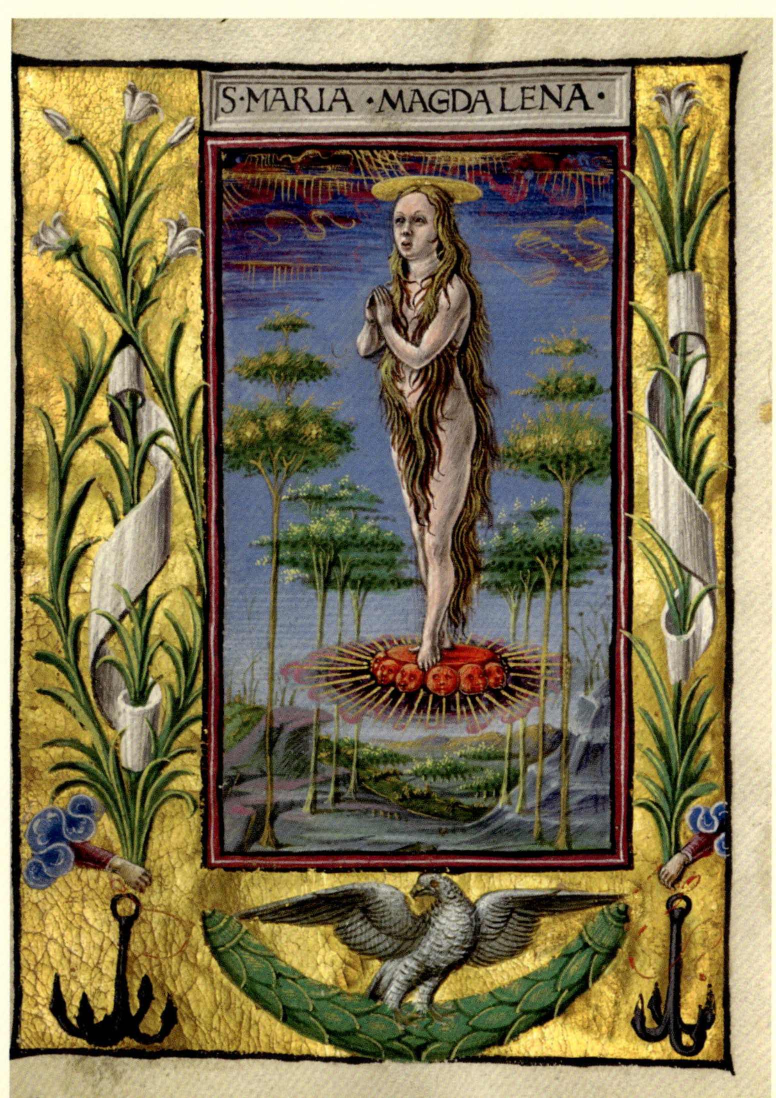

FIGURE 76 | *Mary Magdalene Borne Aloft*, Ferrara, Italy, ca. 1469, Taddeo Crivelli, Gualenghi-d'Este Hours, 10.8 × 7.9 cm (4¼ × 3⅛ in.), Ms. Ludwig IX 13 (83.ML.109), fol. 190v

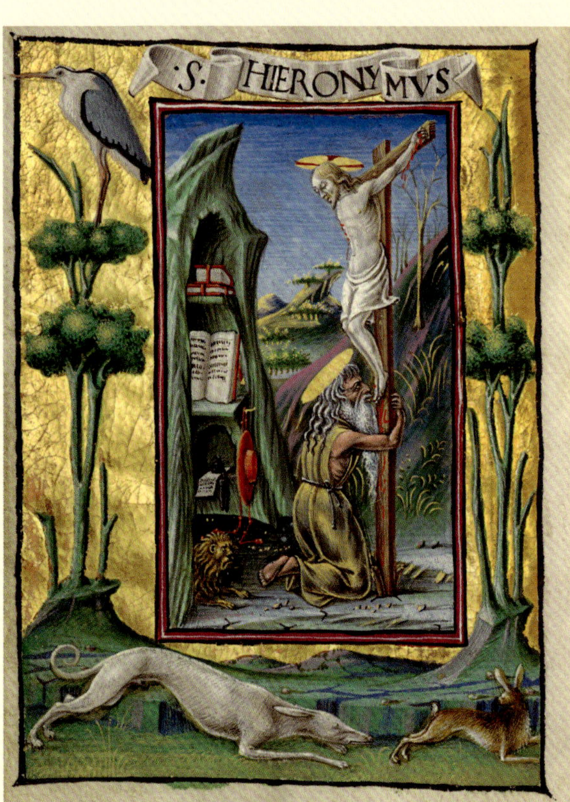

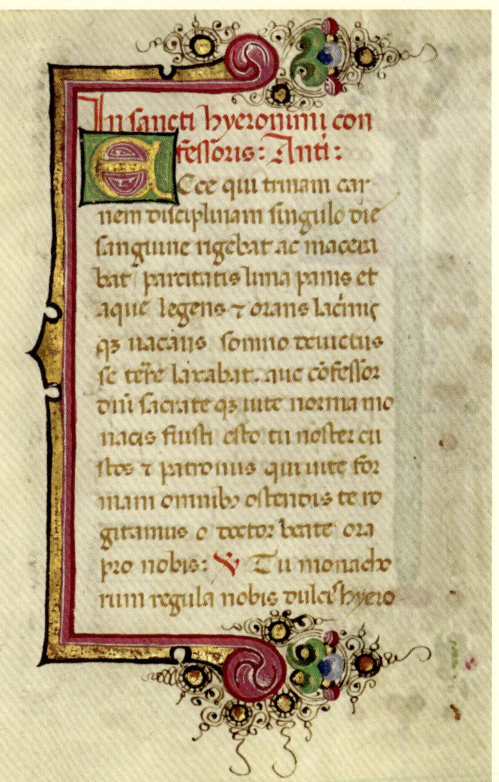

In sancti hyeronimi confessoris: Anti:

Ece qui trinam carnem disciplinam singulo die sanguine rigebat ac macerabat parcitatis lima panis et aque legens ⁊ orans licinic qz vacans somno devictus se terre librabat. ave confessorum sacietate qz vite norma monacis fuisti esto tu noster custos ⁊ patronus qui vite formam omnibus ostendens te rogitamus o doctor beate ora pro nobis: V Tu monachorum regula nobis dulcis hyero

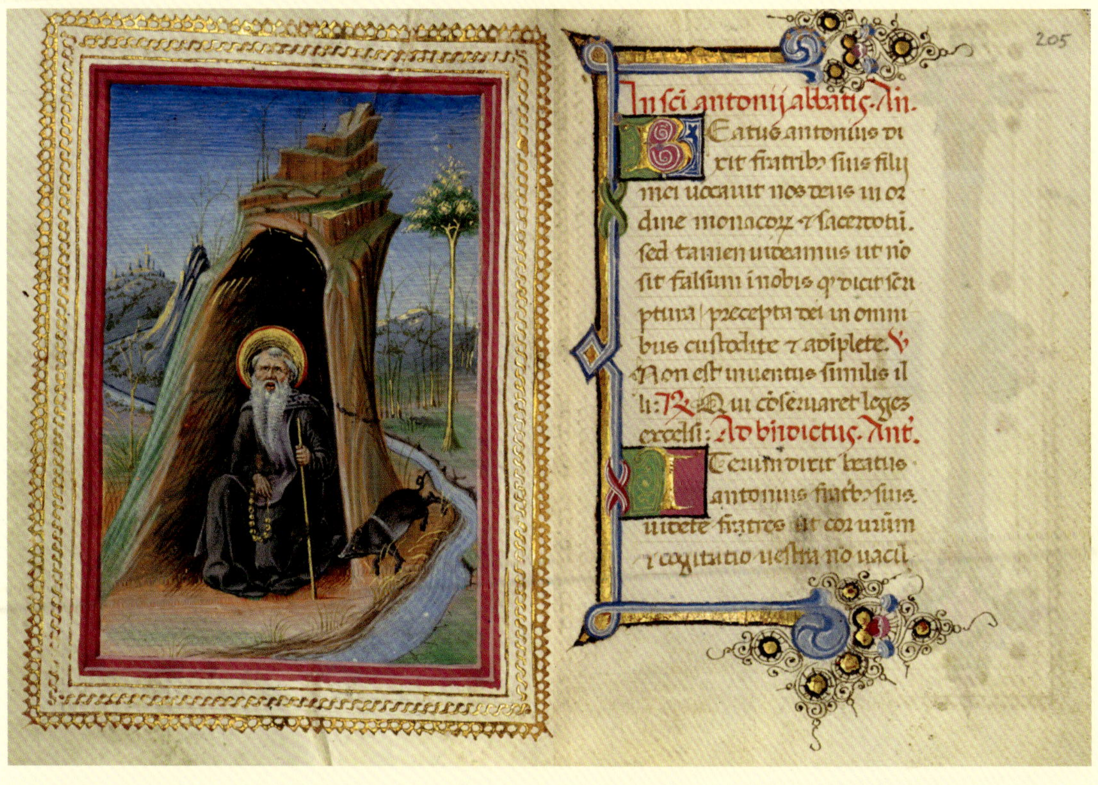

In sci antonij abbatis. An.

Eatus antonius dixit fratribus suis filij mei vocavit nos deus in ordine monacorum ⁊ sacerdoti. sed tamen videamus ut no sit falsum in nobis qd dicat scriptura precepta dei in omnibus custodite ⁊ adimplete. V Non est inuentus similis illi: R Qui conseruaret leges excelsi: Ad bndictus. Ant.

Terum dixit beatus antonius fratribus suis. videte fratres ut cor vnum ⁊ cogitatio vestra non vacil

song. Lilies, symbols of purity and chastity, grow skyward, framing a penitent Magdalene and driving both the narration and devotee's prayers heavenward.

Taddeo Crivelli (active 1451–79) and Guglielmo Giraldi (active 1445–89) produced this manuscript around 1469 on the occasion of the marriage of Andrea Gualengo and Orsina d'Este, a member of one of the wealthiest Italian families. Symbols of the Este house—such as the anchor and the eagle—are included throughout the manuscript, along with numerous scenes of hermit saints and blessed individuals whose time in the wilderness served as a model of piety and prayer for the owners.

The subject of *Saint Jerome in the Desert* (fig. 77), for example, can be connected to humanist circles throughout the Italian peninsula. The Este dukes emulated Jerome's qualities of mental prowess, spiritual conviction, and compassion for the environment. Crivelli added a courtly splendor to the page and provided additional details suggesting a sylvan retreat: a greyhound hunting a rabbit, below, and an exotic crane perched on a tree, above. Jerome's cave filled with the accoutrements of his profession (and a tiny lion) contrasts with Saint Anthony Abbot's dark and foreboding grotto painted elsewhere in the manuscript by Crivelli (fig. 78). A place of temptation and torment, the cavernous mount isolates Anthony from the world beyond. His only companion is a striped pig, symbolizing the saint's ability to heal infirmities, as lard was used as a remedy for a skin disease called "Saint Anthony's fire." The wilderness was therefore here represented as a spiritual retreat or site of divine visionary experiences. ❧

FIGURE 77 | *Saint Jerome in the Desert*, Ferrara, Italy, ca. 1469, Taddeo Crivelli, Gualenghi-d'Este Hours, 10.8 × 7.9 cm (4¼ × 3⅛ in.), Ms. Ludwig IX 13 (83.ML.109), fols. 174v–175

FIGURE 78 | *Saint Anthony Abbot*, Ferrara, Italy, ca. 1469, Taddeo Crivelli, Gualenghi-d'Este Hours, 10.8 × 7.9 cm (4¼ × 3⅛ in.), Ms. Ludwig IX 13 (83.ML.109), fols. 204v–205

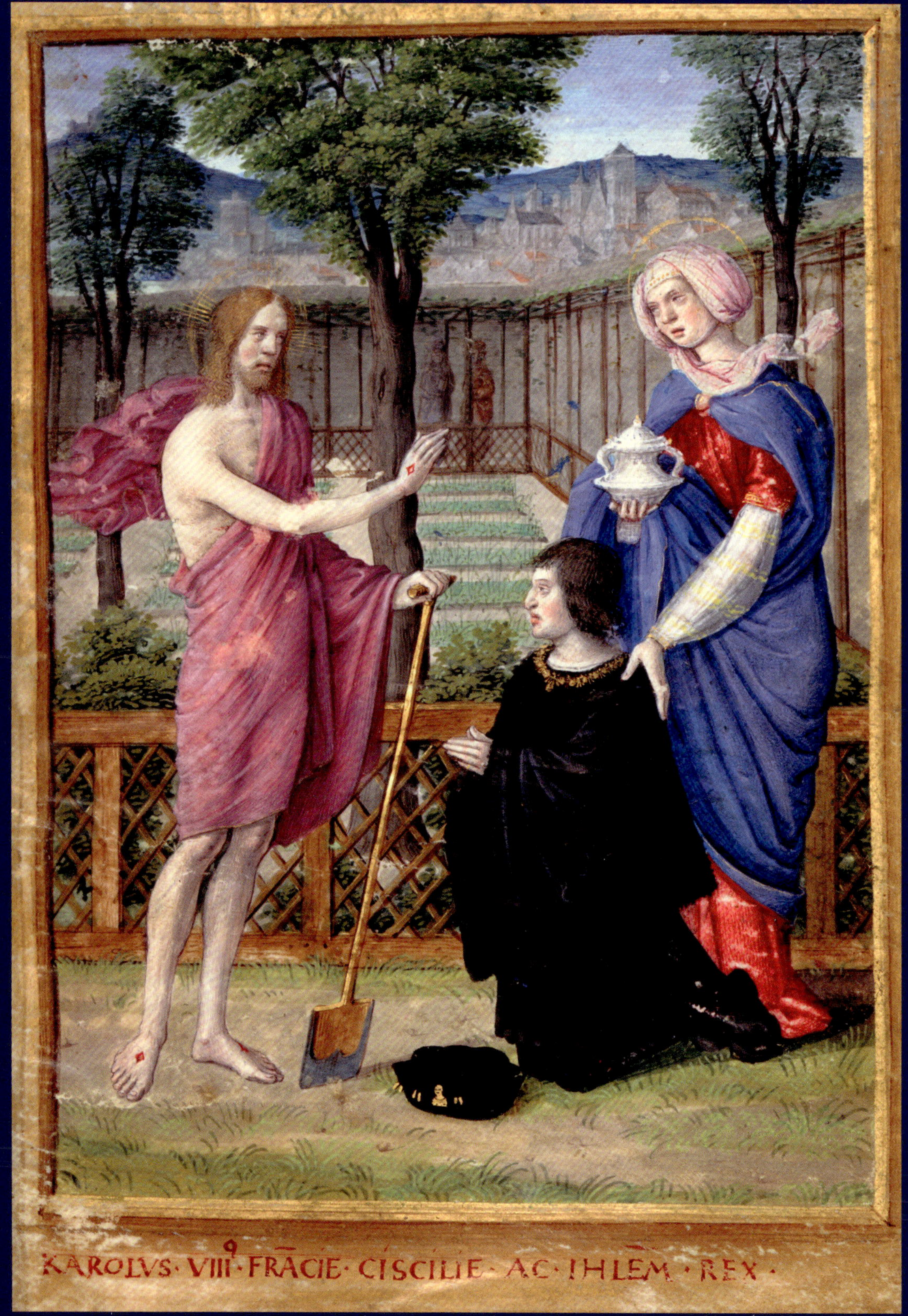
KAROLVS · VIII · FRACIE · CISCILIE · AC · IHLEM · REX ·

EPILOGUE

THE PREVIOUS CHAPTERS HAVE CONSIDERED THE DEVELOPMENT OF LAND-
scape painting and the deep interest in nature and the environment in
Renaissance art, primarily in France, Italy, and the Netherlands but also in
Germany and England.[34] The period of the Italian Wars (1494–1559) forever
changed the history of political relations among Italy, France, and the rest
of northern Europe. On a cultural level, the movement of people and ideas
over the Alps sparked new approaches to landscape architecture and garden
design. The books of hours made for three generations of French kings who
reigned during this conflict—Charles VIII (r. 1483–98), Louis XII (r. 1498–
1515), and Francis I (r. 1515–47)—are each embedded in a visual program that
emphasizes the throne's relationship with the natural world.

On a bifolio inserted into a slightly later manuscript, Charles VIII
kneels before the risen Christ in a garden, presented by Mary Magdalene
(fig. 79). This act of supplication and the setting in a Renaissance cloister
garden position the regent as heir to the life-giving hope of Christ's resurrection. The gardens of the royal residence at the Château d'Amboise, on
the banks of the Loire River, were designed by the Neapolitan horticulturist
Pacello da Mercogliano (ca. 1455–1534), whom Charles brought back with him
to France. The pages of the Hours of Louis XII (fig. 80; see fig. 49) and the
Hours of Anne of Brittany (Anne was Louis's wife and consort)—often referred to as "twin manuscripts"—feature some of the greatest *florilegia* (com-
pendiums of flower studies) of the time.[35] In fact, the plants in Anne's book
are labeled in Latin and French, highlighting the important role she played
in shaping garden culture in France, specifically at the Château de Blois. And

FIGURE 79 | *Noli me tangere*, perhaps Berry, France, ca. 1510, Jean Poyer, book of hours, 29.5 × 23.3 cm (11⅝ × 9³⁄₁₆ in.). New York, Morgan Library & Museum, MS M.250, fol. 14r

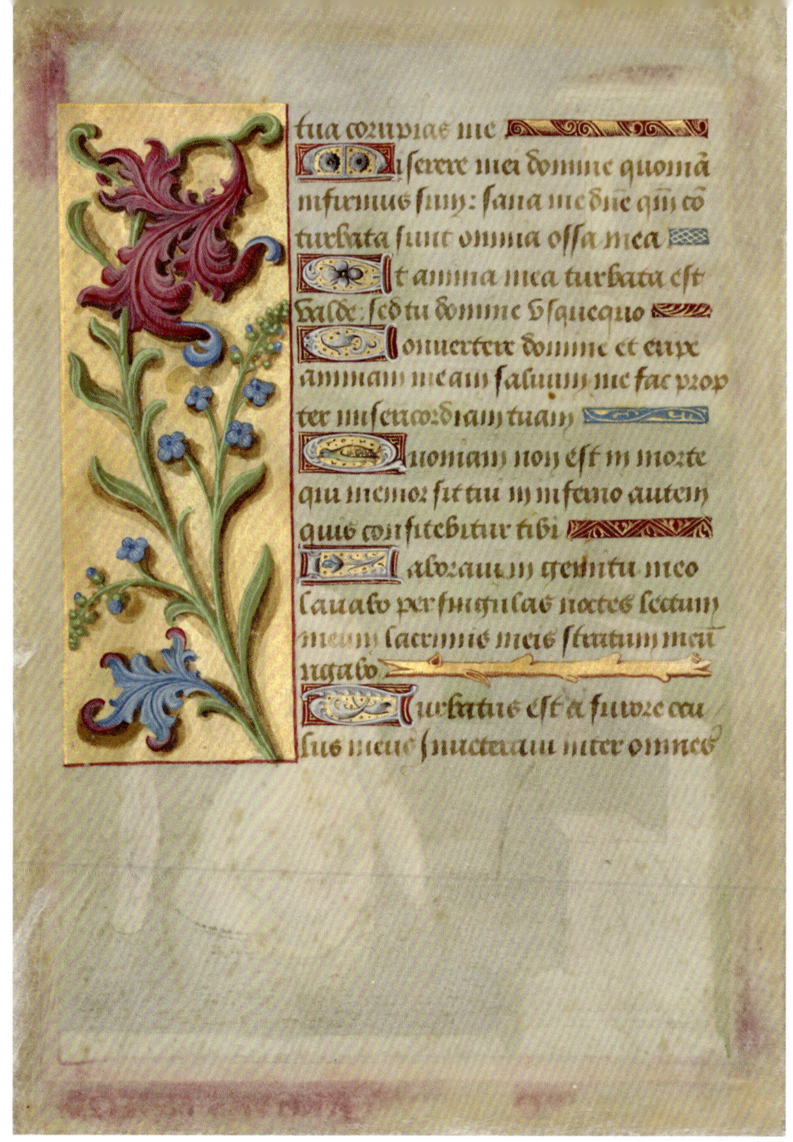

finally, in the little-known Hours of Francis I, the ruler kneels before Saint Marcoulfe, a healing saint in the presence of whose relics the French kings were thought to receive the ability to heal scrofula, or tuberculosis of the neck (fig. 81). With full force, Francis ushered in the Italian Renaissance on French soil by recruiting an entourage of central Italian artists, including Primaticcio (1504–1570) and Rosso Fiorentino (1494–1540), to work at the Château de Fontainebleau. The artists responsible for these manuscripts—Jean Poyer (active 1465–1503), Jean Bourdichon (1456/57–1521), and the Master of François de Rohan (active ca. 1525–46), respectively—were each influenced by Italian art, and their patrons were quite knowledgeable about Italian garden

FIGURE 80 | *Decorated Text Page with Speedwell*, Tours or Paris, ca. 1490s, Jean Bourdichon, leaf from the Hours of Louis XII, 24.3 × 17 cm (9⁹⁄₁₆ × 6¹¹⁄₁₆ in.), Ms. 79 (2003.105), verso

design and pharmacopoeia and sought to transform the French biocultural landscape during their reigns.

These Renaissance devotional books—like the rest of the manuscripts discussed throughout this volume—witnessed the emergence of landscape painting, at times based on classical precedents and at others derived from contemporaneous interest in science, humanist philosophy, and new approaches to naturalism in painting. Regardless of the confines of architectural space or the temporal variances of each passing season, viewing landscapes bound within the pages of a codex afforded readers an evergreen opportunity to connect with nature and experience divine transcendence. ❦

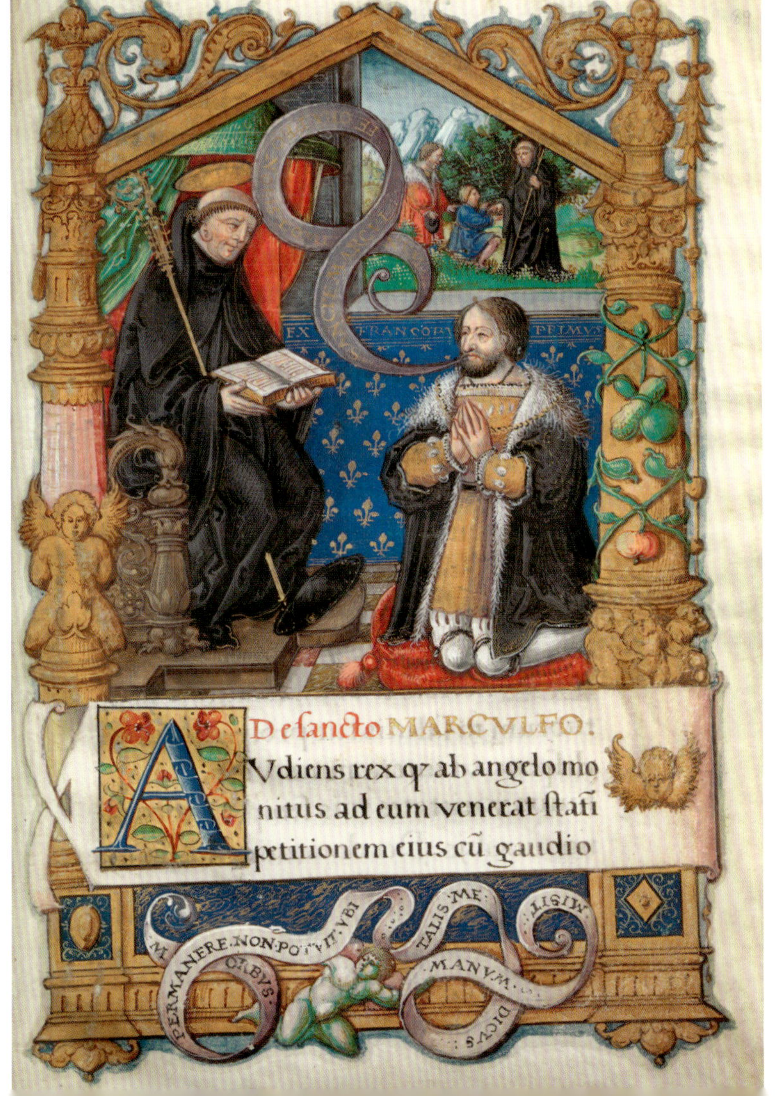

FIGURE 81 | *Francis I before Saint Marcoulfe*, Tours or Paris, 1539–40, Master of François de Rohan, Hours of Francis I, 20.8 × 14.6 cm (8³⁄₁₆ × 5¾ in.). New York, Metropolitan Museum of Art, 2011.353, fol. 89

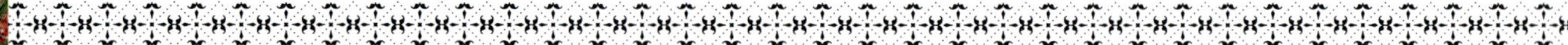

NOTES

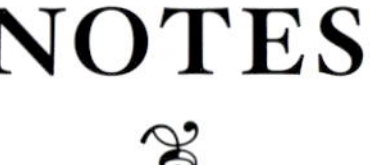

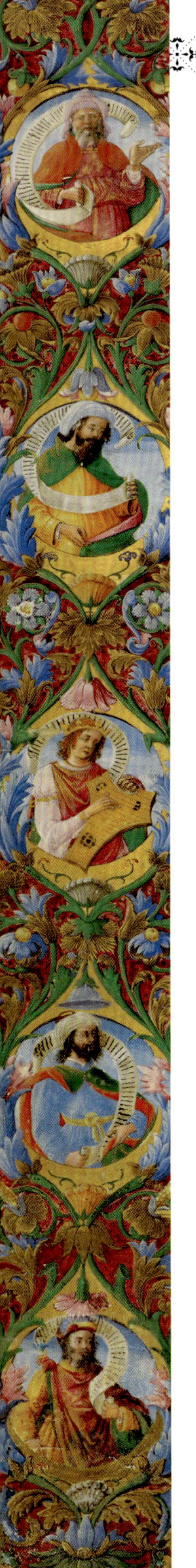

1   The Douay-Rheims Bible, translated from the Latin Vulgate, is generally cited in scholarship on the Middle Ages. The translation there of John 20:17 as "Do not touch me" is widely known, though "Do not hold on to me" is a more proper one, as found in the New International Version.

2   Numerous saints were believed to have experienced transcendence in nature, as recorded in Jacobus de Voragine, *The Golden Legend: Readings on the Saints*, trans. William Granger Ryan, 2 vols. (Princeton, NJ: Princeton University Press, 1993).

3   For a complete reproduction of the book of hours by the Spitz Master and a study of the manuscript, see Gregory T. Clark, *The Spitz Master: A Parisian Book of Hours* (Los Angeles: J. Paul Getty Museum, 2003).

4   For a study of the manuscript, see Patricia Stirnemann et al., *Les Très Riches Heures du duc de Berry et l'enluminure en France au début du XV siècle*, exh. cat. (Paris: Somogy; Chantilly: Musée Condée, Château de Chantilly, 2004). For a complete look at the illuminations, see Jean Longon and Raymond Cazelles, *The "Très Riches Heures" of Jean, Duke of Berry* (New York: G. Braziller, 1969).

5   Medieval medicine is the subject of Monica Helen Green, "The Transmission of Ancient Theories of Female Physiology and Disease through the Early Middle Ages" (PhD diss., Princeton University, 1985).

6   Paula Nuttall, *Face to Face: Flanders, Florence, and Renaissance Painting* (San Marino, CA: Huntington Library, Art Collections, and Botanical Gardens, 2013), 16n10.

7   For a facsimile edition, see James H. Marrow with François Avril, *The Hours of Simon de Varie* (Malibu, CA: J. Paul Getty Museum; The Hague: Koninklijke Bibliotheek, 1994).

8   Pacino's illuminations are reproduced and discussed in Bryan C. Keene, "New Discoveries from the Laudario of Sant'Agnese," *Getty Research Journal* 8 (2016): 199–208. They are also the subject of several essays and catalogue entries in Christine Sciacca, ed., *Florence at the Dawn of the Renaissance: Painting and Illumination, 1300–1350*, exh. cat. (Los Angeles: J. Paul Getty Museum, 2012).

9   Laurence Kanter and Pia Palladino, *Fra Angelico*, exh. cat. (New York: Metropolitan Museum of Art, 2005), 234–36, no. 41, fig. 41, entry by Laurence Kanter.

10   For the manuscript, see Millard Meiss and Edith W. Kirsch, *The Visconti Hours, National Library, Florence* (New York: G. Braziller, 1972). On Belbello, see Fabrizio Lollini, "Giovanni Belbello da Pavia," in *Dizionario biografico dei miniatori Italiani: Secoli IX–XVI*, ed. Milvia Bollati (Milan: Sylvestre Bonnard, 2004), 275.

11   For a biography of Pisanello, see "Gentile da Fabriano (ca. 1370–1427) and Antonio Pisanello of Verona (1395–1455)," *Giorgio Vasari's "Lives of the Artists,"* part 2, http://members.efn.org/-acd/vite/VasariLives.html. This website, created by Adrienne DeAngelis, is in progress; it is intended to offer the unabridged *Lives* in English.

12   Gino Castiglioni, "Primo Quattrocento, il Tardogotico," in *La parola illuminata: Per una storia della miniatura a Verona e a Vincenza tra Medioevo e età romantica*, ed. Gino Castiglioni (Verona: Fondazione Cariverona, 2011), 107, 109–11, 114–15, fig. IV.30.

13   Elena De Laurentiis and Emilia Anna Talamo, *The Lost Manuscripts from the Sistine Chapel: An Epic Journey from Rome to Toledo*, exh. cat. (Madrid: Centro de Estudios Europa Hispánica; Dallas: Meadows Museum, 2010), 332, 345, 357, 365–66, fig. 8.

14   Alessandra Zamperini, *Le grottesche: Il sogno della pittura nella decorazione parietale* (San Giovanni Lupatoto, Italy: Arsenale, 2007), 118–19.

15   See Sara Taglialagamba, *Leonardo and Nature* (Poggio a Caiano, Italy: CB Edizioni, 2010).

16   James H. Marrow describes manuscript painting from the fifteenth and sixteenth centuries as "pictorial illusionism" and "illusionist mastery" (James H. Marrow, *Pictorial Invention in Netherlandish Manuscript Illumination of the Late Middle Ages: The Play of Illusion and Meaning*, ed. Brigitte Dekeyzer and Jan van der Stock [Paris: Peeters, 2005], 2); Paula Nuttall calls it a "new pictorial language" (*Face to Face*, 18).

17   For an overview of painting and illumination in northern Europe during the Renaissance, see Susie Nash, *Northern Renaissance Art* (New York: Oxford University Press, 2008).

18   For a discussion of Van Eyck and the establishment of the Netherlandish canon of painting, see Erwin Panofsky, *Early Netherlandish Painting, Its Origins and Character*, 2 vols. (Cambridge, MA: Harvard University Press, 1953).

19   The relationship between Memling's continuous narrative paintings and portraiture are discussed in Till Borchert, with contributions by Maryan W. Ainsworth, Lorne Campbell, and Paula Nuttall, *Memling's Portraits*, exh. cat. (Ghent and Amsterdam: Ludion; New York: Thames & Hudson, 2005). See also Nuttall, *Face to Face*.

20   The painting is discussed in Sally Whitman Coleman, "Hans Memling's *Scenes from the Advent and Triumph of Christ* and the Discourse of Revelation," *Journal of Historians of Netherlandish Art* 5, no. 1 (Winter 2013), doi: 10.5092/jhna.2013.5.1.1.

21   The most thorough overview of Flemish naturalism during the Renaissance is Marrow, *Pictorial Invention*.

22   For a facsimile edition, with commentary, see Eric Inglis, *The Hours of Mary of Burgundy: Codex Vindobonensis 1857, Vienna, Österreichische Nationalbibliothek* (London: H. Miller, 1995).

23   Ludolph of Saxony, *The Hours of the Passion: Taken from the "Life of Christ,"* trans. Henry James Coleridge (London: Burns and Oates, 1887), 2, 10. See also Isa Ragusa and Rosalie B. Green, eds., *"Meditations on the Life of Christ": An Illustrated Manuscript of the Fourteenth Century, Paris, Bibliothèque nationale, Ms. Ital., 115*, trans. Isa Ragusa (Princeton, NJ: Princeton University Press, 1961).

24   The most essential assessment of Simon Bening's role in the development of Flemish manu-
      script painting is Thomas Kren and Scot McKendrick, eds., *Illuminating the Renaissance:
      The Triumph of Flemish Manuscript Painting in Europe*, exh. cat. (Los Angeles: J. Paul Getty
      Museum, 2003).

25   For another look at the meaning of flowers in Renaissance art, see Celia Fisher, *Flowers of the
      Renaissance* (London: Frances Lincoln, 2011).

26   For a look at the many ways in which gardens permeated Renaissance literary and visual
      culture, see Bryan C. Keene, *Gardens of the Renaissance* (Los Angeles: J. Paul Getty Museum,
      2013), and "Green Leaves," *Apollo* 177, no. 610 (June 2013): 68–72. See also the blogs by and
      about the Met Cloisters and Gardens, a branch of the Metropolitan Museum of Art, New
      York: http://blog.metmuseum.org/cloistersgardens/ and http://www.metmuseum.org/blogs/
      in-season.

27   For a consideration of how attitudes toward the wilderness developed in the premodern
      period, see Albrecht Classen, ed. *Rural Space in the Middle Ages and Early Modern Age: The
      Spatial Turn in Premodern Studies* (Berlin: De Gruyter, 2012).

28   All of the manuscript's miniatures are reproduced in Antoine de Schryver, *The Prayer Book
      of Charles the Bold: A Study of a Flemish Masterpiece from the Burgundian Court*, trans. Jessica
      Berenbeim (Los Angeles: J. Paul Getty Museum, 2008).

29   Hildegard of Bingen, "Hildegard of Bingen: 'Book of Divine Works,' Part I, Vision I,"
      trans. Nathaniel Campbell, 2n2, https://www.academia.edu/3597758/Hildegard_of_
      Bingen_Book_of_Divine_Works_Part_I_Vision_I.

30   A. Richard Turner, *The Vision of Landscape in Renaissance Italy* (Princeton, NJ: Princeton
      University Press, 1966), 39.

31   Nash, *Northern Renaissance Art*, 255.

32   Philip Schaff and Henry Wade, eds. *A Select Library of Nicene and Post-Nicene Fathers of the
      Christian Church: Second Series* (Grand Rapids, MI: W. B. Eerdmans, 1952), 7:391.

33   Bernard of Clairvaux, *Epistola* CVI, 2, quoted in Edward Churton, *The Early English Church*
      (New York: D. Appleton, 1842), 288.

34   For an in-depth discussion of the development of landscape painting north of the Alps
      during the later Middle Ages and the Renaissance, see Jacob Wamberg, *Landscape as World
      Picture: Tracing Cultural Evolution in Images*, trans. Gaye Kynoch, 2 vols. (Aarhus: Aarhus
      University Press, 2009).

35   For a facsimile edition, see *A Masterpiece Reconstructed: The Hours of Louis XII*, ed. Thomas
      Kren with Mark Evans (Los Angeles: J. Paul Getty Museum; London: British Library,
      2005).

SUGGESTIONS FOR FURTHER READING

Andrews, Malcolm. *Landscape and Western Art*. Oxford: Oxford University Press, 1999.

Bakker, Boudewijn, and Diane Webb. *Landscape and Religion from Van Eyck to Rembrandt*. Farnham, Surrey: Ashgate, 2012.

Barstow, Kurt. *The Gualenghi-d'Este Hours: Art and Devotion in Renaissance Ferrara*. Los Angeles: J. Paul Getty Museum, 2000.

Belting, Hans. *Likeness and Presence: A History of the Image Before the Era of Art*. Chicago: University of Chicago Press, 1994.

Bernard of Clairvaux, Saint. *Epistola* CVI, Section 2. In *The Early English Church*, translated by Edward Churton, 288. New York: D. Appleton, 1842.

Borchert, Till, with contributions by Maryan W. Ainsworth, Lorne Campbell, and Paula Nuttall. *Memling's Portraits*. Exh. cat. Ghent and Amsterdam: Ludion; New York: Thames & Hudson, 2005.

Burckhardt, Jacob. *Italian Renaissance Painting According to Genres*. Los Angeles: Getty Research Institute, 2005.

Campbell, Stephen J., and Michael Wayne Cole. *Italian Renaissance Art*. London: Thames & Hudson, 2012.

Castiglioni, Gino. "Primo Quattrocento, il Tardogotico." In *La parola illuminata: Per una storia della miniatura a Verona e a Vincenza tra Medioevo e età romantica*, edited by Gino Castiglioni, 91–137. Verona: Fondazione Cariverona, 2011.

Clark, Gregory T. *The Spitz Master: A Parisian Book of Hours*. Los Angeles: J. Paul Getty Museum, 2003.

Classen, Albrecht, ed. *Rural Space in the Middle Ages and Early Modern Age: The Spatial Turn in Premodern Studies*. Berlin: De Gruyter, 2012.

Collins, Minta. *Medieval Herbals: The Illustrative Traditions*. London: British Library, 2000.

De Laurentiis, Elena, and Emilia Anna Talamo. *The Lost Manuscripts from the Sistine Chapel: An Epic Journey from Rome to Toledo*. Exh. cat. Madrid: Centro de Estudios Europa Hispánica; Dallas: Meadows Museum, 2010.

De Potter, Filippe, ed. *Savery: Een kunstenaarsfamilie uit Kortrijk*. Edited by Filippe de Potter. Kortrijk, Belgium: Koninklijke Geschied- en Oudheidkundige Kring van Kortrijk, 2012.

De Schryver, Antoine. *The Prayer Book of Charles the Bold: A Study of a Flemish Masterpiece from the Burgundian Court*. Translated by Jessica Berenbeim. Los Angeles: J. Paul Getty Museum, 2008.

Eco, Umberto. *Art and Beauty in the Middle Ages*. Translated by Hugh Bredin. New Haven, CT: Yale University Press, 2002. First published 1986.

Eco, Umberto, and Costantino Marmo. *On the Medieval Theory of Signs*. Amsterdam: John Benjamins Publishing Company, 1989.

Falkenburg, Reindert Leonard. *The Fruit of Devotion: Mysticism and the Imagery of Love in Flemish Paintings of the Virgin and Child, 1450–1550*. Amsterdam: John Benjamins Publishing Company, 1994.

Fisher, Celia. *Flowers of the Renaissance*. London: Frances Lincoln Ltd., 2011.

——. *The Medieval Flower Book*. London: British Library, 2007.

Green, Monica Helen. "The Transmission of Ancient Theories of Female Physiology and Disease through the Early Middle Ages." PhD diss., Princeton University, 1985.

Hendrix, Lee, and Thea Vignau-Wilberg, eds. *"Mira Calligraphiae Monumenta": A Sixteenth-Century Calligraphic Manuscript Inscribed by Georg Bocksay and Illuminated by Joris Hoefnagel*. Los Angeles: J. Paul Getty Museum, 1992.

Hildegard of Bingen. "Hildegard of Bingen: 'Book of Divine Works,' Part I, Vision I." Translated by Nathaniel Campbell. Accessed July 21, 2016. https://www.academia.edu/3597758/Hildegard_of_Bingen_Book_of_Divine_Works_Part_I_Vision_I.

——. *Hildegard's Healing Plants: From Her Medieval Classic "Physica."* Boston: Beacon Press, 2001.

Inglis, Eric. *The Hours of Mary of Burgundy: Codex Vindobonensis 1857, Vienna, Österreichische Nationalbibliothek*. London: H. Miller, 1995.

Kanter, Laurence, and Pia Palladino. *Fra Angelico*. Exh. cat. New York: Metropolitan Museum of Art, 2005.

Keene, Bryan C. *Gardens of the Renaissance*. Los Angeles: J. Paul Getty Museum, 2013.

——. "Green Leaves." *Apollo* 177, no. 610 (June 2013): 68–72.

——. "New Discoveries from the Laudario of Sant'Agnese." *Getty Research Journal* 8 (2016): 199–208.

Kren, Thomas, and Scot McKendrick, eds. *Illuminating the Renaissance: The Triumph of Flemish Manuscript Painting in Europe*. Exh. cat. Los Angeles: J. Paul Getty Museum, 2003.

Kren, Thomas, ed., with Mark Evans. *A Masterpiece Reconstructed: The Hours of Louis XII*. Los Angeles: J. Paul Getty Museum; London: British Library, 2005.

Landau, David. *The Renaissance Print, 1470–1550*. Edited by Peter W. Parshall. New Haven, CT: Yale University Press, 1994.

Lollini, Fabrizio. "Giovanni Belbello da Pavia." In *Dizionario biografico dei miniatori Italiani: Secoli IX–XVI*, edited by Milvia Bollati, 273–76. Milan: Sylvestre Bonnard, 2004.

Ludolph of Saxony. *The Hours of the Passion: Taken from the "Life of Christ."* Translated by Henry James Coleridge. London: Burns and Oates, 1887.

Mansfield, Elizabeth. *Too Beautiful to Picture: Zeuxis, Myth, and Mimesis*. Minneapolis: University of Minnesota Press, 2007.

Marrow, James H. *Pictorial Invention in Netherlandish Manuscript Illumination of the Late Middle Ages: The Play of Illusion and Meaning*. Edited by Brigitte Dekeyzer and Jan van der Stock. Paris: Peeters, 2005.

Marrow, James H., with François Avril. *The Hours of Simon de Varie*. Malibu, CA: J. Paul Getty Museum; The Hague: Koninklijke Bibliotheek, 1994.

Meiss, Millard, and Edith W. Kirsch. *The Visconti Hours, National Library, Florence*. New York: G. Braziller, 1972.

Morgan, Nigel J. *Illuminating the End of Time: The Getty Apocalypse Manuscript*. Los Angeles: J. Paul Getty Museum, 2012.

Morrison, Elizabeth. "Marriage, Death, and the Power of Prayer: The Hours of Denise Poncher." *Getty Research Journal* 6 (January 2014): 143–50.

Nash, Susie. *Northern Renaissance Art*. New York: Oxford University Press, 2008.

Nuttall, Paula. *Face to Face: Flanders, Florence, and Renaissance Painting*. San Marino, CA: Huntington Library, Art Collections, and Botanical Gardens, 2013.

Othoniel, Jean-Michel. *The Secret Language of Flowers: Notes on the Hidden Meanings of Flowers in Art*. Boston: Isabella Stewart Gardner Museum; Arles: Actes Sud, 2015.

Panofsky, Erwin. *Early Netherlandish Painting, Its Origins and Character*. 2 vols. Cambridge, MA: Harvard University Press, 1953

Patinir, Joachim. *Patinir: Essays and Critical Catalogue*. Edited by Alejandro Vergara. Exh. cat. Madrid: Museo Nacional del Prado, 2007.

Pearsall, Derek, and Elizabeth Salter. *Landscapes and Seasons of the Medieval World*. London: Elek, 1973.

Ragusa, Isa, and Rosalie B. Green, eds. *"Meditations on the Life of Christ": An Illustrated Manuscript of the Fourteenth Century, Paris, Bibliothèque nationale, Ms. Ital., 115*. Translated by Isa Ragusa. Princeton, NJ: Princeton University Press, 1961.

Ruff, Allan R. *Arcadian Visions: Pastoral Influences on Poetry, Painting and the Design of Landscape*. Oxford, UK: Windgather Press, 2015.

Schaff, Philip, and Henry Wace, eds. *A Select Library of Nicene and Post-Nicene Fathers of the Christian Church: Second Series*. Vol. 7. Grand Rapids, MI: W. B. Eerdmans, 1952.

Sciacca, Christine, ed. *Florence at the Dawn of the Renaissance: Painting and Illumination, 1300–1350*. Exh. cat. Los Angeles: J. Paul Getty Museum, 2012.

Smith, Bruce R. *The Key of Green: Passion and Perception in Renaissance Culture*. Chicago: University of Chicago Press, 2009.

Stannard, Jerry, and Katherine E. Stannard. *Pristina Medicamenta: Ancient and Medieval Botany*. Edited by Richard Kay. Aldershot, UK; Brookfield, VT: Ashgate Publishing Group, 1999.

Stirnemann, Patricia, François Autrand, Emmanuelle Toulet, Inès Villela-Petit, and Antoni Gonzalez Dizz. *Les Très Riches Heures du duc de Berry et l'enluminure en France au début du XV siècle*. Exh. cat. Paris: Somogy; Chantilly: Musée Condée, Château de Chantilly, 2004.

Taglialagamba, Sara. *Leonardo and Nature*. Poggio a Caiano, Italy: CB Edizioni, 2010.

Turner, A. Richard. *The Vision of Landscape in Renaissance Italy*. Princeton, NJ: Princeton University Press, 1966.

Voragine, Jacobus de. *The Golden Legend: Readings on the Saints*. Translated by William Granger Ryan. 2 vols. Princeton, NJ: Princeton University Press, 1993.

Vasari, Giorgio. "Gentile da Fabriano (ca. 1370–1427) and Antonio Pisanello of Verona (1395–1455)." In *Lives of the Artists*. Part 2. http://members.efn.org/-acd/vite/VasariLives.html.

Wagner, Michael F., ed. *Neoplatonism and Nature: Studies in Plotinus' "Enneads."* Albany: State University of New York Press, 2002.

Wamberg, Jacob. *Landscape as World Picture: Tracing Cultural Evolution in Images*. 2 vols. Translated by Gaye Kynoch. Aarhus: Aarhus University Press, 2009.

Whitman Coleman, Sally. "Hans Memling's Scenes from the Advent and Triumph of Christ and the Discourse of Revelation." *Journal of Historians of Netherlandish Art* 5, no. 1 (Winter 2013): 1–23. doi: 10.5092/jhna.2013.5.1.1.

Zamperini, Alessandra. *Le grottesche: Il sogno della pittura nella decorazione parietale*. San Giovanni Lupatoto, Italy: Arsenale, 2007.

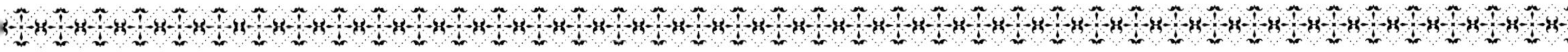

INDEX OF ARTISTS
AND ARTWORKS

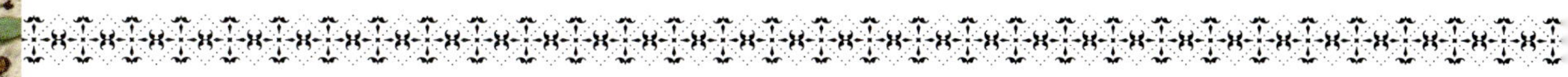

ABOUT THE AUTHORS

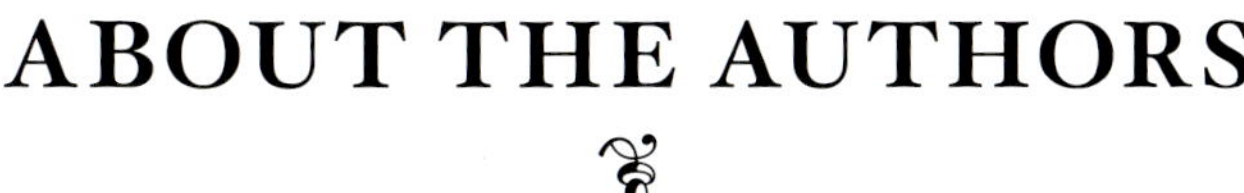

BRYAN C. KEENE is assistant curator in the Department of Manuscripts at the J. Paul Getty Museum. He is the author of *Gardens of the Renaissance*, contributing author to *Florence at the Dawn of the Renaissance: Painting and Illumination, 1300—1350*, and editor of the forthcoming *The World in a Book: Manuscripts and the Global Middle Ages*, all from Getty Publications. He specialized in Italian choir book illumination at the Courtauld Institute of Art, and he is adjunct professor of art history at Pepperdine University.

ALEXANDRA KACZENSKI is former graduate intern in the Department of Manuscripts at the J. Paul Getty Museum. She completed an Andrew W. Mellon Fellowship at UCLA and specialized in Flemish manuscript illumination at the Courtauld Institute of Art. She has presented papers at the Oxford Medieval Graduate Conference (2015) and the Medieval Academy of the Pacific (2016). She currently works as a cataloguer of antiquarian books and manuscripts at Bonhams.

This publication is issued on the occasion of the exhibition *Sacred Landscapes: Nature in Renaissance Manuscripts*, on view at the J. Paul Getty Museum at the Getty Center, Los Angeles, from October 10, 2017 to January 14, 2018.

Published by the J. Paul Getty Museum, Los Angeles
Getty Publications
1200 Getty Center Drive, Suite 500
Los Angeles, CA 90049-1682
www.getty.edu/publications

Elizabeth S. G. Nicholson and Rachel Barth, *Project Editors*
Jane Bobko, *Manuscript Editor*
Catherine Lorenz, *Designer*
Amita Molloy, *Production*

Distributed in the United States and Canada by the University of Chicago Press

Distributed outside the United States and Canada by Yale University Press, London

Printed in Italy

Library of Congress Cataloging-in-Publication Data
Names: Keene, Bryan C., author. | Kaczenski, Alexandra, author. | J. Paul Getty Museum, host institution, issuing body.
Title: Sacred landscapes : nature in Renaissance manuscripts / Bryan C. Keene and Alexandra Kaczenski.
Description: Los Angeles : J. Paul Getty Museum, [2017] | "This publication is issued on the occasion of the exhibition Sacred Landscapes: Nature in Renaissance Manuscripts, on view at the J. Paul Getty Museum at the Getty Center, Los Angeles, from October 10, 2017 to January 14, 2018."—ECIP galley. | Includes index.
Identifiers: LCCN 2017012819 | ISBN 9781606065464 (hardcover)
Subjects: LCSH: Illumination of books and manuscripts, Renaissance—Exhibitions. | Nature in art—Exhibitions. | Landscapes in art—Exhibitions.
Classification: LCC ND2990 .K44 2017 | DDC 700/.46—dc23
LC record available at https://lccn.loc.gov/2017012819

FRONT COVER: *The Assumption of the Virgin*, ca. 1510–20, Master of James IV of Scotland (detail, fig. 34)

BACK COVER (left to right): *Saint Jerome*, ca. 1528–30, Master of the Getty Epistles (detail, fig. 72); *Saint Christopher Carrying the Christ Child*, ca. 1420, Spitz Master (detail, fig. 35); Initial *T*: *Saint Louis of Toulouse*, ca. 1453–63, Franco dei Russi (detail, fig. 37); Decorated Initial *D*, ca. 1480–85, Master of the Dresden Prayer Book or workshop (detail, fig. 60); *Scenes from the Creation*, 1525–30, Simon Bening (detail, fig. 47); *Saint Anthony Abbot*, ca. 1469, Taddeo Crivelli (detail, fig. 78)

PAGE 1: *Scenes from the Creation*, 1525–30, Simon Bening (detail, fig. 47)

PAGES 2–3: *Villagers on Their Way to Church*, ca. 1550, Simon Bening (detail, fig. 29)

PAGE 4: *The Flight into Egypt*, ca. 1420, Spitz Master (detail, fig. 6)

PAGE 6: *Decorated Text Page*, Tours, Paris, ca. 1528–30, Getty Epistles, 16.5 × 10.3 cm (6½ × 4¹⁄₁₆ in.), Ms. Ludwig I 15 (83.MA.64), fol. 2 (detail)

PAGE 8: *Saint Julianus and His Wife*, Bruges, Belgium, ca. 1510–20, Master of James IV of Scotland, Spinola Hours, 23.2 × 16.7 cm (9 ⅛ × 6 ⁹⁄₁₆ in.), Ms. Ludwig IX 18 (83.ML.114), fol. 256v (detail)

PAGE 63: *The Annunciation to the Shepherds*, Tours, ca. 1480–85, Jean Bourdichon, Katherine Hours, 16.4 × 11.6 cm (6 ⁷⁄₁₆ × 4 ⁹⁄₁₆ in.), Ms. 6 (84.ML.746), fol. 55 (detail)

PAGE 104: *The Crucifixion*, 1484–92, Giuliano Amadei (detail, fig. 14)

PAGE 111: *Job on the Dung Heap*, ca. 1480–85, Jean Bourdichon (detail, fig. 45)

ILLUSTRATION CREDITS
Every effort has been made to contact the owners and photographers of objects reproduced here whose names do not appear in the captions or in the illustration credits listed below. Anyone having further information concerning copyright holders is asked to contact Getty Publications so this information can be included in future printings.

Figs. 7, 8: © RMN–Grand Palais / Art Resource, NY / René-Gabriel Ojéda
Fig. 12: Courtesy of the Ministero dei beni e delle attività culturali
Fig. 17: Photo by Robert Wedermeyer
Fig. 18: © Lukas – Art in Flanders VZW / Photo by Hugo Maertens / Bridgeman Images
Fig. 19: © Lukas – Art in Flanders VZW / Bridgeman Images
Fig. 20: bpk Bildagentur / Alte Pinakothek, Bayerische Staatsgemälde-sammlungen / Art Resource, NY
Fig. 22: ÖNB Vienna: Cod. 1857, fol. 43v
Fig. 23: ÖNB Vienna: Cod. 1857, fol. 44r
Fig. 51: De Agostini Picture Library / G. Dagli Orti / Bridgeman Images
Fig. 69: www.lacma.org
Fig. 79: The Morgan Library & Museum / Art Resource, NY
Fig. 81: www.metmuseum.org

NOTE TO THE READER
The two primary types of manuscripts discussed in this publication are books of hours (private prayer books) and choir books (graduals containing the sung portions of the Mass and antiphonaries composed of chants for the Divine Office).

Manuscripts are made of parchment (treated animal skin) embellished with metallic leaf and painted with tempera colors. The front or face of a single manuscript page (leaf) is referred to as the recto, whereas the back or underside of this page is called the verso (abbreviated as *v* throughout).

Unless otherwise noted, all objects are from the J. Paul Getty Museum. The Getty Open Content program allows online users to download high-resolution images of the permanent collection, free of charge. All Getty objects in this book fall within this initiative. Visit http://www.getty.edu/art/collection/.

The images in this book are not to scale.